THIS IS GOING TO HURT

THIS IS GOING TO HURT

Following Jesus in a Divided America

Bekah McNeel

WILLIAM B. EERDMANS PUBLISHING COMPANY
GRAND RAPIDS, MICHIGAN

Wm. B. Eerdmans Publishing Co.
4035 Park East Court SE, Grand Rapids, Michigan 49546
www.eerdmans.com

Book design by Lydia Hall

Printed in the United States of America

30 29 28 27 26 25 24   1 2 3 4 5 6 7

ISBN 978-0-8028-8348-3

Library of Congress Cataloging-in-Publication Data

A catalog record for this book is available from the Library of Congress.

Unless otherwise noted, Scripture quotations are taken from the New International Version of the Bible.

For the helpers, especially Lewis

CONTENTS

FOREWORD

The cure for hubris (religious, political, scientific, or otherwise) is, I think, to experience God through failure, beauty, tragedy, community, and love. Sometimes our learning curve away from self is forced on us, if not by God then by God's angels—say, by a writer with the authentic skill and grace needed to reach us. Bekah McNeel is that kind of writer.

Too serious? Maybe my opening of this foreword is. So, if you are now wondering if *This Is Going to Hurt* will be a readable book, I offer you this quote from page 33 as proof that you will actually enjoy reading about suffering and redemption because McNeel writes vividly and entertainingly: "The major world religions have had their wilderness eras, their empire eras, their reformation eras, and their nationalistic eras. Like Taylor Swift, but instead of burning their ex-boyfriends, they burned heretics."

She has a sense of humor, but McNeel also writes with clarity and compassion—for instance with these lines: "When no one is shouting about the dangers of immigrants, we find it difficult to care about immigration. We rarely notice their suffering until someone is blaming them for ours" (p. 48).

Those two sample quotes offer a glimpse of the powers of observation, humor, and quiet rage that make every page of *This Is Going to Hurt* light up. Above all, it is the lives this book mines that power the author's conclusions woven around the life stories she explores.

We evolved as caring sharers. When we forget this, McNeel reminds us, things go badly. Honesty, kindness, and commitment are not about ethics but about evolutionary survival basics as practiced by all human cultures, at least by the ones that survived. These "moral" attributes are the basics of the human species' longevity and have been for our entire evolution.

Before the era of language, writing, and—last of all—religion, we learned to survive by cooperating. All that the moral teachings of all the religions of the world represent is simply the codification of what we humans already knew about survival—for instance, that loving care of others works best at motivating the loving care by others of ourselves.

According to a story that may or may not be true, the anthropologist Margaret Mead was asked what she thought was the earliest sign of a civilized society. Mead said that the first sign of civilization is a healed human femur. Mead explained that a healed femur is a sign that a wounded person must have received help. Mead is reported to have said, "Helping someone else through difficulty is where civilization starts."

If we are to survive as a species (a big *if*), it will take faith in evolution's truth-telling, Mead-like lessons, and the faith McNeel offers us herein in our continuing ability to help others. She advocates for a renewed willingness to sacrifice for each other in order to overcome the destruction we have wrought against our planet and against one another in the name of religion and various forms of nationalism.

McNeel argues that if religion is to help rather than hinder the civilizing process, then we must reject the cruel "certainties" that coexist with all religious forms of fundamentalism and ideology. The point, she says, is not to argue over *how* we got here but to agree on a better vision of where we want to evolve to now. The implicit manner outlined by the stories and conclusions offered herein reveal a humane project that religious believers, and those who find they are best defined as agnostics and atheists, can all share: what I'll call the theology and politics of Mead's healed femur.

I think that McNeel's book also reflects something of the spiritual mysticism espoused by Saint Maximos the Confessor. His teaching on the meaning of the Eucharist is one example. (Maximos lived in the sixth and seventh centuries and was a monk, a theologian, and a scholar.)

Maximos says that "lovers of God" are granted to "see with inner eyes the Word and God Himself." Maximos might be describing the "inner eye" that McNeel "sees" through in this book, where outward differences disappear in significance compared to the unity all humans have in our shared spirit and aspirations for dignity, care, and love.

Maximos teaches that the soul is granted to "see the Word," who leads it to the spiritual understanding that is "immaterial, simple, immutable, divine, free of all form and shape." In other words, authentic spiritual experience is the exact opposite of intellectually organized theology.

McNeel calls us to the highest sacrament of all: the sacrifice of self for another. The promise of sacrificial mercy she offers is unconditional, based only on faith and love. And that alone is the answer to suffering.

In the book of Hebrews we read of Jesus sharing our suffering, "who for a little while was made lower than the angels, crowned with glory and honor because of the suffering of death, so that by the grace of God he might taste death for everyone" (Heb. 2:9).

Saint Evagrius, also called Evagrius the Solitary (AD 345–399), was a Christian monk and ascetic from Heraclea. Like Saint Maximos, Evagrius captures something of the rule of love trumping theology as well as racial, gender, and nationalistic hubris. For instance, in his commentary on the book of Proverbs he writes, "There was a time when evil did not exist, and there will be a time when it no longer exists; but there was never a time when virtue did not exist and there will never be a time when it does not exist. For the seeds of virtue are indestructible." McNeel seems to think this is true, in that even her stories about suffering eventually point to meaning found in virtue.

McNeel has offered us a prayer for those who suffer and for the clarity of redemption that believers and unbelievers alike may share. There is a name for the redemption this book advocates: empathy. And empathy is (it seems to me) the original virtue Evagrius speaks of. McNeel sums up this historic call for empathy: "it should be clear that in this healing narrative there is no 'us' and 'them.' Just us" (p. 56).

FRANK SCHAEFFER
author of *Crazy for God:*
How I Grew Up as One of the Elect,
Helped Found the Religious Right,
and Lived to Take All (or Almost All) of It Back

Introduction

FUN AT PARTIES

Every party needs a pooper, that's why I'm inviting you.

—"Party Pooper," a 1950s parody song that would later be
made famous by Martin Short in *Father of the Bride Part II*

I f you need to find me at a party, check the corners. Listen for the voice that's
a little bit too intense for cocktail hour, using words with too many suffixes.
That's me. And once you find me, you probably need to rescue the person
trapped there with me, because I assure you, I'm bumming them out.

That's because at most parties people want to know "So, what do you do?"
I'm a journalist.

"Oh really?!?," they say, usually thinking I'm going to spill all the tea on
local politicos. "What are you writing about?"

If I were a more naturally accommodating person, I could mine my port-
folio and come up with a handful of party tricks. I could pull something from
the files entitled "petty gossip" or "heartwarming kid stories."

Instead, I sigh a little and gather up my internal petticoats to step right
into the social shit.

My sparkling banter in recent years has included why we should pay more
for fruit, fetal abnormalities, the mechanics of the GOP stranglehold on Texas,
the failure of the humanitarian parole process for Afghans, and three reasons
a school bus first aid kit should include a chest seal.

So again, if you see me at a party and I'm speaking, you need to come
rescue the person I'm talking to, because they are not having a good time.

Or better yet, I would like to invite you, the reader, into the corner with
me to talk about the issue at the root of all my party fouls, the story I write
over and over again: People are suffering.

People reach out to me with their suffering stories, and I put them into writing, using the best skills available to me. Like all journalists, I put these stories out into the world hoping that thousands of people will read them and be moved. Ideally, I write what I write hoping that politicians, churches, and businesspeople will read the stories of suffering and take action to relieve the suffering. Journalists don't tell you how to act, and we aren't activists ourselves. But every journalist wants their work to inspire action. We don't report on corruption, injustice, and suffering just for kicks. We're trying to give you, the public, the facts and stories you need to change the world for the better.

So imagine my frustration when—after sitting with a young mom and her crying child at the US-Mexico border, interviewing lawyers who clearly outline what needs to happen for this mother and child to have a chance at a stable living situation, and then spending days crafting a story that contains all this information in gut-punching detail—someone responds to my story with an email about how immigrants just need to respect the laws. Or someone in the comment section of a social media post calls the story liberal propaganda and regurgitates some sound bite about the threat immigrants pose to the United States.

Well, if you're the unlucky soul stuck in the corner with me at a party, you don't have to imagine my frustration. You can hear it in my voice. You can hear the weariness and cynicism of someone who spends half of her day listening to stories of profound suffering and the other half of her day listening to people respond to those stories with other stories, stories that justify their lack of compassion.

That's what this book is about: stories of suffering and the competing stories we tell in response that lead us to tolerate that suffering. It's also about the healing stories we could be telling instead, and what those stories would cost us. I'm a journalist who wants people to act on the stories they read and hear. But I'm also a person of faith who believes we have no other righteous choice.

I'll pause here so you can grab a strong drink or a pint of ice cream.

Welcome back.

To introduce the book, I'm going to use some of the basic questions that guide every narrative: who, what, how, and why. Where and when are very important questions too, but if this book is in your hands the answer is, obviously, here and now.

WHO (IS THIS BOOK FOR)?

I assume you're here, reading a book about suffering, because you're either a pretty intense person yourself, or because you're perplexed by the state of the world. Maybe you're a person of faith, trying to figure out where the hope is hidden. Maybe you blame it all on religion. I'm assuming that if you picked up a book by a Christian author about how the stories we tell ourselves about suffering influence our national discourse, then you're probably trying to reconcile something. You've either read *Parable of the Sower* and are sure we're living in the apocalypse, or you watched *Squid Game* and are now alarmed by the cavalier use of phrases like "late-stage capitalism" all over social media. Or maybe you're tired of every family text thread devolving into aggression over Greta Thunberg or March for Our Lives or Joe Biden's electability. (All those examples will be antiquities by the time this book comes out, but I will bet my career on Americans' ability to produce adequate replacements.)

I expect there are some of you, readers, who thought you were pro-life until *Roe v. Wade* fell and women started suffering from sepsis before they could get medical attention in Texas. A few more have probably observed the sweeping teen mental health crisis in the wake of the pandemic and are now rethinking those 2020 social media posts castigating schools for reopening too early. Maybe not. Maybe the last sentence offended you, because you totally stand by that post from 2020.

At least one of you just wants to mind your own business, but now your activist cousin is telling you that silence is complicity and that you are, therefore, a white supremacist. And somewhere there's an activist reading this who doesn't understand why their cousin won't engage in the most pressing issues of our time.

If any of those people is you, then welcome. You are either me or someone I love, and we need to talk about the suffering at the heart of all that divides us. I promise to be earnest, but also humanely humorous. I promise to consider issues from a more productive angle than "Right vs. Left."

I've had a lot of practice looking at suffering from various angles—after all, it's been my job for over a decade. Actually, it's been my job to ask good questions, so more than anything I promise to ask and answer the question, What stories could alleviate both the suffering in the world and our alienation from each other?

Most of the news we read, watch, and discuss has to do with suffering and alleviating suffering. Politicians promise to alleviate our suffering by stimulating the economy and securing our borders. Scientists warn of coming climate catastrophes, but they also have ideas about how to mitigate the effects. We read about crime and punishment, economic busts and relief efforts. Our eyes are glued to images of both devastating poverty and wealth so extreme all waiting or wanting seems to have disappeared.

Even movie reviews, restaurant openings, and fashion are, to a degree, about adding pleasure to our lives to avoid boredom, creating a want and filling it, or helping us avoid the pain of missing out. I'm not going to get too deep into that philosophical quagmire, though. We've got enough going on with just the front page.

We read about a child who was kidnapped, and we want to read about how she was safely returned.

We read about a pandemic, and we want to read about a vaccine.

We read about a heat wave, and we want to know when it will be over.

Problems and solutions. Conflict and resolution. Suffering and relief. That's what engages us in both news and novels.

Often, when I wax on for hundreds of words about school funding formulas or refugee caps or other details I find self-evidently fascinating, my editors write, "Why should I care?" in the margins of my stories. What they are really saying is, "Make me feel the suffering," or "Make me feel the relief."

(News editors are also fun at parties.)

As I've reported on education, immigration, tragedy, and policy over the past twelve years, people have laid their stories of loss bare on the table. Brave people have opened their wounds in public. Early in my career I believed that translating palpable, demonstrable suffering to the page was a mighty act, bringing evidence to the masses. I believed that showing the suffering would inspire someone else, maybe even a lot of people, to alleviate it.

I've also pursued an approach called *solutions journalism* precisely because it seeks answers to our biggest problems and holds people accountable for applying those answers. I was drawn to solutions journalism from day one, because it allowed me to cultivate a more hopeful, redemptive practice. I'm still not fun at parties, but without a solutions lens, I'd probably just avoid society altogether.

The reason I'm still no fun at parties, though, is that every true solutions journalism story acknowledges the limitations of the proposed solution. No panaceas, no silver bullets. So while I am an avid seeker of practical solutions, I recognize that a lot of times solutions are limited by the popularity of a counternarrative, by their political viability, and by the cost they would carry for people who are not willing to sacrifice an ounce of comfort for a pound of healing.

While sharing them is still necessary for an open society, the stories of suffering and solutions alone rarely change minds, let alone hearts, along our most intractable divides. Often, suffering has been already accounted for, and some readers have deemed it tolerable. They've decided it was merited, necessary, or they have simply given it a shrug and a "meh." They have a counternarrative, a story of their own that allows them to remain unmoved. When readers have decided that certain kinds of suffering—poverty, unwanted pregnancy, family separation—are tolerable, then even stories about solutions draw ire. Not only have we, as a society, made peace with some people's suffering, we expect it. Some of us demand it.

But not always. A lot of the responses to my stories seemed to fall into a chasm of politics and apathy, but a couple responses made the leap to compassion or moral outrage, and when they did, when the suffering was deemed intolerable, people demanded it be alleviated at any cost. Readers would demand action in the comment section on social media, followed by prayer hands and lots of exclamation marks. This has happened twice in my entire reporting career: a missing preschooler, and cyberbullying middle schoolers. "Do something!" everyone demanded on social media. Then the moment of agreement was over, and the fights began over who was to blame.

More often, the suffering we describe is deemed intolerable to some and tolerable to others. Half the response is some version of "Omg fix this!" Or the more condescending "Do better." The other half of responses will be along the lines of "The law's the law." Or "They got what they deserved."

We are not inherently and incurably apathetic as a people. But we do have a high tolerance for certain kinds of suffering.

So, when is suffering tolerable and when is it intolerable? The answer to that question has come up repeatedly in my reporting career, particularly on the six subjects we're going to get into in this book: immigration, school curriculum, abortion, climate change, COVID-19, and mass shootings. There are plenty of other topics we could and should discuss; most notably absent from the list here are capital punishment, transgender rights, and universal healthcare. These topics merited more thorough discussion than my reporting could support so far. Each of these topics could be its own book, and the discussion here will not be exhaustive, but with the six selected topics, I have spent enough time in the narratives to capture the heart of things (she said, with more confidence than she felt).

When I pitched this book, I had a complex set of philosophies and frameworks to make sense of when suffering was deemed tolerable or intolerable. I considered nature, human agency, blame, religious hierarchies, power structures, economic liability.

My editor listened patiently before telling me I was overthinking it. Isn't the answer obvious? he asked. It wasn't about some complex formula; it was just about who was doing the suffering. Your suffering is tolerable. Mine is not.

The end.

Just kidding. He's right, of course, but there's a lot of complexity in that obvious statement, hence he agreed to work on this book with me.

HOW (IS THE BOOK ORGANIZED)?

In the first two chapters of this book I explore the elements of stories about suffering. These elements are present in stories that depict the actual suffering and the stories we tell in response to suffering, the counternarratives. Stories are how we make sense of the world, so if a person is telling us a story that makes the world seem unjust or broken, we either accept their story or refute it with a counternarrative that accounts for that perception of injustice or brokenness. Here is a quick example: An immigration attorney claims that asylum seekers suffer as a result of border policy. If you don't want to fix border policy, then you have to counter with a narrative in which the policy is not the problem. You can blame the asylum seekers for their own suffering, or you can claim that the situation would be even worse without the policy.

The first chapter will identify key elements of those stories: judgments, context, and trade-offs. The second chapter will chart the various dividing lines that create the "us" and "them"—a cast of characters—in suffering stories, and the distance we put between them.

Once we've established these elements of suffering stories, the next twelve chapters will examine the hot topics mentioned above—immigration, school curriculum, abortion, climate change, COVID-19, and mass shootings—and explore how the suffering stories we tell determine where we stand on those topics, all of which have divided our country in significant ways. Not every story is the same. Some are character driven, others are driven by the conditions of the world. In some cases, the suffering of some is met with a justification for their suffering, as in immigration. In others, the suffering of one group is countered with the suffering of another group, as in abortion. Sometimes both sides have legitimate concerns, as in COVID-19 school closures; sometimes one side is arguing in bad faith, as in the critical race theory (CRT) curriculum debate. As I looked at the suffering stories for this book, I found, as in all storytelling, the various elements mixing and matching, merging and diverging, becoming more or less significant in different circumstances.

To keep us from thoroughly depressing ourselves, each of these chapters will be followed by another chapter on the same topic, in search of a better story. Think of each chapter pair like an evil twin and a good twin. The evil twin is telling us what's wrong, identifying the business-as-usual entrenchment we find around stories of suffering. Telling these stories isn't evil. I'm just going to call these evil-twin stories because they don't make you feel very good. They're more like the killjoy twin. The good twin chapters will be based on stories from the gospels and the work of people proposing alternative points of view to what is most frequent in our current discourse. As we revisit each hot topic, we will challenge ourselves to look at immigration, school curriculum, abortion, climate change, COVID-19, and mass shootings in light of Jesus's ultimatum in Luke 9:23, "Whoever wants to be my disciple must deny themselves and take up their cross daily and follow me." While I'm not going to suggest that a giant revival or evangelistic effort is the only hope for a compassionate society, I am going to suggest that the gospels contain stories that would revolutionize our public discourse if we let them.

I'd also like to consider how the ethic of cross-bearing might open a new response to the suffering of others and new possibilities for conversation and, dare I say it, democracy. By cross-bearing, I mean taking up the challenge laid out by Jesus in the three Synoptic Gospels, Matthew, Mark, and Luke: if you want to walk in the Way of Jesus, you have to take up your cross *daily*. He's not talking about grand martyrdom, here. He's talking about lives that put our self-interest aside and choose self-sacrificial love in a way that is not rewarded, in fact may be punished, by the power structures of the day. Taking up your cross and following Jesus means not capitulating to exploitation and power hoarding just because that's "the way it's done." And when you realize, "Oh shit, that's going to cost me something"—a promotion, an election, some profit, some power—the gospels are there to agree with you. "Right. Because it's a *cross*."

The goal is not to reduce the Christian life to a series of good works or social positions. To take up one's cross does require us to embrace abundance when the world screams scarcity at us. Spiritual transformation is, on some level, necessary. But a full doctrinal embrace of Christianity is not. No honest person could say that only Christians can be compassionate and just. (In fact, given the current evidence, you might be able to find some who would say the opposite.) There's a need to debate what it means to follow Jesus's Way, or even what it really means to have faith in Jesus, or to be responsive to the Spirit. I'm not going to do that here. Instead, I'm going to suggest that at whatever level you encounter the stories of Jesus and the Way the gospels describe, there's an invitation to dignified sacrifice and nonviolence. I'm not concerned right now with the "Way" being the "Way to heaven." This book is about the Way of life, or *shalom*, a major theme of not only the gospels but also the Hebrew Scriptures they drew from and the letters to the early church groups that expand on Jesus's ministry.

Shalom—wholeness and harmony throughout our interconnected world—is key to understanding what is referred to throughout the good-twin chapters as "healing." By healing I do not mean making everything perfect, finding panaceas, and conforming life to our preferred standards of comfort and control. Healing, in this context, means reconnecting what has been torn apart or exiled, making whole what has been depleted. To heal is to remove barriers between us and respond to suffering with compassion.

Which reminds me. I need to tell you what I mean by "compassion." Here's what I mean: solidarity. As Walter Brueggemann told me during an interview, when you have compassion for someone, you are suffering too.[1] He told me that the Greek word for Jesus's compassion in the New Testament implied a physical upset at what he was encountering. Compassion moves us to act, because it hurts us. It's a solidarity so deep that when it happens to our neighbor it is as though it is happening to us.

Compassion erases the false line between loving thy neighbor and loving thyself.

Maybe the compassion is emotional; we really feel the suffering. Maybe it is ethical; we are disquieted and unable to ignore the suffering. Sometimes it leads us to take direct action to end the suffering. Sometimes it leads us to share the suffering so that it is not compounded by isolation. Compassion works differently in different relationships, but it is always uncomfortable, and it is never inert.

Narrative reorientation is necessary, I believe, because the instinctual position that my suffering is less tolerable than your suffering has led to, predictably, a lot more suffering and entrenchment. It leads to and is fed by tribalism, racism, xenophobia, and homophobia—beliefs and systems that protect me and mine from incursions by you and yours. We also see a gravitational pull around power, because powerful people can protect themselves really well, and so if we hunker down around them, we think we, too, can avoid suffering. Powerful people, who like having us hunkered around them, feed our sense that we are suffering and that loyalty to them and their ideas and products will alleviate that suffering. This in turn makes us even less willing to consider sacrificial love for those not in our tribe.

What a cycle, right?!?

In a series of essays that became his book *The Cruelty Is the Point*, journalist Adam Serwer pointed out over and over again that this sort of safety-seeking mob loyalty was at the heart of Donald Trump's appeal to white, Christian conservatives. It wasn't that they were actually marginalized or oppressed—the so-called Calamity Thesis that Trump had found some actual suffering hitherto ignored by elites—it was that these voters live on a steady diet of fear that they will lose their dominance, which feels like suffering. Serwer writes. "The Republican Party . . . has grown more racially and religiously homogeneous and its politics more dependent on manufacturing threats to the status of white Christians."[2]

Serwer goes on to point out that not only does this kind of mob become cruel in an effort to avoid suffering for themselves, but in the process they actually begin to *delight* in the suffering of others as a group ritual. "Their shared laughter at the suffering of others is an adhesive that binds them to one another, and to Trump. Taking joy in suffering is more human than most would like to admit. Somewhere on the wide spectrum between adolescent teasing and the smiling white men in the lynching photographs are the Trump supporters whose community is built by rejoicing in the anguish of those they see as unlike them, who have found in their shared cruelty an answer to the loneliness and atomization of modern life."[3]

Safety at the center and vulnerability on the margins is exactly how our world doles out suffering. It is a comfortable story. But I think we need something different, and I think Jesus pitched the better story. As a riddle.

The Jesus we meet in the gospels is all about the ironic and mysterious. "Whoever wants to save his life will lose it" (Matt. 16:25). "The last will be first and the first will be last" (Matt. 20:16). "Whoever wants to be great among you will be your servant" (Matt. 20:26).

As someone who really likes to understand the rules of the game, I sympathize with any disciples who were frustrated by this sort of talk. I'm sure there were some. You know who else was frustrated? The rule makers and rule enforcers. The chief priests. The Sanhedrin. Rome.

But wise people ever since have pointed out this sort of radical irony was not a momentary political movement. It was a reorientation of our instincts, and as such, is just as radical today as it was on the edges of the empire two thousand years ago. Jesus wasn't being coy; he was being fundamental. It's up to us to gain clarity by putting the riddle in context.

In every situation we have to ask what it means to take up our cross.

Before the groaning overwhelms us, this is not a call to martyrdom. The gospels' irony isn't just a buzzkill. The writers' main takeaway from the Jesus message was not "You want to be happy, but God wants you sad." The gospels are saying there's something better than the pursuit of happiness. The inside-out approach to suffering isn't neglect of self; it's the reorientation of self. Psychology bears this out, and other wisdom traditions like Buddhism and Stoicism affirm it as well: we're happier when we aren't obsessed with being happy.

Jesus's ironic statements in the gospels assume we do want to save our lives, ultimately. That we are headed somewhere, whether we are first or last. That we do want to be great. He's not on some subreddit debating whether there's such a thing as a truly selfless act. Nor is he inviting us to try to win awards for piety and philosophical consistency. The gospels are saying that redemption is real and felt and experienced by all when we all stop adding to the suffering of others by trying to avoid it for ourselves. We stop over-consuming, we stop denying history, we stop over-policing, we stop hoarding, we stop leaving others unprotected. Instead we conserve, we repent, we repair, we share, and we shelter. This ironic Way is felt and lived, which is why I think we need to look at it in the context of real things happening now, to see what kind of abundance it offers.

At this point your cocktail glass or ice cream bowl probably needs a refresher.

Chapter 1

INTO THE DESERT WE GO

You're crying for somebody's wasted time,
There are sadder stories I've heard.
Get over the wallpaper, baby,
This house is coming down.

—MIPSO, "Wallpaper Baby," singing about either the end
of a relationship or the end of the world

Every marriage has its lore, and at the heart of my marriage is a story about suffering. Blisters, in particular.

A couple of weeks before our wedding, Lewis went on a bachelors' hiking trip to Big Bend National Park with our quietest and most even-keeled friend, Ben. The day before they left, Lewis bought a pair of those strappy all-terrain sandals worn by every granola person you've ever known. These sandals, not yet broken in, would be his only footwear.

"You sure you don't want to take socks just in case?" I asked. In response I got some sort of dismissive muttering about how any extra weight was blah blah blah and the whole point of the desert blah blah blah minimalism, minimalism, minimalism.

Three days into what was supposed to be a five-day trip with no cell service, my phone rang. It was Lewis's number, but Ben's voice. They were coming home early, he told me, and he asked if I could meet them with some first aid supplies for what Ben described as "blisters." I was a little smug, grabbing a few Band-Aid bandages and a half-used tube of Neosporin ointment from my medicine cabinet. Determined not to belittle his blisters nor say "I told you so," I had a handful of supplies and a condescending smile in place when the men got home. Ben entered first, looking relieved to be back but also uncharacteristically frazzled. He glanced at my first aid supplies. "You're going to need a bigger bandage," he said, grimacing.

Lewis limped in behind Ben, and I understood both the relief and the befrazzlement (yes, I made that word up; there was not a suitable alternative). The "blisters" where the straps of the sandals had rubbed away several layers of skin were puddles of gelatinous pus and subcutaneous tissue. The soles of his feet were rubbed completely raw. I tried not to think about the dirt mixing with the blood and pus, but both men had obviously seen things they would never unsee. To this day the blisters are a reference point between us for how Lewis's minimalism is sometimes self-defeating—a point I make repeatedly. But that's for another book. In this book, we're more interested in the blisters themselves, the stories Ben told about them while I bandaged, and the stories Lewis told himself while trudging until he could trudge no more.

LEWIS IN BIG BEND: THE POWER OF STORIES

Human beings are what psychologist Jerome Bruner calls story-making creatures. We collect sensory data through our ears, eyes, nose, mouth, and skin and send them to our brain, which constructs a story about the meaning of the sensory data. New stories are integrated into old stories, which is why we don't (usually) wake up confused about the person in the bed with us, the bright light pouring through our windows, or the sound of cartoons coming from the den at 6:00 a.m. on a Saturday.

Stories are how we know which changes in our environment are threats and which are rewarding opportunities, explains journalist Will Storr in *The Science of Storytelling: Why Stories Make Us Human and How to Tell Them Better.* "We're surrounded by a tumult of often chaotic information. In order to help us feel in control, brains radically simplify the world with narrative," Storr writes.[1]

As the sandal straps sawed through Lewis's feet, he tried ignoring them, looking at the desert vistas instead. He tried telling himself they were ordinary blisters that would go away, that a little pain was worth it, because his feet weren't hot and sweaty in boots with *socks* (Oh, the excess!). He could jump in the river in these sandals and hike in them, simplifying his packing. Plus, he didn't want to be a wimp, and he didn't want to ruin Ben's trip. He told himself stories about beauty, idealism, opportunity, and friendship that allowed him to tolerate the pain. For a while.

Meanwhile Ben was telling a different story that went something like this: "Dude, your feet. We have to go home."

The pain was growing, and eventually Lewis had to acquiesce to his suffering story.

Storytelling determines how we relate to our own suffering, as Lewis found out. It also determines how we relate to the suffering of others. Our story about homelessness will probably determine our response to the woman asking for money on the subway. Our story about school will influence how we react to our child's begging to stay home. Our story about dogs will determine whether we are drawn to pet the Rottweiler or run from him.

We tell stories as individuals and groups, as system builders and culture makers and agenda setters. At our best, the suffering of others informs where we stand on an issue, to help us get clear on the moral imperatives. At our worst, we tell stories to justify where we already are, to muddy what should be clear, to quench the Spirit. People who study narrative—narratologists!—typically talk about its power for good, said Jim Phelan, a professor at Ohio State University and editor of the International Society for the Study of Narrative's journal called, you guessed it, *Narrative*. Stories help us develop a system of ethics that includes caring for one another, persevering through challenges, and other prosocial behavior. But, he warned me over the phone during our interview, "That same power makes it available to be a force for evil. It's dangerous."

Narrative helps us to understand the world and also to *shape* the world, Phelan told me. A person can craft a narrative to persuade an audience that the world is not as they once thought it was but as the storyteller says it is. To persuade a crowd of voters that America needs a change, a politician may tell the story of a country adrift. To persuade investors, a CEO may tell the story of a breakthrough. Such narratives can lead to ethical shifts and shifts in power. A religious narrative of marriage might vest power in the Bible or Qur'an to determine who may and may not marry. A narrative in which marriage is a social institution might shift that power to the government.

During his campaign and time as president, Donald Trump used narratives about immigrants to change the ethical priorities of many evangelical Christians, who in the past had been moved by the individual stories of suffering and had believed in the need to show compassion to refugees.

(This next part gets a little academic, but it's really important, because when we talk about hot-button issues, people often toggle between two different types of stories to justify their positions and persuade us to join them. We will be wiser if we understand that there are big, general truths and messy, particular exceptions. Also, know that I deleted about fifteen hundred words getting further into the ethics and neuroscience of storytelling. So, you're welcome.)

For many evangelicals, the stories that moved them to compassion for refugees and asylum seekers were *mimetic*—they reflected the real circumstances faced by the real people they met or heard about through various ministries. They might learn about a family fleeing war or disaster and, from that specific story, reflect on the biblical call to welcome the stranger. But Trump, Phelan explained, was able to present a competing narrative about immigrants, one that was *thematic*—immigration was a threat to safety and, more potently, culture. Instead of immigration policy that spoke to evangelicals' narrative about compassion and welcome, Trump connected immigration to a white supremacist longing for a white, Protestant America. His anti-immigrant narrative gave people a story—a way to make sense of what could have been seen as illicit longings. You're not racist or xenophobic for wanting fewer Spanish-speaking people in your neighborhood, you're patriotic. You're sensible. You want to make America great again.

I was reporting on pro-immigrant Christian ministries during the Trump administration. I saw them struggle with funding cuts, opposition from former allies, and accusations that they were aiding and abetting criminals. Trump's story worked. White evangelicals had not by and large embraced the thematic story of the special place immigrants have in God's heart. Those who supported refugees were used to welcoming individuals based on individual worthiness. They might have felt sympathy for a handful of people, but most apparently didn't connect that instance to an important biblical theme or to some deep reservoir of their own identities and imaginations. Thus the thematic story was there for the taking, and Trump took it. And while Trump rarely deigned to provide evidence for his wild claims, outlets like Fox News were more than ready to highlight the mimetic stories of immigrants who committed crimes (which they do, on occasion, just like people born in the United States) to back up the anti-immigrant thematic narrative.

Compelling storytellers have to harmonize mimetic stories of people's real, messy lives and thematic stories where a person represents something bigger, Phelan said. Trustworthy stories do not ignore either one. Not every immigrant, pregnant woman, COVID-19 patient, teacher, or shooting victim will fit within our narrative about who is suffering and how. Good journalists learn to avoid the words "all" and "none." Always hedge, my editors taught me, by saying "many" or "few." Within data sets and community statements, we have to allow room for outliers and detractors. Outliers and detractors add nuance to the thematic narrative but don't negate it. Sometimes a Black state representative writes the anti-anti-racism bill. His identity adds complexity to the narrative of how white supremacy works, but the bill itself still prolongs the suffering of children of color whose stories are erased from history.

When we meet people—whether they are our doctors, teachers, house-cleaners, or characters in a news story—whose unique stories contradict what we thought we knew, we are invited to learn more. Learning how a Black law-maker comes to support a racist law teaches us something about how identities are negotiated in the United States. When a teacher opposes a program that would result in a pay raise, we are invited to learn more about that program and its liabilities. We also have the opportunity to look at the thematic idea of "Black people" and "teacher" and remind ourselves that people's lives have a lot of intersections and facets. Not only are the parts that make up the whole quite different from one another, but we almost never understand the whole as well as we think we do.

Potawatomi writer Kaitlin B. Curtis wrote about the pressure to choose between creative writing and social work as an academic field. Poetry and literature invited her into the beautiful particulars of the human experience. Social work exposed the systems and structures that shape community. She could not choose one or the other. "I now understand that to get to the macro, we have to spend time in the micro; to understand how we got here as a whole, we have to understand who we are, each one of us, and the stories we tell."[2]

So as you're reading these chapters about hot-button issues, and your in-ternal debater brings up a story about this one lady you heard about who regretted her abortion, or the good guy with the gun who saved someone's life, remember that those stories do not override the suffering described; they add nuance to it. They pull us back from extremes, give us a healthy tension to resolve. Lewis's experience with his sandals did not lead him on an anti-sandal crusade. But he now knows the difference between well-broken-in sandals and brand-new sandals. He also packs socks.

When a person's suffering story doesn't align to our overall narrative about how the world works, I hope that we can be wise enough to discern whether that story is a shade of gray in a larger truth or evidence demanding we reconsider our position. My reporting puts me up close with many mimetic stories of suffering. But I tell those stories within the context of society's thematic stories, and the thematic stories, more than the mimetic ones, determine who continues to suffer and whose suffering—or perceived suffering—is alleviated.

Some thematic stories make it easier to respond to mimetic stories of suffering with compassion, healing, and acceptance. Other thematic stories make it easier to respond to mimetic stories of suffering with blame, defensiveness, and scapegoating.

ELEMENTS OF CONFLICT

So what are the elements of thematic stories that help us make sense of suffering? Well, probably the same as most other stories. Every creative writing student has learned the elements of story: plot, characters, tone, setting, etc. My daughter recently told me that every story needed a hero, a problem, and a one-true-love.

I am going to modify the eight-year-old's analysis and focus on the conflict and the characters—not the hero and their one-true-love but rather the "us" and "them" inherent in our response to suffering stories. More on that in chapter 2. But first, let's look more closely at how we describe the central conflict. The suffering itself isn't the entirety of the conflict. If it were, then the resolution would be simple: alleviate and prevent suffering at all costs. But the conflict also includes the context in which suffering is happening, the judgments we make as a result, and the trade-offs that would be required to eliminate the suffering.

How Suffering Is Defined by Context

Most of us can intuit when context changes suffering and when it doesn't. Most of us will try to comfort a crying child, but we will also say that the child's cries are easier to endure if they are the result of not being allowed to drink laundry detergent or stick their hand in the fire. Very few people—no people, hopefully?—would make the argument that I should be able to run over a pedestrian, no matter how badly I need to get home to pee.

But not every context is so clear. In the abortion debate, it's easy to see "pregnancy" as the context for a woman's suffering without understanding how different pregnancy is for different bodies in different social situations. When we address climate change, we are often asking people to imagine a context of constant disaster and limited resources, from a context where paying more and driving less feels like suffering.

Dramatic inequality makes it more difficult to discern our context as well. Writer Toni Morrison pointed out how difficult it was to even create a context for what paradise might look like in her 1998 novel *Paradise.* Among other things, paradise is often associated with plenty, with having enough and knowing you will have enough tomorrow. But equating plenty with paradise seemed wrong in a society that had accepted both the perceived "never enough" of extreme wealth and the actual "never enough" of extreme poverty.

"In this world of tilted resources, of outrageous, shameless wealth squatting, hulking, preening itself before the dispossessed, the very idea of plenty, of sufficiency, as utopian ought to make us tremble," Morrison said in a 1998 lecture at Princeton University.[3]

How do we tell a person in poverty that their dreams of a stable home are idealistic, when they watch Bezos, Branson, and Musk race to the moon? We faced these contextual dilemmas when we tried to make COVID-19 protocols in a world where our risks, economic safety nets, and access to healthcare were dramatically unequal. Compelling people to wear masks or stay home depended on the stories we told about suffering, and those stories struggled to account for the varied and unequal contexts Americans live within.

Even writing this book, I have had to consider the tone deafness of proposing we all open ourselves up to suffering in a world where some already suffer constantly and others not at all. I'm still going to do it, because I think the justice and abundance of Jesus's way is radical enough to take care of the cringe, but the cringe was real.

Suffering stories also take place in a social and political context. All the topics this book addresses are taking place in what journalist Amanda Ripley calls "high conflict." High conflict is the backstory to much of what looks like bad faith arguments or inherent enmity. It happens when, as Ripley writes, "conflict clarifies into a good-versus-evil kind of feud, the kind with an 'us' and a 'them.'"[4] In the next chapter we will get more into how high conflict creates a cast of characters in our suffering stories, but it's important to note that high conflict shapes the context or the setting of our suffering stories as well. Partisan division in the United States has reached a point of intractability and demonizing that reduces our ability to problem solve, because it can be difficult to see value in anything that doesn't support our political position.

In this adversarial, high-conflict context, Ripley writes, "The brain behaves differently. We feel increasingly certain of our own superiority and, at the same time, more and more mystified by the other side. When we encounter them, in person or on a cable news channel, we might feel a tightening in our chest, a dread mixed with rage, as we listen to whatever insane, misguided, dangerous thing the other side says."[5]

This isn't new. In his 1881 essay "The Color Line," Frederick Douglass described the high conflict of racism this way: "Few evils are less accessible to the force of reason, or more tenacious of life and power, than a long-standing prejudice. It is a moral disorder, which creates the conditions necessary to its own existence, and fortifies itself by refusing all contradiction. It paints a hateful picture according to its own diseased imagination, and distorts the features of the fancied original to suit the portrait. As those who believe in the visibility of ghosts can easily see them, so it is always easy to see repulsive qualities in those we despise and hate."[6]

In high conflict, instead of responding first with compassion, we may first ask whether the person's suffering challenges or supports my side of the conflict. We will try harder to explain away suffering that makes our position look inhumane. High conflict is a context that shapes our judgments, and thus our responses.

How Judgments Make Suffering Tolerable or Intolerable

When we are responding to someone else's suffering, we often make a judgment about whether their suffering is worthy of compassion. We look at their situation and hold it up to the things we believe about morality, life, justice, and nature.

Did they deserve it? Many people are okay with the death penalty, because they feel people convicted of a capital offense deserve capital punishment. But we rarely believe that innocent children deserve to suffer, not even in the service of some ideal or greater good. I heard that one a lot when I urged people to put their children in racially diverse public schools.

Is the pain natural? The Greek and Roman Stoics, as well as Buddhists, would argue that when we strive against nature, we suffer, and that if we simply accept nature's way, we may have pain, but we won't suffer. We will endure, or move on, or whatever the most placid course of action may be. There's a reason radical acceptance is considered timeless wisdom, but adopting this as your own life philosophy is different from turning a deaf ear to others, and even some Stoics and most Buddhists agree that injustice, if it is within our control to set right, should be addressed. They teach that injustice is not nature's way, and thus alleviating the suffering caused by injustice is in line with nature.

Is the suffering somehow beneficial? Like the dad in *Calvin and Hobbes* comics who says rainy camping trips and diarrhea build character, sometimes we judge that either the end goal will be worth it or the suffering itself is good for the sufferer. This one gets pushed on women a lot, because childbearing is, frankly, miserable for many of us. Either the baby at the end is always worth the pain, they tell us, or the pain serves some sanctifying purpose. So argue the men who will never have to build that particular part of their character.

Hot topics are hot, often, because we don't agree about what's deserved, natural, or beneficial. One person might argue that it is natural to flee a crumbling government and cross a border, that immigrants should not suffer because of it. Another might argue that obedience to the law, including immigration law, is at the heart of nature, and laws should not be broken. Black kids come home from school having experienced racism at school, and we judge that to be wrong. White kids come home from school feeling sad that their white ancestors enslaved people, and some will judge that this is just as wrong.

Our judgments are informed by a lot of different things: religion, loyalty, greed, fear, compassion, ambition. But one of the biggest factors that influences our judgments is the trade-offs that would have to be made if we were to alleviate the suffering.

The Trade-Offs Inherent to Compassion

One of the central ideas of this book is that alleviating suffering requires some kind of trade. It would be great if it didn't, but it usually does. The trade-offs can be personal, like following a diet to avoid a heart attack. They can be interpersonal, like people risking their lives to save their neighbors in a flood.

They can even be transpersonal, like driving less to cut carbon emissions. Sometimes we frame the trade-off as a loss: Whatever money we donate to the food bank or local shelter is money we don't have to spend on what we want. Sometimes the trade-off is an unspoken positive for us: when we don't discuss systemic racism as a society, those who benefit from it get to feel good about the advantages they have.

I was consulting for a nonprofit as they prepared to launch a campaign to end all the systemic inequality in San Antonio's school system. Ambitious. I like it. They called me in to ask about major drivers of inequality. We identified segregation, funding tied to property values, and rigid attendance zones. These are easy policy fixes. We know how to do it.

Then why weren't those changes happening, the executive director asked me. Who was stopping it? Who benefits from the status quo?

I dramatically grabbed the white board marker, pulled up my cardigan sleeve exposing my pale (almost translucent) forearm, and wrote on the board: "White moms."

"This is who is not going to let you proceed," I said, with decades of history buttressing my confidence.

Now, that's not to say there's not enough prosperity to go around. For instance, policy advocates such as Heather McGhee have helpfully pointed out that mutual flourishing for white and Black people is possible. Her work shows how racism has harmed all of society, not just the Black folks it is intended to oppress, and investing in equality would benefit us all. The moms resisting equitable funding aren't (always) using racist arguments. They are usually talking about the overall insufficiency of public-school funding. I have never met a public school that was not trimming their budget. But that underfunding is the direct result of a society that doesn't want to fund people they deem unworthy. Rejecting white supremacy and racist policies shouldn't even be considered a trade-off. And yet if there weren't some cost to giving it up we would see more movement toward properly integrating schools and addressing police violence. Immigration reform bills would get somewhere.

I hear the argument that in an abundance mindset it's win-win-win-win-win-win. But to get to that abundance mindset, we are first deconstructing a system built on competition. So at the *very least*, the cost might come to you as a sort of psychological discomfort as the vision of "the good life" changes from yachts and private jets to a neighborhood where *every* table has enough food. If far-right media and everyone's grumpy uncles are to be believed, such a psychological reorientation might even feel like a war.

Both sides of the trade aren't always equally costly, but we would have to let go of something we're deeply attached to. That thing may be self-righteousness; it may be an economic advantage; it may be a good feeling or nostalgia. It may be a specific right, like, say, one guaranteed by current interpretations of the Second Amendment. In the healing stories chapters, we will ask what would happen if we made that trade.

Sometimes we do have to trade suffering for suffering. In the chapters on COVID-19 and abortion we'll explore those moral dilemmas. But when we consider climate change and the anti-CRT debate, the trade-off introduces an opportunity to assess our relationship to our own discomfort.

Psychologist Todd Kashdan has written books and spoken on numerous podcasts about our addiction to comfort. Similar to the way extreme wealth distorts our understanding of the context of suffering, comfort addiction has messed with our ability to assess the trade-offs inherent to compassion.

On the Hidden Brain podcast, Kashdan extolled the value of discomfort. The podcast host, journalist Shankar Vedantam, introduced Kashdan's research this way, "In day-to-day life, most of us have an instinctive desire to avoid pain. This makes sense. Pain is, well, painful. The problem, however, is that constantly seeking to avoid pain and distress can cause us to lead constricted lives and keep us from reflecting our deepest values."[7]

Science and many philosophies and religions agree that certain amounts of distress and discomfort are incredibly valuable for spurring needed change and building character. But modern society has capitalized on the human desire to avoid discomfort and is constantly suggesting ways we might buy a product or service that will help us avoid discomfort. Once I learned you could pay $1,000 to have someone essentially stand in line for you at Disneyworld, even the Lightening Lane lines seemed intolerable.

When I operate from my addiction to comfort—and, dear reader, I am indeed addicted—I feel like carrying my own reusable grocery bags is a proportional trade for an ocean's ecosystem. Maybe I'm willing to do it, but I'm going to feel like a saint and martyr. And if I don't do it? Well maybe living in a world with abundant fish and sea vegetation isn't worth it to me if I'm constantly having to schlepp reusable bags around.

It's obvious why the trade-off element of suffering stories is where we get most stuck. No one wants to suffer more than they already are, but we tend to make false equivalencies about who is being asked to do what. We tend to tolerate others' suffering far longer than we should to avoid our own. Compassion changes that. It makes another person's suffering intolerable enough for us to make sacrifices of our own.

Which is why we tend to be very picky about who gets our compassion.

Chapter 2

ONE OF US

> *One of us, thought Gamache. Three short words, but potent. They*
> *more than anything had launched a thousand ships, a thousand at-*
> *tacks. One of us. A circle drawn. And closed. A boundary marked.*
> *Those inside and those not.*
>
> —LOUISE PENNY, *The Brutal Telling*

Allow me to tell you a story about what sociologists call the "narcissism of small differences," or, as I like to call it, doctrinal pettiness.

I grew up in a super conservative evangelical church. It was part of the Presbyterian Church in America (PCA), which is the fundamentalist offshoot of the more familiar country-club Presbyterians. We weren't just any fundamentalists; we were snobby about it. But a weird kind of snobby. We were elitist about our theology and hymns. We put a high value on things like debutante balls and high tea, but we were also too folksy for things like science and "the media." As kids we memorized the Westminster Shorter Catechism; as teenagers we were given books and classes on manners and social decorum. On October 31, we replaced Halloween not with some generic, hokey Harvest Festival but with a robust, assertive Reformation Festival.

Meanwhile, my super conservative evangelical high school was of the more charismatic variety. We sang loud praise music and closed our eyes when we sang contemporary worship music at our weekly chapel. Most people lifted their hands as they sang, but I could never muster the gumption. My church was really judgy about overly emotional worship—we kept the Holy Spirit trapped in the Bible like something from a kids' magical adventure movie.

The major dividing line in my life was between those who believed God chooses who goes to heaven and hell (Calvinism, roughly) and those who believed we choose whether to follow God and thus choose our eternal destiny (Arminianism, roughly). Most of the theologically aware people in my high school were appalled by my church's Calvinism, which I vigorously defended. Most of the people in my church scoffed at the namby-pamby, bleeding-heart Arminianism of my high school peers. My friends and teachers in high school said Calvinism was cruel. The adults in my church kept up an earnest debate over whether Calvinists (we Presbyterians) and Arminians (the local Baptist church) believed in the *same God*.

At my super conservative evangelical college, basic Calvinism was taken for granted. Obviously we are totally depraved from birth! Clearly God does the choosing! However, while my home church believed that the "end times" had been inaugurated with Jesus's first visit to earth (Reformed amillennialism, roughly), the college's doctrinal statement maintained that the "end times" were associated with the second coming of Jesus at some future date (dispensational premillennialism, roughly). Among their many critical, earth-shattering, line-drawing, fellowship-breaking, eternally consequential differences: Reformed amillennialists baptize infants and dispensational premillennialists do not—they only baptize people who request it for themselves. The assumption is that adult baptism is reserved for those making an earnest commitment born of a heart and mind fully focused on the death and resurrection of Jesus, and purely from a desire to make Jesus Lord of their life. Well, hormonal, college-age Bekah proved that assumptions make asses not only out of you and me but out of sacraments too.

In my fourth semester of college, I had massive crushes on two young men, a Reformed amillennialist and a dispensational premillennialist. When I was hanging out with the latter, we went to his church and I considered getting re-baptized, since I only had my illegitimate (per him) baptism to my credit. This upset my parents.

The other young man was part of a rebellious little Reformed amillennial sect within the college. When I took New Testament classes with him, he would insist that "we," the Reformed students, sat together on one side of the class to separate ourselves from "them," the dispensational hordes. This upset my friends among the hordes.

Then I went to a nonreligious graduate school, learned about Edward Said's theory of the "Other," and deconstructed my faith to the point that none of the people from my church, high school, or college would probably claim me as part of their religious "us."

"Us vs. them" thinking is not only common but it can also be based on minutiae, as my conservative evangelical upbringing demonstrates. It is harmful when our suffering stories and counternarratives are shaped by such thinking—which they almost always are.

As I recounted in the introduction, I started this project with a complicated calculus for how we decide when to respond to suffering stories with compassion, and when to allow the suffering to continue. I bought a lot of books. Read a lot of philosophy. I found news stories to illustrate my points about justice, teleology, and virtue. Then my editor pointed out that the complicated calculus was unnecessary, because the answer was axiomatic: my suffering is always less tolerable than your suffering. If one of us is going to get punched in the face, I'd prefer it to be you, always you. So instead of a book, I had a cross-stitch.

Fortunately for me and my desire to write this book, how we decide who is "me" or "us" and who is "you" or "them" in broad social contexts is still complex enough to merit exploration. It's not always as simple as deciding which one of us gets punched in the face.

Identity matters. Ideology matters. Agenda matters. Stories matter. The sometimes-malleable, sometimes-rigid "us vs. them" is an important element of suffering stories, along with the context, judgments, and trade-offs we discussed in the last chapter. While those elements explain the conflict of our suffering stories, the "us vs. them" element tells us who we believe to be in conflict. Who counts as "us" and who counts as "them" tells us whose suffering can be ignored, and whose must be addressed. It puts boundaries around our compassion.

As I told people about this book, several people suggested, as my editor had, that I was still overcomplicating things. Aren't all these issues just political issues? Isn't the real "us vs. them" divide in this country between Republicans and Democrats?

I don't think so.

POWER, NOT POLITICS

On the surface, the major dividing line in our country appears to be Republican vs. Democrat. Right vs. Left. This is really frustrating for people who remember a time when you could be "not that into politics" and get along with anyone. They like Joe Biden and *The West Wing*, and they love that photo of

Michelle Obama hugging George W. Bush. These folks are bothered by the overdramatization of political differences, like when social media pilloried Ellen DeGeneres for talking to George W. Bush at a ball game.

I'm advocating for neither a veneer of niceness nor toxic discourse. I think there's a better way to address the injustices and to heal the suffering. To get there, we have to address our real dividing lines, and I don't think left vs. right politics is the way to do it. The absorbing power of politics plays a trick on the eye. It gives the appearance of balance to unevenly distributed power in the United States. Political framing draws us deeper into the illusion that political parties exchanging power is the way to change the world, when hundreds of years of evidence would suggest otherwise. For instance, no political party at any time has been run by Indigenous people, the original inhabitants of the land. Mass incarceration and restrictive border policies have increased under both Republican and Democratic presidents. We should have fundamental misgivings as to whether a government can, by nature, embrace nonviolence.

Political ideologies are consequential, and each of the issues in this book has a political dimension, a political context, but it would be simplistic to say we should just side with a political party. There's so much more going on when we decide where we stand on abortion, immigration, climate change, curricula, guns, and how to handle a pandemic. And if there's not, if you are just siding with your party, I urge you not to. I urge you to be more radical, in the old sense of the word. "Radical" originally meant "from the root." Like the root vegetable the *rad*ish. Find your radishes.

As we consider how "us" and "them" identities affect our responses to suffering stories, I'm not going to bend over backward to show how "both sides" tolerate the suffering of the other. Because power matters in "us" and "them" relationships. If you have power, then the suffering you tolerate is the suffering that will likely continue, and the suffering you don't tolerate is the suffering that will be relieved. I'm also not going to equate the discomfort of the powerful with the deprivation of the oppressed. Not every position is equally valid or harmful. I'm never going to dignify bunk ideas like reverse racism or anti-man sexism.

And I'm going to reference the Trump presidency and Trumpism a lot. I don't see either of those as political entities as much as they are manifestations of identity-driven tribalism and high conflict. I see Trumpism as a sociological movement, a context, not a political "us" or "them." It's a radish. Treating it like a political entity is how most of us in the media infamously misunderstood and underestimated it.

There's another reason I want to avoid political framing: I don't want to activate any thought-terminating clichés. Our political parties have an increasingly cultish appeal, writes linguist Amanda Montell in her book *Cultish: The Language of Fanaticism*, and one cultish feature is the way we use thought-terminating clichés to dismiss arguments and questions we don't like.[1] Current public discourse on the Right and Left is full of thought-terminating clichés—quick, dismissive assessments of something as "woke" (from the Right) or "problematic" (from the Left). We sniff something that sounds like "the other side" and quickly dismiss it. I have to mine my own heart here. I harbor plenty of tribal instinct. I was very reluctant to express frustration with COVID-19 protocols, or to admit that Biden is almost as bad for immigrants as Trump was. I've had to check my cultist tendencies in order to get down to radishes.

I'm not suggesting some milquetoast "third way" in which we all ignore the controversial suffering in the world and focus on our personal piety and growth. I'll get into radical alternatives more in the second half of the book. For now, I'd ask you to try to read what's coming as a human being who wants less suffering in the world and is willing to do what it takes to get there. We're not hunting bad guys. We're just getting deeper into the characters in suffering stories, and not all of them suffer equally.

US VS. THEM: CHOOSE YOUR FIGHTER

As I've been working on this book, I've been helping an Afghan friend of mine try to figure out how to get her family to the United States. We check in regularly, and with fluent but heavily accented English, Hessena regales me with maddening tales about navigating bureaucracy as an immigrant woman of color and a woman wearing a headscarf deep in the heart of Texas. Not just the immigration bureaucracy, either. Registering for schools, getting insurance, filing complaints with landlords—she never accuses anyone of being Islamophobic or racist, but her experiences often leave me fuming anyway.

They would never be so rude to me, I think to myself as she tells me about some dismissive answer she got from some clerk after either the Department of State or the US Postal Service lost her son's birth certificate and passport application. In the *context* of the clerk's busy day, they *judged* that her concerns were not urgent, and not worth the *trade-off* of spending extra time finding her answers. But underlying that internal story they are telling themselves about the conflict is the fact that Hessena is Other to them. They do not see her as an "us," and so if it's not convenient or required to help her, they just don't.

My friend's experience of the world demonstrates just how many overlapping and intersecting "us vs. them" groups can be active in any given situation.

Nation

Growing up as an evangelical in the United States, the nation seemed absolute, real. It had borders and laws and citizens and buildings. It seemed like an inherent "us" to belong to. Then I moved to London and read Benedict Anderson's book *Imagined Communities*, and the Jenga tower of my identity fell.

Anderson's book digs into the idea of nationalism as something slippery, based not on the material of the state (the borders, buildings, etc.) but on the imagined community we construct when we identify ourselves as American or Peruvian or Ethiopian. Nationalism can exist abroad, as diaspora or expats. Nationalism can exist in contested places like Palestine or Kosovo. It is a group of people to whom we feel loyalty, even if we have never met them, because they uphold our language, our economic system, and our laws.

"It is imagined as a *community*, because, regardless of the actual inequality and exploitation that may prevail in each, the nation is always conceived as a deep, horizontal comradeship. Ultimately it is this fraternity that makes it possible, over the past two centuries, for so many millions of people, not so much to kill, as willingly to die for such limited imaginings," Anderson writes.[2]

Who you imagine to be inside the nation matters a great deal. Imagining Black Americans as rightful claimants to the nation would demand reparations. Instead, some imagine a white nation into which Black Americans should feel lucky to be an addendum. Instead of imagining the United States as the "golden door" or the "Mother of Exiles"—like Emma Lazarus invites us to do in the poem "The New Colossus" on the base of the Statue of Liberty—some imagine it as the birthright of Puritans and colonists. To be welcomed in, an immigrant must be productive, must make us richer. They cannot take our jobs or bring in neediness, regardless of what they are fleeing.

We also imagine a set of shared values as being distinctly "us." When a police officer murdered George Floyd, and before that when the US government separated families at the southern border, social media was filled with a common lament: "This is not who we are." It was countered, of course, by people pointing out that the track record of the United States would indicate that racist violence has always been a pretty big part of who we are. It was a discourse split between the imagination of a good and great America, and an imagination of a United States that still has work to do.

When we start to disagree over the core values and ideas that bind the nation—should we be more welcoming, more isolationist, less surveilled, less beholden to wealth—the tension rises, because the imagination, we realize, is a fragile thing, and if we run out of shared imagination, what happens to the nation? Do we cease to be "one nation"? It's happened before.

Race

When we talk about the various dividing lines in America, one stands out above the rest: the color line. Frederick Douglass coined that term, the title of the aforementioned 1881 essay he published in the *North American Review*. In "The Color Line" Douglass takes aim at the way white people could use things that seemed real (physical characteristics) to create an "us vs. them" system (white supremacy) that went far beyond the morally neutral subject of skin color to imagine all sorts of implications for the genetic differences between people, justifying the suffering of millions. That system has proven itself to be harder to eradicate than backyard bamboo.

Douglass saw this, but he refused to accept that nature was the reason racial divisions were pernicious:

> It is claimed that this wonder-working prejudice—this moral magic that can change virtue into vice, and innocence to crime; which makes the dead man the murderer, and holds the living homicide harmless—is a natural, instinctive, and invincible attribute of the white race, and one that cannot be eradicated; that even evolution itself cannot carry us beyond or above it. Alas for this poor suffering world (for four-fifths of mankind are colored), if this claim be true! In that case men are forever doomed to injustice, oppression, hate, and strife; and the religious sentiment of the world, with its grand idea of human brotherhood, its "peace on earth and good-will to men," and its golden rule, must be voted a dream, a delusion, and a snare.[3]

Though ethnic and cultural prejudice has always existed, systemic racism as we know it was invented to serve an economic purpose during colonial expansion. The treatment of Native Americans was also clearly racialized, as colonial conquest was throughout Africa and Asia as well. It was a way of making the original inhabitants less than human so that killing them *en masse* and taking their land would be more palatable to Europeans who believed they'd moved beyond savagery. This, of course, is also how a white "us" justified the generational enslavement of humans, treating them as animal possessions, or "chattel."

Because Black and Indigenous people have the self-possession inherent to human beings, they have pressed the United States toward treating them as such. Non-white people have a strong sense of "us" as they debate the best course of action for thriving in a country where they are treated as "them" by those in power. (I'm breaking with academia here, in which "us" is always the position of societal power and privilege. I'm using "us" as a perspective with potential for resistance.) When Issa Rae said, "I'm rooting for everybody Black," at the 2017 Emmy Awards Ceremony, she was channeling this "us" that has had to fight for its survival in so many ways. But the more Black and Indigenous people lean into a Black and Indigenous "us," the more white people fight to keep "them" from becoming powerful. There was even this one time in the 1860s when white resistance to Black liberation led half the states to leave the United States, and the country ended up at war with itself. Maybe you heard about it.

Violence and suppression continued as Black people became part of the "us" of democracy, as in "*we* the people"—but non-white immigrants demonstrate just how useful a flexible construction of race can be when trying to maintain control of a multicultural democracy. Historians like Nell Irvin Painter and Matthew Frye Jacobson chart the recruiting of Irish, Sicilian, Slavic, and Jewish immigrants, among others, who were once not included in whiteness. Nineteenth- and early twentieth-century theorists were running to and fro trying to explain this scientifically in an effort to preserve the science-ish basis for who could be white and why white was best. Meanwhile the legal benefits of whiteness gave plenty of incentive for the immigrants to alter their surnames, play up their Anglo features, and do their part for the white "us." More voters, more teachers, more business owners would serve as foot soldiers for white supremacy.

Now, I know this has all been historical, and I know the argument that we've erased the color line. Martin Luther King Jr.! The Civil Rights Act! Obama! My Black friends! Fret not—we'll get deeper into that in a future chapter.

Gender

Like race, gender sounds like a difference based in nature. I mean, penises and vaginas, right? But it also builds an "us" and "them" that goes beyond nature. Penises and vaginas really are different, but there's nothing about your genitals that determines whether you wear a dress or pants, prefer to text or be texted, work inside or outside the home. Gender is the story we tell about sex, and those stories have historically wielded a lot more control over our lives than biological sex itself.

Binary, absolutist gender stories are the basis of discrimination against queer people. From conversion therapy to forced celibacy to bathroom bills and debates over marriage, queer people are expected to suffer complete self-abnegation so as not to corrupt a two-gender hierarchy. Straight women have access to power in these male-dominant, binary gender stories, but it is contingent on good behavior. Women are only "us" in a patriarchy if we accept that we are always the lesser "us." We are the "them" within the "us." We are sheltered, welcomed, and given certain benefits, but we will also be required to suffer.

We learn the stories early. I knew it was flirty to pretend to need a big strong man, or worse, a big smart man to help me. I knew the damsel in distress archetype, but I had not made the connection to suffering. Being helpless, weak, and vulnerable is best demonstrated by actually suffering. Gender is the story we tell ourselves about sex, and suffering is part of the story of femininity.

Of course, the fact that cisgender men carry their most delicate body parts on the outside of their bodies never comes up. Their constant vulnerability to crippling pain doesn't inform the kind of medical care they receive. No one withholds pain relief on the basis that men should be used to pain, what with their sensitive bits just swinging around for all the world to bop. No one makes the argument that a man should not be president because one accidental knock to the nuts could incapacitate him during a national emergency. Nor has the risk of being wounded stopped them from going to war, playing sports, etc. They just wear codpieces. Where there's a willy there's a way.

The narrative that women, who are idealized as mothers, inherently suffer more has led to a societal ambivalence toward pay disparities, rape kits that are used to collect but never verify evidence, and the utter dumbfuckery that is finding affordable childcare. A 2002 collegiate primer on social inequality puts it this way: "The frequent conflicts women encounter between their family and work roles account in large part for the extent to which they lag behind in higher-status and higher-paying occupational positions."[4] The assumption is that the woman will sacrifice, and so no one feels the need to help alleviate her suffering through paid leave, job protection, childcare, or *calling Dad first* when the kid goes to the nurse's office at school.

Of course, if there's an ambivalence toward helping women, then there's outright refusal or opposition to providing medical care, legal protection, and social support for queer folks, especially those who are transgender. From gender-affirming healthcare to bathroom usage, transgender people are often used as a convenient "them" whose suffering is more than tolerable to the "us" who believe in a two-gender world with men in charge.

One of the ways the male-dominant, binary gender story maintains its legitimacy, especially in modern democracies, is religion. Suffering ordained by God is always tolerable.

Religion

For some, the idea that religion divides is a big fat "duh." Furthermore, for those who believe it to be nothing more than a collection of fantasy stories, the division and oppression is extra infuriating. The way one might feel if followers of Santa Claus started rounding up followers of the Tooth Fairy and sending them to the gulag.

Whether or not you believe in a God or gods or karma or hell, there are no precepts in most world faiths that mandate "us vs. them" thinking, consolidation of power, or hoarding of resources on earth. Most sacred texts can be read to encourage the opposite. But it's been more advantageous to power-hungry people throughout history to interpret scriptures and teachings as lines drawn around "us," ensuring that there can always be a "them." A "them" whose riches can be plundered, whose land can be taken, whose lives are expendable. Faith, like everything else, is perfectly peaceable until it becomes the justification for someone else's suffering.

Historically speaking, religion has played a role in plenty of bloodshed, but historian Karen Armstrong points out that it rarely worked alone. The idea of religion as a privately held belief or an identity of choice is relatively modern, she writes in *Fields of Blood: Religion and the History of Violence*. As the earliest societies developed, "premodern politics was inseparable from religion."[5]

To move beyond subsistence farming, ancient societies had to divide into food makers and sit-and-thinkers. A little group of people had time to sit on their tushes and invent math, because they could eat food other people harvested. The food makers had to work twice as hard. But to justify the inequality between the food makers and the sit-and-thinkers, humans couldn't be equals. Someone had to have a higher power on their side to justify which suffering was tolerable and which was intolerable.

"Civilization demands sacrifice, and the Sumerians had to convince themselves that the price they were exacting from peasantry was necessary and ultimately worth it. In claiming that their inequitable system was in tune with the fundamental laws of the cosmos, the Sumerians were therefore expressing an inexorable political reality in mythical terms," Armstrong writes.[6]

This is not to say that religion is merely an invention of a society's elite, a tool for seizing power. Archaeologist John R. Hale, in surveying evidence of religion across ancient cultures, concludes that the search for meaning and the divine is a common and primal part of human history. But historians like Armstrong, Reza Aslan, and many others show us how that inherent awareness of something beyond ourselves has been used by people who step in with self-serving explanations or adapt a religious expression to suit the needs of the community. The major world religions have had their wilderness eras, their empire eras, their reformation eras, and their nationalistic eras. Like Taylor Swift, but instead of burning their ex-boyfriends, they burned heretics.

This religious seal of approval on state ambition has persisted in our era. Most religions have their versions of this, but I'm going to focus on Christianity for our context. European monarchs added "by the grace of God" to their ceremonial titles, to remind the serfs not to get any wild ideas. The United States uses its "Christian nation" origin myths to justify its wars.

But where does the bishop stand on the chessboard? Right next to the king and queen. Religion gets power and influence from its coziness to politics and wealth, so it decks itself out in the culture and economics of the nation—"wrapping Jesus in the flag," as Native American theologian Randy Woodley says in his book *Mission and the Cultural Other*.[7]

In evangelism, the act of trying to convert people to a religion, Christian missionaries have been notorious for spreading Western cultural preferences as much or more than they preach the love of Christ. "For over five hundred years Native Americans and other Indigenous peoples around the world have been told by both government and church that their cultures are inferior to those of Europeans, and that they must abandon their own Indigenous cultures in order to be accepted by society and by God," Woodley writes.[8]

Of course, when you are told you must give something up in order to please God, some of what you're giving up will inevitably be wealth. In absolute terms, the Sumerian food makers were wealthier than their sit-and-think overlords. But that wealth transferred hands through religion. This kept up during the colonial age. As Kenya's first president, Jomo Kenyatta, put it, "When the Missionaries arrived, the Africans had the land and the Missionaries had the Bible. They taught us how to pray with our eyes closed. When we opened them, they had the land and we had the Bible."[9]

This partnership between religion and other forms of power is a relic of the past, but it is hardly gone, as Woodley shows, and as anyone can see watching any of the numerous exposé docuseries on abuse and chicanery in modern mega-ministries. Missionary, colonial, imperial logic still maintains complex borders around our national, cultural, and religious identities at home and abroad. Inside the systems, power protects itself from accountability for the suffering it causes, and without accountability to keep it in check, abuses more. Outside the borders, we can explain away any suffering that would, if we were more compassionate, slow down our conquest. When conquering our religious Others, we point to sin or rejection of God as an acceptable reason for the suffering.

DISTANCE AND BLAME: THE SPACE BETWEEN

"Us" and "them" can be created by these identity-based dividing lines, as we saw above. They can also be created by distance and blame in our storytelling.

Even if we are not divided, even if we are emotionally moved by the plight of the sufferer, if we do not feel close enough to them to see them as some part of "us," evidence says we won't act compassionately. We won't do anything about it.

Media scholar Lilie Chouliaraki studied televised coverage of global disasters—events not typically subject to social divisions or high conflict—and found that the distance created between the viewing "us" and the suffering "them" influences whether we take compassionate action.

"Who we care for is a matter of whether or not their suffering is presented as relevant and worthy of our response," Chouliaraki writes in *The Spectatorship of Suffering*. "It is no doubt good to celebrate global unity when it makes its rare appearances, but it is more useful to examine how and why the sufferings we watch almost always evoke pity for those like 'us.'"[10]

The further the *distance* from the sufferer in the story, the more sufferers are seen as "them." Chouliaraki is looking at global distances, but in my reporting I've seen that distance can be created along any of the lines mentioned in this chapter. When sufferers are presented, either on purpose or inadvertently, as "them" and underdeveloped as humans, it creates distance, and the "us" watching or reading their story is encouraged to consume "them" as almost fictional. When journalists don't present a possible solution, we contribute to that feeling of fictionality. "They" are suffering in a world where "we" cannot help.

We see this kind of reporting in the wake of school shootings, when "senseless tragedy" is the bottom line, and the survivors and bereaved parents are simply nameless images of grief. "They" are the unlucky, the people isolated from the rest of "us" by a grief we don't want to imagine.

On the other hand, if we listen to those who are suffering—if we follow their journeys into activism or calls for accountability, their efforts to rebuild lives, their proposed solutions—the observers are invited to join with the sufferers and make an "us." Solution stories, in-depth profiles, and just plain nuance all have the potential to expand "us" and increase the coalition of people seeking to end a particular suffering, be it the ravages of climate change or the spread of COVID-19.

But getting closer doesn't always lead to compassionate action. Sometimes the stories highlight our connectedness as threats to each other. We are not all in this together, working together to find the solution. "They" are the cause of our suffering, be it real, potential, or invented for political gain. Rather than cultivating compassion, we assign *blame*. Media outlets and politicians know this, and they use blame as a way to bring an issue urgently close, to get people agitated and active. Instead of closeness generating a sense of "us," it just makes "them" scarier, like they are on our doorstep. We often call this process "the outrage machine." Having a "them" to blame for suffering—even imaginary or potential suffering—creates a rally point, a common enemy. It makes us conveniently mobile for those who want our votes and our money.

Phew. There you have it. Context, judgment, trade-offs, "us vs. them" framing, distance, and blame. These are the elements we will use to evaluate our current suffering stories and counternarratives, and then we'll shake it up and use those same elements to build healing stories.

Here's the problem, though. I'm not a theologian or a philosopher. I'm a journalist, and my primary journalistic skill set is figuring out what people are saying, whether it matches the facts, and what are the consequences. So if I want to find healing stories, I first have to find someone telling healing stories. The healing narrative chapters are full of big ideas and strong opinions—but none of them originate with me. They are things I've seen, read, and heard while out in the world, picking up facts. They come from scholars, advocates, and experts, many of whom have lived the stories they are trying to heal.

I also, as a born cynic, believe that for this healing to catch on at a societal level will require spiritual renewal and reformation, and I think that's exactly the demand of the moment. We do not need renewed commitment to the old narrative that together we can do anything, conquer anything, progress further. We need a new story that radically redefines our understanding of who "we" are and what we are here to do—a cultural story to fit the solutions offered by those swimming against our current culture of competition, high conflict, and power hoarding.

Fortunately, I know just the guy. Or rather, I'm re-getting-to-know him. Jesus is not the guy I thought I knew, the one who had been co-opted into preserving the old order and keeping the baddies at bay. We don't know much about historical Jesus, but we know he was executed for sedition and that the lasting impression he left with his followers—the takeaway that led them to worship him as the Christ and live lives of devotion to his Way—was a message of humility, healing, and costly sacrifice for the sake of others. So much so that decades after his death, the message that had been so well preserved as to make it into three different accounts of his ministry was this: take up your cross. That seems like someone to listen to if you're trying to radically reorient your stories.

But first, more ice cream! And maybe a nap—that was a lot of frame building.

Chapter 3

IMMIGRATION—THE LEGAL DRAMA

*We were invented. We were chosen by the Government to serve as
scapegoats for all that they wanted to prevent happening in the 1970s.*

—TOM HAYDEN, antiwar protester,
after he was convicted of crossing state lines to instigate
a riot at the 1968 Democratic National Convention

In the wee hours of July 23, 2017, police found a tractor trailer full of dead
and dying people in the parking lot of a Walmart on San Antonio's Southside neighborhood. They died of heat exposure and asphyxiation as they
traveled from Laredo, on the Texas-Mexico border to San Antonio, and were
left in the trailer without water, proper ventilation, or air conditioning on a
100-degree day.

My phone rang at about 6 a.m., as I was the reporter on call that day for
the *San Antonio Report*. As I gathered details about the ten dead and dozens
of injured, I thought that surely this was one of those turning-point tragedies,
one of those stories that grabs us by the collar and demands action. A "never
again" moment.

But near the bottom of that first piece, the first immigration news story I
had ever written, I have a quote from the San Antonio Chief of Police William McManus.

"This is not an isolated incident," McManus said back in 2017. "This happens quite frequently."

In 2022 it happened again. This time fifty-three people, including teenagers, died. The mass casualty events are upsetting, but they are only a tiny
fraction of the South Texas graveyard.

If you've never been to rural South Texas, let me paint a picture for you:
hot, prickly, and lethal. Whatever doesn't kill you will just slow you down so

that the heat can get you. Over three thousand immigrant deaths have been reported in Texas border counties over the last twenty years. The Strauss Center at the University of Texas at Austin estimated that this was likely a dramatic undercount, because of how many bodies are never found or reported on the sprawling private ranchland that makes up most of the region. Private land also makes the journey even more difficult for the people passing through, because humanitarian groups that would usually leave small tanks of water along immigrants' routes can't get onto the ranches as easily as they can access public land along the Sonoran Desert passageways through California and Arizona.

People trying to get to the United States endure suffering that seems surreal to those of us who will never have to climb on top of a train, walk through snake-infested mountain passes, or climb into the back of a sweltering tractor trailer to get where we are going. At respite centers in McAllen and Del Rio, people described their journeys to me, and I would nod along like this was all normal, and then I'd climb back into my air-conditioned car and attempt to patch up the tear in my perception of reality. Because it seems impossible that those two things could exist in the same world: air conditioning and La Bestia. Smartphones and the Darién Gap. It doesn't seem like walking from Ecuador is something that can be done in a world with airplanes.

If it's difficult to comprehend the suffering inherent in their journey, it's also difficult to comprehend the suffering these humans experienced in their countries of origin. And even when we can comprehend it, we're loath to acknowledge how much of the suffering was wrought by centuries of colonialism and political interference. In my years reporting on immigration, I heard multiple women explain their lives and the lives of their children in Honduran towns run by gangs after the United States repeatedly destabilized the national government. After earthquakes and political unrest in Haiti—a country long ravaged by colonial interests and exploitation—people were cut off from their livelihoods. There simply was no way to put food on the table. People don't leave their homes for kicks. Migration is part of human history, because suffering is part of human history. People have always moved from scarcity and violence in search of relief. Whether they come to the United States as formal refugees or claim asylum after crossing the border without documents, whether they have a green card or a visa or Deferred Action for Childhood Arrivals (DACA) or temporary protective status or none of these things, they are part of a regular movement throughout history that carries people away from suffering and toward respite, health, and plenty.

Rather than acknowledge the natural role of migration in response to suffering, and the unnatural role our own country has played in necessitating it, many in the United States are angry about Black and Brown immigrants coming here. Discrimination is worse for those who are in the United States without legal status, or those whose legal right to cross the border and claim asylum is contested by chaotic border policies. For Black and Brown immigrants in some sort of legal limbo, the nation as a whole is ready to tolerate, even inflict, additional suffering.

One man I met had spent the last of his money on a plane ticket from the Democratic Republic of Congo to Quito, and then walked, hitchhiked, and stowed away from Ecuador to Montreal, Canada. When I met him in the dead of summer—immigration stories almost always happen in the dead of summer—he was sitting on the pavement outside a San Antonio bus station, sweat pouring, eyes suspicious. I was reporting for *Christianity Today* and had a Congolese translator with me. We were also sweaty. Eventually he warmed to us a little, and as we texted over the coming weeks, he gave me permission to share his story as he explained his disappointment in the United States. In the various way stations and offices where he waited for aid or opportunity, he heard about Donald Trump's vicious quotes about "shithole countries." He caught the glares of passersby. As he crossed the United States he was unsettled, even as he was physically more comfortable than he had been in Mexico and Central America. He was thankful for a scrappy network of volunteers, many of them church groups, who meet immigrants at bus stations to deliver food and toiletries, but their kindness was the exception, not the rule, for this dark-skinned man who spoke three non-English languages.

His suffering, to most of the people he encountered, and to many of the talking heads on bus station televisions, was far more tolerable than his presence.

THE ROLE OF THE RULE

When people would explain to me their tolerance for the suffering of immigrants, they often speak in terms of law. "The law is the law," one Facebook user helpfully commented under my story about a ministry to teens who cross the border into El Paso each day for high school.

For some, the idea that people are in the United States illegally justifies a lot of suffering. In breaking a law you forfeit rights, and you *should* then suffer. This is not limited to immigrants. Support for the death penalty and prison labor follow the same lines of logic. The law is sacrosanct, and violating it makes your suffering not only tolerable but necessary.

I saw the same argument when the United States began deporting Iraqi immigrants, many of whom had been in the United States since childhood. They were deporting those with "final orders of removal," meaning they had done something that violated the terms of their legal presence in this country. For most, it meant they had committed a felony. The Chaldeans I spoke to had been convicted on drug charges or domestic violence. With an expensive lawyer, many would have been able to fight the charges entirely, or at least resist the original misdemeanor plea deal that made it more likely that their next offense would be charged as a felony. Alas, like the rest of the country, those without money were more likely to end up with criminal records and prison time. Unlike those born in the United States, however, the Iraqis' felony convictions meant an end to their legal right to be in the country.

Starting deportations with those convicted of felonies was politically expedient for two reasons: first, it furthered the Trumpian rhetoric that immigrants are dangerous, and second, people convicted of felonies garner little sympathy in the United States anyway. The Chaldean Christians I met were the quintessential lawbreakers in the eyes of Americans, so it didn't bother anyone that shipping them to Iraq, where many of them did not speak the language and did not know anyone, meant they would be persecuted and killed.

We're not a nation apt to shed a tear for the death of those we fear, and our justice, military, and political systems reflect that.

A 2021 Pew survey found that 64 percent of Americans supported the death penalty in murder cases. That's a high number. But get this: 80 percent of Americans agreed there was a risk of innocent people being put to death. At the same time 63 percent agreed that the death penalty had little if any deterrent effect. These, for me, are WTF statistics. We're not sure if we are killing the right people, and killing them is not keeping us safer, but yeah, why not? Oh wait, there's another statistic that is quite illuminating. More than half the survey respondents believed (and reality supports this belief) that Black people are more likely than white people to receive the death penalty for similar crimes. Assuming that all survey respondents answered both questions, 23 percent of them both supported the death penalty *and* believed it to be administered in a racially biased way! That really does invite the question whether racial bias is a pro or a con for a lot of people. It certainly implies a certain amount of inherent criminality assumed in relation to Black people.

Black and Brown immigrants are living in that context. They are criminalized in the same way as Black and Brown native-born, with the added complexity of how immigration itself is seen to be fraught with lawlessness. Even visa and green card holders and naturalized citizens often deal with ignorant assumptions about their legal right to be in the United States. For those who are in the country illegally, there is simply no sympathy.

Laws are not immutable of course—our laws change, and the policies that shape our immigration system change quickly. But there's a reverence for the system that creates those laws and policies. I meet a lot of people who give a what-can-I-do shrug and say something to the effect of "We obey the law, even if we don't like it." Then they quote Romans 13 and go back to their coffees.

The law *seems* like a neutral, objective arbiter between the undeniable suffering of immigrants and the fear and anger of those who want them out. But even then—even if you accept the law as a dispassionate arbiter—any good movie buff knows there's plenty of drama to be found in the legal system. There's plenty of room for human emotions and agendas among the letters of the law, which is what gave screenwriter Aaron Sorkin so much fodder for his Netflix film *The Trial of the Chicago 7* about the prosecution of antiwar activists during the Vietnam War. The film is based on the true story of the Vietnam War protesters charged with conspiracy and intent to incite a riot in 1968 Chicago, which exposed real conflict within a system Americans like to imagine as dispassionate. I love Sorkin banter as much as the next logophile, but I found the sentencing statements of the actual defendants to be more compelling, and more relevant to the stories we tell about our legal system—in particular, the way the law is used to prune and control the population. That's why the statement of Chicago defendant Tom Hayden, upon his sentencing, introduces this chapter: *We were invented.*

The court system was established by people who migrated here from another continent, seized land, and later developed property and immigration law to control access to the land and its resources. The law reflects our biases about who should be considered a criminal.

If you look at the process by which immigration-related law and policy is enacted in the United States, it is so much clearer that our disposition toward immigrants drives the law, not the other way around. We create the boundaries and classifications dividing us. In 2017 Texas passed a "show me your papers" law, giving police officers and sheriff's deputies the right to ask for legal documents in the course of any interaction, among other things. I wrote an analysis of the bill before it went into effect, and Texas historian Teresa Van Hoy gave one of the best cautions against appealing to the law as our moral compass.

"Those of us who have the law on our side do well to consider who makes the law," Van Hoy told me in an interview for the *San Antonio Report* in 2017. "Laws have a long history of privileging some at the expense of others. Slavery was once legal. Beating women was once legal. Our own Constitution had to be amended to grant African-Americans and women the right to vote. Legality does not guarantee us a hard-won place on the moral high road. If the moral high road is mapped and paved by those who share our assumptions and secure our privilege, we will need to confirm that our choices are not only legal, but also just."[1]

I DON'T LIKE THE WAY YOU LOOK ON ME

Not all immigrants are fleeing violence and poverty. Not all make a dangerous, miserable journey. Immigrants come to the United States in a variety of ways for a variety of reasons, but the great irony is that those who suffer the least are often those the laws of the United States welcome most readily, like my three girlfriends who had been living comfortable middle-class lives in other countries before they married into green cards. It is easier for an athlete or an investor to get an employment visa than it is for a woman fleeing exploitation to gain asylum. It is easier for those who can afford lawyers to sort through their immigration papers than for those who spend years in refugee camps waiting for their case to process without an advocate. There's a direct relationship between a person's ability to pay and how much of their suffering we, as a society, will alleviate. We debate whether immigrants should be able to access public benefits, and we evaluate their eligibility based on whether they will be a drain on the system.

We also express a societal preference for immigrants who look like us or fit who we wish we were. Even with legal status, poor, Black, Brown, and non-English-speaking immigrants are resented and told to "speak English" or "go back where you came from" by their neighbors. They are treated as a threat, as though in welcoming them the United States was downgrading its cultural, economic, and national security. No one treats my blonde-haired, blue-eyed friend Becky that way. With her posh English accent, they all assume she's brilliant and fancy (she is brilliant, but not fancy).

Anti-immigrant sentiment has long been part of the United States, as has the sorting of immigrants into desirable and undesirable based on class, race, and ethnicity. The Chinese Exclusion Act was the first law putting a cap or restriction on the number of immigrants allowed into the United States. It blocked entry for all Chinese workers for ten years. In 1924—the same year that the Labor Appropriations Act created the Border Patrol—the Johnson-Reed Act set quotas for immigration from the Eastern Hemisphere, and during World War II several more restrictions were added. In 1952 the Immigration and Nationality Act refined those quotas to block more immigration from Communist countries and gave the president the power to impose quotas or block immigration from specific countries whenever he or she found "that the entry of any aliens or of any class of aliens into the United States would be detrimental to the interests of the United States."[2]

The version of that law drafted by Senator Patrick McCarran was a reaction to laws that repealed various restrictions, according to researcher Maddalena Marinari: "Guided by a mix of anti-Communism, nativism, and antisemitism, he believed the acts placed the country at risk from 'a flood of undesirables.'"[3]

In the "omg-we-have-*got*-to-stop-discriminating-against-people" flurry of 1960s legislation, Congress added this line to the Immigration and Nationality Act: "No person shall receive any preference or priority or be discriminated against in the issuance of an immigrant visa because of the person's race, sex, nationality, place of birth, or place of residence."[4] That was followed by a period of relatively reasonable immigration policy, though hawkish foreign policy would soon result in floods of immigrants fleeing destabilized nations, only to be deported by Democratic and Republican presidents alike. Noncitizens cannot vote, so there was little at risk in deporting them by the thousands, and it wasn't an issue most Americans had super strong feelings about until someone made a border wall part of the national imagination.

Donald Trump made limiting immigration the cornerstone of his wall-building, America-first plan to "Make America Great Again," and he kicked it off immediately after taking office. In 2017 Trump proved that the presidential power to set restrictions, granted by the Immigration and Nationality Act, overrode the clear discriminatory intent of his "Muslim ban." The next four years would be a wildfire of suffering at the US-Mexico border, one that would carry over into the next administration. As I write this in 2023, Joe Biden has done relatively little to get people out of tent camps in Mexican border cities, because to do so would look like he was soft on border security. Once "secure borders" are in play as a way to prove you're not some left-wing radical, the lives of thousands become a fair trade.

WOULD YOU RATHER BE INVISIBLE OR HATED?

Between Trump's rhetoric, Texas's "show me your papers" law, and the tractor-trailer tragedy in the summer of 2017, it seemed like immigration was suddenly a hot topic. As an education reporter, covering immigration was adrenaline-inducing compared to writing another paragraph about "What is a charter school?" But as I watched the readership numbers on my immigration stories, I found them far lower than even some of my wonkiest education stories.

At a staff meeting, I expressed surprise to my editor. I thought surely something as human and urgent as the indictment of a smuggler and the possible end of DACA would draw eyeballs and the ever-important clicks. "Nah," my editor said. Immigration stories always pull low readership. It's a complicated system with people who feel really far off, who are inherently different, and whose suffering seems so extreme at times we don't know how to relate to it, so we just ogle and move on. We understand the body counts but not the system that creates them.

Trump was actually changing that, at least in some ways, in 2017. He brought immigration closer to us, but the bridge he used was blame, not compassion. He was using immigrants as a scapegoat for nationalist anxieties and creating a common enemy to unite his base. He made immigrants real characters in our communities, but only as dangerous predators. Two years into his administration, I started seeing job postings for immigration reporters. I took one myself. Reporting, I met people who were trying to adjust to this compressed distance, humanitarians getting hate mail, ministries losing donors. While the biggest struggle in their job had once been getting people to care, now it was defending their work against accusations of lawlessness and national betrayal.

Our job as journalists was to keep the distance compressed but to find facts and truth to replace the specters raised by fear and blame. We invited the people themselves, the immigrants, to introduce themselves as often as they felt safe. We made space for them to share their stories, and we hoped that the audience would deem the suffering of their fellow humans intolerable.

But they didn't. Trump's inflammatory presence spilled over onto immigrants, and without it we've regressed to simply ignoring their plight. Because we were never fellow humans. We were always nation and stranger.

GOOD IMMIGRANTS WELCOME-ISH

The "us vs. them" of immigration is not complicated. The "us" with all the power is the nation, the imagined community that is (twinkly stars, wistful face) America. In our national imagination, the country is made up of citizens and immigrants who "did it the right way."

The right way could mean any of the following:

1. You colonized the native lands that are now the United States.
2. You arrived on a boat when showing up without tuberculosis was a legal pathway.
3. You fit into one of the groups deemed advantageous by the United States government.
4. You had both the time and means to navigate the process of legal immigration.

This imagined community is law-abiding and English-speaking. This "us" believes in opportunity for those within its borders and thus can be a little prickly about who gets in. This "us" believes that the violation of national laws cannot be tolerated. It is an injury against the stability of the country. The "us" also privileges the opportunities and prosperity of those already inside the nation over those outside.

Which brings us to "them." In terms of immigration, "they" are those who are not yet here, and who want to be. To join the nation, to become "us," they must in some way enhance the prosperity of the nation and affirm its vision of itself as both great and good. There is a range of opinions on how much assimilation is necessary, but at the very least the nation expects that immigrants will not try to change the nation. They will not change the way we speak or worship, the holidays we observe or what our children learn in school. Oh, and they will be thankful to the point of obsequiousness for the privilege of breathing our democratic air.

An immigrant from Latin America, Asia, or Africa has to do a lot more work—they have to be more of a "good immigrant"—than a European immigrant does to become part of the national "us" because they will never be part of the white racial "us." Nation and race become really hard to pick apart.

Most of all, though, "they" cannot pose any harm or threat. Any harm inflicted from outside the nation is intolerable. It's like it is in a family. I can call my sister an idiot, but you can't. Speaking as the nation, some are very sensitive to the idea that immigrants will take jobs or require public benefits—taking "our" money. Most statistics say the violent crime rate among undocumented immigrants is the same as the general population. But in the logic of a nationalistic "us"—one that prioritizes the nation above all else—thousands of innocent sufferers should be barred from entry to prevent the one of "them" from entering who will cause suffering to one of "us."

Salient to this conversation is the fact that this country was built by people who came from other countries in Europe and killed thousands and thousands of members of the "us" who was already here. It's almost like we're scared that we've set a dangerous precedent, or, more likely, as Nigerian immigrant writer Chigozie Obioma observed in a painful essay about his first encounters with American inequality, "America was the naked man who hid himself behind the cloak he held up for others to take."[5]

We Americans who are pro-immigrant often try to argue our position based on the same self-serving relationship between "us" and "them." When I was the immigrant communities editor at *Christianity Today*, a lot of the pitches that came to me fell along these dividing lines, without questioning them. Support immigrants because they work hard. Because they love America. Because so many are Christians. Support a path to citizenship for those who have proved their loyalty. We were constantly reading statistics and pitches about all the good that immigrants did for "us" and how they were part of a religious "us." Now, I love these stories. I love immigrants living their lives doing great things, loving their families, starting churches. I love to challenge America's assumptions about itself and others. But even more, I was thankful for writers like Karen González questioning the myth of the "good immigrant" criteria by which we determine whether immigrants are an "us" whose suffering should be alleviated or a "them" whose suffering could or should be tolerated. "Subscribing to the rhetoric of the good and bad immigrant reduces our neighbors to objects that either benefit or don't benefit us. But God sees us all as his beloved children and friends. Do we see as God sees?"[6]

THE BROKEN BONES OF OUR IMMIGRATION STORIES

We tolerate the suffering of immigrants—those in tent camps at the southern border and those being made to prove themselves continually by being "good enough" in our schools and cities—because of a story we tell about the United States, who belongs here, and who threatens it.

Context: We are a legalistic society, and we expect rulebreakers to suffer. Some Americans believe that we live in a delicate ecosystem held together by good behavior and market principles, and that non-white, non-Christian, non-American people threaten the good thing we've got going. The desire to preserve America as is—including the laws that guide us—has created a high-conflict context for deciding who belongs in the nation.

Judgments: Change = suffering. Nationalism tells us that those inside the nation *should not* have to suffer for the sake of the outsider. Whether it's lost jobs, cultural adjustments, or the chance of a rise in crime, people inside the nation judge that they *should* be spared.

Trade-offs: There are two trade-offs underpinning our story in response to immigration. First, many believe that the aforementioned judgment is inevitable, that every immigrant allowed in is a native son crowded or somehow endangered. Some immigrants can become less threatening by assimilating, if they are willing to suffer the loss of their home cultures. The other trade-off is the one we make for the good of the nation, when visas, advocacy, and status are afforded to immigrants who will enhance the nation through their economic contribution. Ironically, this means those who suffer most in their countries of origin are most likely to be excluded.

Us vs. them: The United States has a really high view of itself. Our imagined community is not a ragtag crew with mixed motives and rough edges. No, in our imagination we are "a city on a hill" to quote Ted Cruz quoting

John Winthrop quoting the gospels. So to be part of us we have all kinds of criteria. Some are explicit (like legality), some are implicit (like assimilation), and some become clear only once the Black or Brown immigrant has done it all "right" and is still treated as an outsider.

Distance and blame: When no one is shouting about the dangers of immigrants, we find it difficult to care about immigration. We rarely notice their suffering until someone is blaming them for ours.

Chapter 4

AN IMMIGRATION AUTOBIOGRAPHY

And then I see myself as a twenty-seven-year-old, walking through
my neighborhood, remembering the changes I saw on those streets. . . .
We became disposable. We became invisible.

—JARRETT ADAMS, ESQ., reflecting on life after
exoneration in his autobiography, *Redeeming Justice*

In the gospels, Jesus had an admirable repertoire of ways to express his dis-
approval. We have table flipping, dirt scribbling, irony, and insults. But my
very favorite is when he shows total disregard for what the religious leaders
are saying and just does his thing.

I love contemptuous Jesus.

He's on full display in Mark 2, when the scribes appear to be following
him around nitpicking every unlawful thing he and his disciples do. They
critique his forgiving of sins, hanging out with tax collectors, refusing to fast,
and finally, picking grain to eat on the Sabbath. I imagine his response in
Mark 2:25–28 (NIV) to be uttered with all the eye-rolling disdain of someone
who has been pestered until they could be pestered no more. He references a
story about King David, a nice I-know-the-Scripture flex, then drops the mic:
"The Sabbath was made for man, not man for the Sabbath." It's the perfect
brush off, but it's also a summary of Jesus's whole approach to the law: The
point of the law was to protect people and keep them from terrorizing each
other. The Sabbath in particular was to protect people from lives of unrelent-
ing toil. God knows our little exploitative hearts. We will work each other to
death if someone doesn't step in and stop us. Sabbath and practices of rest
were part of the creation story and the story of the Jewish people. Jesus's sim-

ple statement references a story they knew well, while still challenging their hierarchical, legalistic application.

When Jesus reminded them of the story behind this most holy law, I think he was replying to all their complaints about his rule breaking. When he said, "The Son of Man is Lord even of the Sabbath," he wasn't just underscoring, he was telling us to get ready to rethink our rules and laws according to his inside-out kingdom.

The first time we looked at immigration, we considered how the law was used as a buffer between "us" the nation, and "them" the foreigner. Standing at the center of the nation, our laws look just. They look just because they serve us well. But the law looks different from the outskirts of power and wealth. The law looks a lot more arbitrary, like something that might work for you one day and against you the next. We cannot see the full effects of laws aligned to our nationalist center, because from where we stand, the benefits eclipse the injustice. But from where de-centered people stand, there is no eclipse. They see the gaps clearly.

So it matters who tells the story. Legal nonprofits such as the Innocence Project and Equal Justice Initiative also ask us to rethink our laws by telling the stories of wrongly convicted people whose economic statuses and racial identities led to their incarcerations. I led into this chapter with a quote from Jarrett Adams's autobiography because I think it demonstrates the difference we hear when we listen to people telling their side of encounters with the justice system rather than the supposedly neutral position at the center of power.

We have a high tolerance for the suffering of immigrants, because we have put "us" as a nation at the center and crafted laws to protect what we think the nation should be. The laws then dictate the context, judgments, trade-offs, and distance between "us" the nation and "them" the foreigner. But the Lord of the Sabbath has his own story to tell, and the "foreigner" is very close to the center. The inside-out stories of the gospels give us clarity on what it would mean for the law to be made for man, not man for the law, with regard to immigration.

IMAGINATION REBOOT

Like the rest of humanity, the nation of Israel has a migratory history. God was regularly telling them to pack up and go. Individuals like Abraham were sent in search of promised land. Sometimes those instructions were part of a liberation movement, as in Exodus. Sometimes the nation was taken involuntarily into exile. Sometimes they were moving around in other people's territory (I'm with those who doubt the historical accuracy of the great military conquests). But throughout their history, the Israelites always had in their civic and religious code an acknowledgment that a foreigner was to be treated as one of the tribe. "The foreigner residing among you must be treated as your native-born. Love them as yourself, for you were foreigners in Egypt. I am the Lord your God" (Lev. 19:34).

The gospels also place Jesus himself in the position of the foreigner. His instructions to offer welcome are not based on Israel's history, "for you were foreigners," but on *his* identification with those in need, "I was a stranger" (Matt. 25:35).

The foreigner, in the biblical narrative, is not a corruption of group purity. He is not a threat. He is suffering, but he is also entitled to move toward safety anywhere on the earth. The earth, the place imagined communities carve up into states with borders and laws, belongs to God and all of God's people who dwell on it, explains public theologian and immigrant Karen González in her book *Beyond Welcome: Centering Immigrants in Our Christian Response to Immigration*: "In God's economy, the land should never become a source of disillusionment, dispossession, exploitation, enslavement or death."[1]

God's people are called to become the foreigner's new nation, his security and protection. Treating foreigners as native-born means they will be expected to participate as native-born—working, sharing, giving input. It means not assimilation but integration, González points out. We could imagine a community where newcomers do not shed the traditions and culture that give them strength, but they will lend that strength to the flourishing of their new home and neighbors. (I just have to insert one aside here to acknowledge that this is *not* how the colonizing European foreigners behaved upon arrival in what is now the United States. Just saying.) And even if we are different in color, clothing, or tradition, the immigrant's new neighbors will not see the immigrant's suffering as more tolerable than their own. The newcomers arrive with a voice, and they, as part of the nation, use that voice. As they add their celebrations, traditions, languages, and priorities, newcomers do change the nation, the imagined community, because that community isn't based on shared nativity, race, or culture. It has to be based on something more essential, with room for us to mix without dissolving.

Just as inclusion in the just nation is not based on socially constructed things like culture and race, it's also not based on performance. González warns us about the idea of "good immigrants" who never take, never screw up, and are an improvement to the nation. That's not where their dignity and belonging comes from, she writes. It comes from their being created in the image of God. They are as messy as anyone else in the nation, but we, their imagined community, care for them as well as we would care for our brothers and sisters, because that is what they are.

For Christians in the twenty-first century, the world is bigger than it was for anyone in the Bible. We are connected by commerce, militarism, and information to the entire world. An inside-out approach to foreign and domestic nationhood means that we have an "us" that encompasses the whole world, and near to our center are those same foreigners—those stateless people moving away from suffering in search of hope as humans have always done—who need protection and support from the big "us" of humanity.

States will have to work out a lot of details. The United States, Iran, Brazil, Madagascar, and Mongolia have borders and laws and citizen obligations that allow them to function. But the kingdom of God—those operating according to the Way of Jesus—can operate within their states in a way that preserves the dignity and health of all humanity. The imagination of the nation will influence the laws of the state. It will be more complicated in a hyperconnected, globalized era, and there are just more people to deal with—but immigration reform, should we ever really try it, can be guided by a different imagination of a community within a state committed to doing good for the big "us" of humanity moving forever across its borders.

DESIRE PATHS

Now that you have reoriented the fundamental relationship of the nation and the foreigner, turned that "us vs. them" inside out, and enveloped all of humanity in your "us" (oh, is that all?), you can make a new judgment. Instead of judging that lawbreaking merits suffering, we will say, with Jesus—both the one in the gospels and the one executed for rebellion—where the law increases suffering, the law needs to be reconsidered.

You don't have to oppose the rule of law to reimagine how it works in relation to immigration. You just have to rethink how we get the laws we get. In an inside-out story of immigration, we would be less focused on laws that keep others out and more concerned with keeping them safe on their way in.

I live across the street from a university, and all around our neighborhood are apartments, duplexes, and houses full of students who walk to campus. Unfortunately, we also live in a car-based city, so sidewalks are usually incomplete and uneven, where they exist at all. In place of smooth cement, there are what urban planners call *desire paths*. These narrow, moderately straight dirt trails, worn bald by foot traffic, occur where people have made a way outside of existing infrastructure. Smart urban planners use them to place sidewalks, bike lanes, and bus stops.

In our neighborhood, the desire paths show us where a commonsense sidewalk should be and yet is not. They highlight the failure of the city to provide.

When I was at a private college in another city, the two halves of campus were divided by a sports complex, and a diagonal desire path across the outfield of the baseball diamond was an endless frustration to the athletics staff. "Use the marked path!" the athletic director would urge the student body in email after email. But the marked path was ridiculously long. It was made to preserve the attractiveness of facilities used by a handful of student athletes. The desire path from third base to the top of right field was the path of the people.

Both the accusatory paths beaten by college kids in my neighborhood and the defiant paths beaten during my own college experience are opportunities for authorities to adjust their plans and meet the needs of people.

When I look at the southern border of the United States, I see desire paths leading from suffering to relief. I see them in the two-year wait times for an immigration hearing. I see them in the Greyhound bus routes and commercial air routes carrying immigrants from San Antonio to cities across the United States. If we were wise, we would allocate resources accordingly, because desire paths are persistent, as any urban planner knows. We would accept that this is where human history, including our own foreign policy, has brought us, and we would create systems to accommodate, in cooperation with the people who are using them.

As González advocates for hospitality, she makes a distinction between the highly conditional, condescending, even begrudging welcome we often show immigrants and the dignified hospitality of a host who really does want to include and honor the newcomer. "What I am referring to is the kind of hospitality that is truly engaged, where nonimmigrant Christians listen to and learn at the feet of immigrants they have welcomed into their countries—the kind where immigrants are asked to give feedback and evaluate services they receive, including resettlement; the kind where immigrants are at the table and asked to speak into the planning of programs and services that service their own communities; the kind where their dignity and choices are respected and decisions are not made on their behalf."[2]

If we followed the desire paths of those seeking safety and relief in the United States, we would pave the sidewalks of immigration. We would not obsess over the changing face of the outfield. We, the people who get to vote, would reward lawmakers who write and vote for such things; all the while we would use what autonomy we have as private citizens to ease the process through generosity and help.

But to do that, we have to change our relationship to the law. We have to see it not as a tool of the privileged but as a servant of the vulnerable. Where the law is not just, where it is being used to hold up a hierarchy or consolidate power with an elite, we have to challenge it, as Jesus did. If we are really thinking about an inside-out world, we bear the risk of suffering under the law. We break it, or we refuse to condemn those who do.

"Perhaps rather than condemn immigrants who enter the country unlawfully, we should applaud them for subverting an unjust system, for obeying God's laws above human-made ones," González writes.[3]

WRONG SIDE OF THE LAW

In 2019 a federal court found volunteers with the humanitarian aid group No More Deaths guilty of "abandoning personal property" inside a wildlife refuge after they dropped food and water along a known route used by people coming into the United States on foot, a desire path. They were fined $250 and sentenced to fifteen months' probation. It's hardly comparable to deportation or life with a felony conviction, but the punishment also illustrates exactly what we are called to do in a world where the law harms our human neighbors.

Those who find the suffering of immigrants, asylum seekers in particular, to be intolerable will seek to change the immigration system—either working within it, alongside it, or against it. They will take up the cross of self-righteousness and self-protection granted to them by unjust policies.

There are a lot of people who see the suffering and ask what can be done to alleviate it, but the ones who will ultimately do the work are the ones who are willing to suffer alongside. My reporting has introduced me to humanitarian aid workers who spend their days in the hot sun and freezing rain, caring for those living in tents in Reynosa, Mexico, waiting for their numbers to be called to cross the border. I've talked to advocates and lawyers who are making much less money than they could be in other sectors. I've attended protests and read petitions. The ones who are paving the desire paths are the ones who give up time to help navigate a system designed to weaponize inefficiency, making the waits unendurable. They give up money in a system designed to be expensive, weeding out the poor. They give up the secure, cozy feeling we get when we think all our neighbors are just like us. They risk being punished by the same system punishing immigrants who did not come here "the right way," because they believe that the law should be made for humans, not humans for the law.

HEALING OUR IMMIGRATION STORY

Compassion and dignity for immigrants becomes much more plausible if we change the elements of our nationalistic story. It's not that we must disregard the nation, but we do have to reckon with the way we've imagined it—and how that imagination creates suffering. The best part about imagination is that it can change, and so can the elements of our immigration story.

Context: A healing story happens in the context of our obligation to show love to one another—a focus on our truest loyalty. No human being is more or less human than another, but we are of different nations, classes, networks, and net worths.

Judgments: In the context of a global humanity, the paths charted by immigrants are legitimate and deserving of attention. We can judge that any law that increases the suffering of the people with the least to protect them is a law that should be reconsidered.

Trade-offs: If we are going to tell a story that protects the hopeful human activity of immigration, we have to be prepared to trade our legal perfectionism, and that might involve some suffering. Unless you like fines and jail. We have to trade in our safe place under the umbrella of laws that benefit us and harm others, and we have to engage in the dangerous work of solidarity with people outside the law.

Us vs. them: By now it should be clear that in this healing narrative there is no "us" and "them." Just us. That's going to keep happening. It's not that we're erasing differences—it's that differences no longer make a chasm between "us" and "them."

Distance and compassion: Cosmically, we share a tiny speck in the universe. We have all been given one planetary home to share, and those of us who believe in a Creator do not have the right to deny our neighbors access to what God has given to all of us.

Chapter 5

CRITICAL RACE THEORY– THE MOCKUMENTARY

When Mr. Lincoln died in exile in Canada he was a lonely and bitter man, disgraced, abandoned, almost entirely forgotten by history. Today he's only remembered as the man who lost the war of Northern Aggression.

—The alarmingly familiar faux historian in
Kevin Willmott's line-walking mockumentary
C.S.A.: The Confederate States of America

Most of my life in journalism has been on the education beat, or the broccoli beat as we like to call it, because knowing what's going on in education is good for you, even if it's not the most exciting thing to read about. Early on, as a white woman living in a segregated city (as we all do!) I had not really interrogated the gaps I was seeing. I didn't need to, because I'd been given stories about those gaps all my life. They came down to values, work ethic, two-parent families, all the coded ways we talked about the differences in test scores, graduation rates, degree attainment, and ultimately income for white, Black, and Latino students.

So I reported on the fairly bland, fairly bureaucratic efforts to close those gaps using school choice, educational technology, experiential learning, and a whole recipe book full of jargony sauces for the broccoli. Along the way I met a few people who offered me a different explanation for the northside of San Antonio being so much whiter than the rest of the city, and the houses on the near westside being built small and crowded together with no broadband internet access, and the schools on the eastside not having windows. As I met education

57

crusaders on the southside and concerned parents on all sides and kids waking up at 4 a.m. to take city buses across town for Advanced Placement classes, I had to rethink those easy, self-serving narratives I'd believed my whole life.

It felt nice to believe that my family and friends had comfort and options—and a few had considerable wealth—because we were hard workers who took education seriously, while those who did not have money were lazy, immoral, or irresponsible. It is nice to have your material cake with moral icing and eat it at a party with all the authority figures whose approval you were raised to crave.

But the narrative didn't hold up. It didn't match the facts I was seeing on the ground. I was doing the slow work of questioning one narrative and considering another, writing my way through a city carved into over a dozen heavily unequal school districts. Occasionally I wondered if I was just buying into activist rhetoric, because I, like so many other white millennial women, just wanted to be woke.

Then on the four-hundredth anniversary of the arrival of enslaved people trafficked into the American colonies, a better education journalist, Nikole Hannah-Jones, led the *New York Times Magazine* publication of The 1619 Project and explained that our segregated schools were just the tip of the iceberg. The project asserted that racism is baked into the entire American project and denying this only exacerbates the ongoing inequality. Shortly after its publication, Hannah-Jones announced that it would be made into a curriculum for schools.

The official story-keepers of the nation came after the scholarship, the underlying philosophy, the intention, and the politics of Hannah-Jones and the other contributors. The 1619 Project questioned the virtue of a country that claims it is "great because it is good," casting a shadow on its authority. Once the shadow is cast, it calls into question our wars, policing, tax laws, immigration policy, mandatory minimums, and unquestioning veneration of capitalism. But even that bickering over the legacy of slavery was nothing compared to what would happen in the summer of 2020 when protests broke out over the suffering and death of Black people at the hands of police. Suddenly more people started using the term *systemic racism*, and teenagers stuck at home because of the pandemic were making cute social media graphics about defunding the police. Wokeness went mainstream.

The backlash, or "whitelash" as one Black educator called it, was made just as accessible, and soon it was not historians and journalists debating the narrative but everybody all the time. In September, Donald Trump commissioned The 1776 Project to refute The 1619 Project. He issued Executive Order 13950 which prohibited federal funds from going toward the promotion of "divisive concepts," such as anti-racism. Political moderates felt the need to email a bunch of people to explain that their opposition to "the Black Lives Matter agenda" was based not on racism but on the need to be historically accurate. My inbox became a library of hyperlinks and attachments explaining how misguided or insidious, antidemocratic or Democratic, and liberal or illiberal all of this "critical race theory" (CRT) is. "Woke" was now an insult. Try to keep up.

For a while I just watched it all unfold in the streets and op-eds while my reporting on the education beat was wrapped up in back-to-school drama and COVID-19 protocols. Then, across the country, state legislatures—which control the bulk of education—started passing laws banning the use of The 1619 Project, sometimes echoing the language of Executive Order 13950, the new boilerplate for anyone looking to prohibit teaching and learning of how racism has shaped the United States.

One particular piece of borrowed language came to the forefront as states debated and passed these laws, known as "anti-CRT" laws (we'll get to the weirdness of that moniker later). The laws prohibited the teaching that "any individual should feel discomfort, guilt, anguish, or any other form of psychological distress on account of his or her race or sex."[1]

Historians can debate historians about the dates and names in American history. They can ensure accuracy of places and quotes. But history isn't just dates, places, and names, as The 1619 Project clearly showed. History includes suffering stories. To counter the suffering story of Black Americans in particular, but also Indigenous, Latino, and Asian Americans, white Americans needed a suffering story of their own. Wounded national pride was certainly part of it, but in order to make the narrative really compelling, those opposed to anti-racist education had to show that specific people would actually suffer as a result of learning that racism did not have a tidy end date sometime in the 1960s. So they argued that children would suffer if they learned a non-white perspective of race in the United States.

DON'T HURT THE KIDS, OBVIOUSLY

Imagine this scene: My phone rings, and it's a Texas State Representative.

Lawmaker: "Hey Bekah, I have an education story to pitch you. We just introduced a new bill prohibiting teachers in Texas from telling kids they should feel bad about their race."

Me: "That sounds wholesome. I mean, most of the teachers I've met would never in a million years tell any of their students to feel bad about themselves for any reason at all, much less their race, but I've heard some wild stories. In a world where teens still spray-paint the N-word on lockers, crowds chant anti-Latino slurs at basketball games, and young gunmen burst into houses of worship to massacre Black and Jewish worshippers, I can see why some might think we need to remind teachers that racism is . . . bad."

Lawmaker: "Well, right. But the real damage is being done by woke teachers who are teaching white kids that they should feel bad about their ancestors owning slaves. White kids need to be protected."

Me: "What's that you say? The students we're trying to protect from racial suffering here are *white*? Is that necessary? Has there been an incident?"

That scene is imaginary, but it summarizes the general conversation between conservative lawmakers and reporters while Texas's anti-CRT bill was working its way through the legislature.

In most of the places where conservative education groups like Moms for Liberty have been most active, there are claims that anti-racist curriculum will hurt kids. This was at the heart of the infamous Southlake, Texas, conflict, which became the subject of an NBC podcast. The conflict began when part of the community tried to respond to the real, current, documented suffering of children of color within a majority white district, where they are regularly harassed and bullied. Parents, teachers, and students tried to form a diversity council, and all hell broke loose, with opposing parents saying that any anti-racist modifications to curriculum or training would cause emotional harm to their white children.

Writing for the *New Yorker*, journalist Paige Williams reported on the activities of Moms for Liberty in Tennessee. Following their anti-CRT agenda to the statehouse, Williams reported that one assemblyman argued the case by claiming "that he'd heard about a seven-year-old Williamson County girl who had had suicidal thoughts, and was now in therapy, because she was ashamed of being white." Williams notes that no such family ever corroborated the assemblyman's claims.[2]

Look, no sane person can argue that kids should be made to feel personal guilt and anguish over something they cannot help—whether skin color or sexuality or the systemic injustice they were born into. Such suffering should not be tolerated; the judgment is sound. But is it—for the straight, white males on whose behalf anti-CRT bills are written—a necessary battle to fight? Is that really what anti-racist curricula inherently do?

WHY KIDS USE THE N-WORD

We're being told by cultural commentators that our white kids will suffer harm if this stuff is taught in schools, but people of color can already point to real, documented instances of suffering because the country's racial history has not been accurately taught.

Fairly frequently we on the education beat would have to cover some kind of racist incident at a public school—graffiti, viral videos, pep-rally signs. After one such scandal, another education journalist in San Antonio, Krista Torralva, demonstrated the direct link between the offensive words used in a viral video and that school district's long history of exclusion and racism.[3] The systemic issues and the interpersonal ones often pop up in the same areas. Not always, but often enough to take notice.

There's an argument that anti-racist education actually *re-creates* the divisions between white people and people of color. But I think the real concern there is that white "us" doesn't want their kids to see the divide from the perspective of the racial "them." That's got to be what white "us" is trying to prevent, not racial awareness. Because, I promise you, "our" kids know exactly how "we" feel about our racial "them."

Kids are so well tuned to our in-group and out-group sentiments that we don't need to use slurs or even make derogatory jokes for our kids to pick up on the reason we like the schools we like or the reason we protest public housing being built in our neighborhoods. Maybe you didn't teach your kid the N-word or how to draw a swastika, but if you weren't actively working against it, society was teaching them the concept of the N-word, the shock value of Nazism, and the idea of a lesser race to be feared. Moving to a whiter school is a good example of the flight response, so you shouldn't be surprised when your teenage boy shows a fight response. Whenever a story breaks about racist bullying at a "good school," I will rant, to whomever will listen, that the kids are just putting a transgressive, reckless, teenage face on what they learned from their parents. As Krusty the Clown did on the Simpsons, they are "saying the quiet part out loud."

So when a white mom tells me she doesn't want her child to feel bad, citing some right-wing media account of a rogue teacher who did a terrible job with their anti-racism lesson, I have a hard time agreeing that her concern is worth the trade-off of continuing to subject children of color to a school system where the root cause of racist bullying—the thematic narratives of a culture that devalues the lives of people of color—is not addressed.

But I also don't believe that anti-racist teaching has to make white children despair! They will feel the discomfort of growth and facing hard truths, sure. They absolutely should. But good anti-racist teaching doesn't turn white kids inward. Good anti-racist teaching pushes kids toward solidarity. I know it does, because I have done it with my own kids at home through books, marches, museums, and monuments. Together with the kids, we critically reflect on things they hear at school, in movies, or catch in glimpses of news articles. I have visited schools with courses dedicated to anti-racism, where white children thrive. I have read the memoirs of white Freedom Riders and abolitionists. White people who have supported Black liberation efforts are not evidence that systemic racism doesn't exist. They are examples of how white people can choose to behave when they know that it does.

The trade-off between the suffering of white children and the suffering of children of color is the argument we are having on the surface. But it is a proxy conflict for something much deeper, much older. It's not only the suffering of white children motivating the systemic racism deniers, but also—I would say more so—all that would be lost by admitting that systemic racism exists and is ubiquitous throughout our institutions. It's more politically and socially palatable to debate the suffering of the current generation of children, but that conveniently decontextualizes the ongoing effort of white Americans to distance themselves from the suffering caused by racism without alleviating it and to continue benefiting from inequality.

HISTORY CLASS

The nation already had a sprawling, enshrined national narrative when Hannah-Jones came along and challenged it. It already accounted for atrocities of slavery and Jim Crow as either "a different time" or the isolated actions of hateful people. The Civil War and the Civil Rights Movement are held up now as atoning works, victories for the nation in its battle over hate, the end of racial suffering. Even in Executive Order 13950, the Trump administration participated in this revision, citing Abraham Lincoln and Martin Luther King Jr. as great Americans who ended racism in the United States.

No one better represents the ravages of revisionism than Martin Luther King Jr. Pulled from the context of his life and goals, King's words have been used to gloss over the suffering caused by colorblind approaches to history and social studies. His words urging white supremacists to lay down their obsession with racialized power—by, for instance, not judging people by the color of their skin—are now being turned on communities of color, demanding that they stop calling for reparative action, anti-racist curriculum, and acknowledgment of ongoing racial injustice. King's hope in an "arc of history" that "bends toward justice" has been quoted to prematurely declare victory over racism. His reminder that we are woven into a "single garment of destiny" is misused to erase the uniqueness of the Black experience. It's like something Christopher Guest or Kevin Willmott would dream up for a mockumentary, like the one quoted at the beginning of this chapter, *C.S.A.: The Confederate States of America*. Willmott's satirical reimagining of American history as if the South won the Civil War is stomach churning and may be too offensive for many viewers. But for those of us who grew up immersed in the Lost Cause—the mythology of a virtuous Southern goal in the Civil War—it's the kind of upset we need. It also invites the question of how much hasn't changed, and, in ways only satire can, interrogates the competing spirits of American history and culture. I can't recommend the mockumentary to everyone—like I said, it's strong medicine. But I do encourage you to seek out the real King, the radical critic of capitalism and militarism. The King hunted by the FBI, hated by many.

In the revisionist narrative, individual racists, whether grumpy old uncles or mass shooters, are aberrant violations of United States values, rather than being products of it. By contrast, CRT teaches racism as a system that affects our institutions—something we cannot escape as individuals because we have to live, work, spend money, and obey laws in a society still marked by racism. It's a huge threat to the revisionist narrative. But is it being taught in schools?

CRT is a way of looking at laws, media coverage, policies, social movements, and cultural products through the lens of race. It's one of numerous critical theories used to isolate the variables when trying to figure out what is shaping our society. It's a convenient bogeyman because of its origins in academia, which, as we have been told over and over again, is basically a Marxist bot factory. CRT came into popular vernacular through the work of conservative journalist Christopher Rufo, who has made a concerted effort to link any and all terminology associated with anti-racism—for example, *white privilege*, *systemic racism*, and *implicit bias*—back to a specific set of 1960s academic writings by a very left-leaning group of scholars.[4]

The origins of language and terminology are tricky things. Just because a term originated in scholarly work, as many terms do, doesn't prevent it from evolving to encompass a broader or narrower, more adaptable or more specific range of ideas. For example, *pro-life* was coined in the 1960s to refer to cultural nonviolence. *Popular culture* began as an academic term used to study cultural objects that are not limited to a particular institution. Now we use it to mean TikToks and Marvel movies. People generally understand this, but when Rufo and others said that anti-racist concepts had their "origin" in Marxist theory, it also roused Americans' lingering fears about Communists and Satan worshippers embedding ideology into seemingly benign cultural artifacts so that one day our children would hear a code word on the radio that would turn them into a zombie army of horoscope-checkers and labor activists.

So, are second graders really practicing critical race theory as it was originally developed, by conducting rhetorical analysis of case law? No. Are they learning that injustice is something in society, not just personal hateful actions? Possibly. But that's been Rufo's explicit, well-documented endgame all along, supported by conservative think tanks like the one he works for, the Manhattan Institute: to smear Marxism like stinky fish guts all over anti-racist and anti-homophobic teaching. And if the stench of Marxism doesn't get you, how about the fear that your child is going to be publicly shamed for being white?

Eventually we will move on from the CRT boogeyman, but the underlying tactic isn't going anywhere. It's too effective, like a little black dress that pairs well with pearls, diamonds, or a sassy brooch. The little black dress of white supremacy is to convince parents that their kids are being physically, academically, or emotionally endangered by anti-racist efforts.

I can't speak for every training program and teacher doing anti-racist work in their classrooms, but having met hundreds of teachers in the course of my career, it is hard for me to imagine a qualified elementary or secondary teacher delivering the infamous "you are either oppressor or oppressed" lesson cited by conservative activists, without offering the students an understanding of how we work together to end oppression, freeing all of us from those designations. I don't know a single teacher who is trying to make their classroom a more hostile place, because they are the ones who have to be there every day.

Considering teachers as conduits of anti-racist thought brings up a sore question: Who *should* decide what is helpful and appropriate to teach kids about race? Some of the people I have interviewed suggest that anti-racism, social emotional learning, and any kind of value system have no place being taught in school. School is for academics. But wherever you stand on that, you still have to deal with history, and you still have to deal with segregation, and you still have to deal with the history of segregation. That's why schools have always been one of the primary institutions for the battle over the national narrative, said historian Rebecca Brückmann, when I was interviewing her for a story on Moms for Liberty. "They found education, K-12, a very easily accessible and influential arena for their activism," she said. "This is where maternalism really can shine."

From southern textbook committees to northern anti-busing campaigns, white parents, particularly mothers, have always played a role in keeping the shape of racism in schools, even as it became illegal to be explicit about it. Now, Brückmann said, conservative parent groups are recycling some of that "concern for the children" rhetoric to keep kids from learning about southern textbook committees and northern anti-busing campaigns.

She points to the effort to ban a book about Ruby Bridges because it points out that white moms were among those harassing Ruby Bridges on her walk to school. In this lifetime! "They are trying to cover up the work of their mothers and grandmothers," Brückmann said.

No longer wanting to be seen as explicitly racist could be considered a form of progress, but the new insistence on color blindness creates distance between race and the society formed by it. Our discussion of racism as individual animus pulls race, for the first time in the history of the United States, up out of the banks and schools and housing market and federal laws, decontextualizing it and putting distance between racism and the millions of people still living in communities that look remarkably similar to when George Wallace declared, "Segregation now, segregation tomorrow, segregation forever."[5]

If we want to insist that there is no racial "us" and "them," we still have to bridge the lived difference between white and non-white people, supposedly part of the big, colorless "us." We have to explain the suffering.

YOUR OWN DAMN FAULT

So if someone really wants to go with this narrative that the United States is post-racial, that there is no racial "us" and "them," then they have to find someone to blame for the suffering that disproportionately falls on the backs of people of color.

"I've got it!" cries the ghost of racism past, jumping from his rocking chair so quickly that his Veterans of the War of Northern Aggression hat topples from his head. "Let's blame non-white people."

All the other ghosts groan. "No, no, no, we're not doing that anymore. You can't bring race into it," says the ghost with the anti-Semitic tattoo.

"Okay, but hear me out," the first ghost drawls. "What if we say that the suffering—the alcoholism, the drugs, the poverty, the imprisonment—is the reason they are suffering."

The ghosts sit in silence for a moment, trying to figure out if the first ghost has had a stroke. Until, one by one, their faces open up into glee.

"By Jove! You're either a moron or a genius," says a professorial ghost, looking up from his book on the superiority of European literary traditions. "Because that plan makes no sense. Which means it'll probably work."

Obviously I made this scene up, but it is just about as plausible as the way we explain the war on drugs, the removal of Native American children from their families, and the general logic of erasing racism as the root cause of suffering for pretty much everybody who isn't white. When we see Black Americans are five times as likely as white Americans to be in prison, or a high rate of alcohol-involved death in Native American communities, we are quick to attribute it to moral failure—rather than societal failure. We don't look at the history of prisons or alcoholism in the United States. We don't consider those statistics in the context of other statistics that show white people use drugs or alcohol at similar rates. It's a convenient explanation for their suffering, and one that requires no emotional suffering on the part of the nation.

The scapegoating of Black and Indigenous people in particular, but all people of color, really, allows the nation to maintain its virtue. It gives us a good excuse to spare our kids the suffering of anti-racist learning. If the gaps and disparities reveal not a suffering story but a moral failure story, then we are off the hook. Even better, it makes room for well-meaning white folks with nonprofits and ministries to come in and save people of color from themselves and to suggest that the end of suffering lies in following a specific set of ethics. That morally upright living—not social justice—will end suffering.

THE BROKEN BONES OF OUR HOW-TO-TEACH-KIDS-ABOUT-RACISM STORY

The fight against white supremacy, from plantation rebellions to Black Lives Matter, has seen great progress. But the backlash narrative has evolved right alongside it to ensure that white people never have to suffer a loss in moral, social, or economic status. Unfortunately, white folks cling to a moral status that requires us to deny responsibility for the suffering wrought by white supremacy. Many Americans take comfort in racially stratified social statuses—including communities of color. And our economic status is inherently insecure thanks to capitalism run amok and the disappearing middle class, giving us lots of free-flowing anxiety looking for a vessel to fill. Racism was a vessel created to hold just such anxieties, mixed in with the avarice and egotism that keep capitalism striving once bellies are full. The current iteration of the backlash story is the CRT debate.

Context: The current CRT debate gets its intensity and tone from our high-conflict political moment. But the real context is a long history of using school curriculum to control the national narrative about race, and our insistence that there's no experiential distance between white and non-white. It is not only high conflict but old conflict, and fundamental conflict.

Judgments: The judgment that kids shouldn't be made to feel bad about their race or sex is sound. But who is being made to feel bad? The reality is that anti-racist curriculum does not inherently denigrate white children the way that a white supremacist reading of history reinforces the way society still devalues the lives of non-white people. It's up to us to help kids process collective shame and repair (more on that in the next chapter).

Trade-offs: Learning your forefathers were not the Christ figures you thought they were is uncomfortable for all of us. Being disabused of a lie you'd believed for a long time is, yes, painful. Even more uncomfortable, our kids will know better and do better than we did, which means they are going to look back at our choices and have . . . feedback. But continuing to believe the current justifications and explanations for the way wealth, health, and opportunity are allocated in our society will uphold the barriers we put in place long ago—segregation, voter suppression, criminalization, etc. We have to get real about our inability to tolerate discomfort for ourselves while we tolerate generational suffering in others.

Us vs. them: The racial "us vs. them" is sneaky. It plays out in the way individual bodies are treated differently, but it is fostered and maintained by an agenda that promises to protect any body who buys in.

Distance and blame: We see the obvious disparities around us, the distance between racialized experiences of the United States. We reconcile these disparities with our imagination of the nation, and our desire to see ourselves as righteous, by blaming people for their own suffering.

Chapter 6

A CRITICAL RACE THEORY MEMORIAL

For the hanged and beaten,
For the shot, drowned, and burned.
For the tortured, tormented, and terrorized.
For those abandoned by the Rule of Law.
We will remember.
With hope because hopelessness is the enemy of justice.
With courage because peace requires bravery.
With persistence because justice is a constant struggle.
With faith because we shall overcome.

—Poem inscribed on the wall of the Memorial for
Peace and Justice in Montgomery, Alabama

O f all the sanitized Jesus stories we grew up on, probably the most deradicalized is Zacchaeus, the wee little man who climbed up in a sycamore tree. It's a short story about a short man, a tax collector, who climbs up in a tree to see Jesus, only to have Jesus invite himself over for lunch, inflaming the religious leaders and prompting Zacchaeus to make amends and receive a blessing.

As a kid, I was reasonably baffled by the story from Luke 19, understood primarily through the lens of the Wee Sing Songbook, which mentioned Zacchaeus's stature but not his job. Was it radical of Jesus to be kind to a small man? Or was Zacchaeus an "everyman" chosen as the lucky winner of lunch with Jesus—like Charlie, from *Charlie in the Chocolate Factory*? (That story really did shape my childhood religion.) One well-meaning children's choir director explained to us that the point of the song and story was that we were not supposed to let our small stature get in the way of our excitement to see Jesus. You know, in case he ever came to town.

Duke Kwon and Gregory Thompson restore the relevance to the Zacchaeus story in their book *Reparations: A Christian Call for Repentance and Repair*, pointing out that Zacchaeus was a villain's villain, chief tax collector, who had gotten rich off extorting, stealing, and exploiting his people on behalf of the occupying Roman empire. He wasn't just a thief—he was Rome's thief. Jesus would have scandalized the religious leaders when he went to the tax collector's house, but that was just the knife going in. The gospel writer twists the knife when Jesus calls Zacchaeus a "Son of Abraham" after Zacchaeus declares that he will pay back all he has stolen with interest.

"It is easy, upon hearing the Zacchaeus story, to imagine that this offer of restitution was an example of singular magnanimity, a spontaneous gesture of abundant good will," Kwon and Thompson write.[1] But the authors point out that Zacchaeus's pledge was a recitation of the Hebrew law regarding restitution, in Numbers 5:6–7: "Tell the Israelites that when a man or woman acts unfaithfully against the Lord by committing any sin against another, that person is guilty and must confess the sin he has committed. He must make full restitution, add a fifth to its value, and give all this to the one he has wronged."

It wasn't charity. It was justice.

Zacchaeus pledges to give half his possessions to "the poor" as well. Again, it's tempting to see this as an act of private generosity—like donating 1 percent of company profits to charity. But in the context of restitution, not charity, it is more likely that Zacchaeus is acknowledging his participation in a systemic sin. He has contributed to a world in which people don't have enough. He accounts for both the names and faces of those he knows he has wronged and the amorphous ripples of injustice in society.

We will get into the actions Zacchaeus took later in this chapter, but I want to start with his acknowledgment. He doesn't hem and haw about the difference between being a tax collector and a rogue thief. He doesn't throw away his culpability just because there's a much larger problem—the Roman empire—to be addressed. He acknowledges the personal and systemic nature of the harm and connects it to the kind of harm addressed by Hebrew law hundreds of years earlier.

It makes me think of the storytelling work of Bryan Stevenson and the Equal Justice Initiative (EJI), challenging social discourse about race and criminality and rooting their stories in history. At the end of many of their most challenging social media posts, EJI includes this statement: "To overcome racial inequality, we must confront our history." This chapter opens with the poem emblazoned on EJI's Memorial to Peace and Justice in Montgomery, Alabama, which commemorates the thousands of victims of lynching in the United States.

That memorial is one of the few attempts in the United States to confront the suffering stories wrought by white supremacy in a way that doesn't immediately move them to the scrap bin of history. It turns the narrative of the prosperous nation inside out, prioritizing the stories of Black men and women who were violently exploited to build our national wealth and then excluded from partaking in its abundance. The national healing story will emerge from that center. It will be told by Black people, by Indigenous people, and by all those pushed to the margins in a power-hungry system. It is not for me to say what it could or should entail. But, for the white people interested in promoting a healing story—marching in solidarity, if you will—we have some prep work to do. Before we are ready for the healing story, we have to tell a repentance story.

Owning the real suffering story makes repentance possible. White people are going to have to first take up our crosses and die to the myth, accepting the material cost that could come with that, and the shame that absolutely will.

ESTABLISHING FACTS

American philosopher Susan Neiman is a Jewish woman born in the Deep South, a multilayer identity she brings with her in her role as director of the Einstein Forum. Her book *Learning from the Germans: Race and the Memory of Evil* was published in 2019 as the United States was in the throes of a debate that has cycled through alongside curriculum debates: monuments.

Plenty of Germans feel that the shaming over the Holocaust needs to end, Neiman chronicles in her research, that enough is enough with the amends-making. Her quotes and observations sounded similar to things one might hear in an anti-CRT statement at a school board meeting, with one critical difference: German grumblings are not legitimized by the German state. "All told, since 1945, Germany has spent more than a billion dollars building monuments to commemorate the Holocaust and many millions every year to maintain them. What's absent is any monument to those who created and fought the war."[2]

Similarly, in German schools, one would not find any version of World War II history that glosses over the Holocaust. While there can be some debate about what is age appropriate for children to discuss and see, the Germans have taken a stalwart approach to passing on the fullness of their national shame. In 2020 Euro News surveyed how the Holocaust is taught to school children around Europe, in both curricula and field trips. (As a child who grew up going on yearly field trips to the Alamo, I can only imagine what kind of hell would be raised if American school children visited sites less amenable to revisionism, such as, say, Auschwitz.)

> In Germany, the teaching of the Holocaust is the one educational matter
> on which each of the 16 federal states, which set their own curricula, col-
> laborate. It is mandatory in history and civics classes, and will most likely
> also be covered in literature and religion lessons, and possibly in biology,
> art and music. Most schoolchildren will at some point visit a concentration
> camp—although this is not compulsory, except in Bavaria.
>
> On the subject of Holocaust education in Germany, the [International
> Holocaust Remembrance Alliance] says: "Germany knows the magnitude
> of its responsibility for the worst crimes in European history and strives
> to come to grips with this legacy. If there is anything Germany can share
> from its own experience, it is this: facing up to the grim truth of what took
> place is the only path to reconciliation. A past that is not examined fully
> and honestly will remain a burden for the future."[3]

Reconciliation commissions around the world have found that to be true, even where they fall short of the desire to see full reparations. Tangible effects are difficult to get to. South Africa put a hard number on apartheid repara-tions but fell short. Despite a few high-profile cases, criminal prosecutions were difficult to secure in postwar Germany and even more difficult in South Africa. But giving younger generations time to grow up inside the repentance narrative, separated from their nation's version of Lost Cause mythology or their parents' ambivalence about racial others, helps to preserve some progress. The next generation might be bolder in pursuit of amends if they are not so unsure about facts. Of course, that means the facts must live in society as facts, not as propaganda or activism, as conservative news likes to frame it. We must reach a basic agreement.

Canada's Truth and Reconciliation Commission, formed as part of a legal settlement with First Nations and groups of Residential School survivors, was given ninety-four action items, most having to do with recognition and making the truth known throughout the country. The commission findings are available to the public, allowing Canadian businesses, governments, and churches to respond appropriately.

These are not easy conversations, but liberation and reconciliation rarely are. Obviously here I have to point to another thing Jesus said, as he urged us toward lives of repentance and healing: "If you hold to my teaching, you are really my disciples. Then you will know the truth, and the truth will set you free" (John 8:31–32).

We know freedom is the destination, but we still have to wrestle with what we are willing to trade to get there.

THIS IS WHY WE MARCH

Kwon and Thompson assert that owning the past and present racism in our society is essential to the work of repair: "The ability to open one's self to truth, especially when the truth is painful and requires change, is a hard-won skill of the heart. The challenge is greater when one's nation, and even church, embraces romanticized autobiographies that obscure the truth."[4]

Acknowledgment is just the first step, but for many it's a step too far. I'm not going to make any argument for material reparations here (though I'm happy to do that elsewhere if you want to take me out to dinner). However, material reparations are relevant to our discussion on anti-racist curricula and CRT because it is probably the biggest trade-off white folks fear. They resist the suffering stories, because if all the suffering stories are real, the situation clearly demands repair, and we should feel shame until we make those repairs. The financial cost of repair is a huge topic we absolutely should take up, but let's talk for a minute about the shame we seem to fear almost as much.

To make "*if* reparations" more like "*when* reparations," we have to allow ourselves to be discomforted by the pain of others.

White parents, I want to speak for a moment to this fear that our white children will be harmed by seeing themselves as oppressors, or that they will have self-loathing if they believe white privilege exists. Many of us are so uncomfortable with a repentance narrative, we don't know how to talk about it to our children. We take in the activist Instagram and the buzzwords, and instead of understanding the real aims and goals of people harmed by white supremacy, we become anxiously self-focused and perfectionistic. We confuse a suffering narrative fighting to be heard with a repentance narrative. Instead of sitting with the truths being told, letting them take center stage, we start looking for the new criteria for being good white people, which in this context seems to require us to be self-abasing and speak in big grad school words our children won't understand.

But how we see ourselves is really not the point of anti-racism. The point of anti-racism is how we understand the social system we are in and how it affects people. We acknowledge the disparate effects on people based on race, culture, class, generational wealth, and ability. We own the intentionality behind it, and the benefits we have because of it. But then we get to make a choice. We acknowledge how the system relates to us, then we choose how we relate to the system. Do we protest the curriculum with the difficult truths, or do we advocate for it? Do we vote for the candidate who wants to expand unjust laws or the candidate who wants to change them? Do we call the police, or do we march in the streets? Do we choose a school that will give our kids all the advantages, or do we choose a school where our children will be part of a movement to integrate and balance our schools?

Let me tell you another story about a child's ability to see this clearly, and with hope. Because when we decide that the truth is worth the discomfort we might have to accept in trade, we are often surprised to find the discomfort comes with a hefty side of hope.

We have taken both of our children, separately when they were four and six years old, to the Memorial for Peace and Justice in Montgomery. It is a lot for a child to sit with. We followed good guidance on how to keep the experience from being overly salacious or traumatizing, but we felt strongly that they should see it. My son's response to the Legacy Museum was delightfully male. He moved through the museum silently and at a pretty good clip, leaving my husband to wonder how much he was taking in. Then he stopped at a photo mural of Massive Resistance, in front of an image of a white little boy holding a sign saying something like "No Negroes in my school." Loudly, but to himself, he said, "Well, that sucks." And he moved on, bought a journal in the gift shop, and wrote down his thoughts, which he keeps to himself.

My daughter Moira's response has been much more conversational. After the lynching memorial, we went to the Freedom Riders museum and learned about the role that white people can play supporting our Black neighbors in their self-liberation.

Shortly after her trip to Montgomery, Moira participated in our local Martin Luther King Jr. commemorative march and was ready to begin her career as a protester. But she also learned about the 1963 Children's Crusade and how the peacefully protesting children were arrested, blasted with hoses, and terrorized by police.

"Would the police arrest me at a march?" she asked.

"Maybe. Everyone has the right to march peacefully, but getting arrested is always a possibility if people start fighting, or if the police don't like what you're doing," I said.

"I'm not scared to get arrested," she decided. Then she thought a little more. "But they wouldn't kill me," she said slowly, tilting her head like she was reasoning with herself over the risks she would be taking.

"No, they probably wouldn't even hurt you," I agreed.

"They hurt the people on the bridge," she said. "But they wouldn't hurt me, because they would see my light skin."

"You're probably right," I concurred, thinking about Portland's "wall of moms," the white women organized by Black mom Teressa Raiford to stand with linked arms during the police violence protests of 2020 as both a shield and an indictment on the high value placed on white women but not on women of color.

"Everybody has the right to march," she said slowly, reasoning this out. "People with light skin have . . . super-rights."

"This is true," I said. "And it's not fair, is it? That's why we're marching."

Taking up your cross in the context of racial reconciliation means dying to the agenda of advantage and rising to the agenda of justice. It means dying to self and rising to solidarity. If we can be the repenting generation who embraces history early and often, we will spare our children the grief of deconstructing their understanding of society. Instead of a painful disillusionment, we will offer them a future built on truth. But more importantly, we can stop inflicting fresh harm on our neighbors and unite behind their healing stories. My friend Anashay Wright, who runs the nonprofit Disruptive Partners, often tells white people to stop asking what they can do, stop asking Black people to help brainstorm a better future from scratch. Black people have been clear about their agenda, she tells me. It's out there for anyone to hear and read. If white people want to get on board, great.

GUILT, SHAME, AND KINSHIP

I grew up in a southern, evangelical, Reformed church. We talked about sins of the fathers and corporate sins all the time as we bemoaned the secularization of America, the weakening of the family, and all the other ills of the godless 1980s and 1990s. However, during the summer of 2020 protests against police violence moved a handful of white pastors—Tim Keller and Max Lucado among the highest profile—to suggest corporate repentance for the systemic racism of the United States. The blogs! The blogs, they did erupt! Suddenly God was not visiting anything on anyone's children or grandchildren. Then we were focusing on the verses that insist we all stand individually responsible for our sins before God—we do not need to repent for Indigenous genocide, land theft, American chattel slavery, the trail of tears, convict leasing, whitecappers, Jim Crow, lynching, involuntary sterilization, redlining, restrictive housing covenants, Japanese internment, Hiroshima, destabilizing interference in Latin America, massive resistance, anti-miscegenation laws, the war on drugs, or police violence. Unless we did the actual violence, we cannot be blamed.

But where communities have gotten serious about reconciliation, where they have moved from repentance to healing stories, the repentance story had to be adopted corporately. On a 2022 trip to Canada the Pope apologized for the role of the Catholic church in the Indian Boarding School movement.

A papal apology is pretty powerful stuff, but even that is not as instructive as President Nelson Mandela—perhaps the most famous opponent of apartheid in South Africa—apologizing for apartheid as part of the Truth and Reconciliation Commission's efforts in that country. If repentance narratives were about personal culpability and individual guilt, Mandela would be the last person to owe an apology. However, in his role as head of state, he was instead leading the nation to own its collective shame.

I'm squeamish about shame myself. In the theological, somewhat psychological way I usually use it, shame means a feeling of unworthiness. When I feel that I am essentially bad and merit exclusion from the group, I say I am wrestling with shame. But my therapist and others use *shame* differently, distinguishing it from *guilt* in a helpful way. In her book, Neiman discusses this contrast during an interview with Stevenson: "Without shame, you don't actually correct," Stevenson says in the interview. "You don't do things differently."[5]

Guilt, Stevenson explains, is connected to the harm we ourselves have caused. Or the rules we have broken and the consequences of our infractions. It can also be felt in private, and a person can decide on their own how to deal with it. If I knowingly checked the racial makeup of an elementary school to make sure there were no Black kids before enrolling my kid, I might feel guilty. But I don't feel guilty for the racist things my grandfather did.

Shame, in the sense that Neiman and Stevenson discuss it, is social. It is, Neiman writes, "when you see yourself reflected through others' eyes and you cannot bear to let that image stand. To overcome shame, you must actually do something to show others you are not inevitably caught in your, or your forebears' worst moments."[6]

People decry anti-racist curriculum because it puts uneasy facts not just on a government website, or better yet, a nonprofit website, but in the school down the street. If we need it in every school, it implies that the problem is widespread, maybe even, as the Racial Equity Institute teaches, in our "groundwater." It reveals the deepest reason we, unlike the Germans, have a hard time getting our monuments and memorials right: we didn't go astray for twelve weird years. We are centuries deep in shit. We built our nation on stolen land. That nation got rich off human exploitation. Some of us got ahead because others were held back. Germany's shame is acute, and still they struggle. The United States' shame is chronic. We're daunted by the scope of the shame and what would be required to overcome it, so we do nothing but hunker down and wait for people to get over it. The irony, of course, is that without allowing that shame to do its productive work in our society, the next generation just continues the harm.

In her book *Becoming Kin*, Anishinaabe-Ukrainian writer Patty Krawec shows us that in moving toward solidarity kinship with the people our ancestors dispossessed, murdered, and enslaved, we are offered a way out of that shame as well. "You can transform the ancestors who gave you heartache," she writes. "You transform them by writing against the things they, and you, benefitted from, the legacy they gave you, not by transforming them into somebody they are not."[7]

Krawec maps out the inescapably communal and corporate path toward repair between settlers and Indigenous people. Inasmuch as we continue to

repeat the settlers' myths of uninhabited lands, savages, and the civilizing effects
of colonialism, we ourselves are settlers. To the extent that we live unmoved
by the continued demands of Indigenous people and Black people, we are still
living in the settlers' ways. "Being confronted with racist behavior—our own
or in the systems we're part of—is hard, but it's not the worst thing," Krawec
writes. "The worst thing is being unwilling to listen, unwilling to do better."[8]

It's common, of course, for individual white people to insist that they have
not even benefited from white supremacy or the exploitation of people of color.
However, white America collectively has. Remember, each white person has
a mimetic story, our own personal history, but our culture also has a thematic
story, one that does have historical, legal, and financial evidence to support it.
White Americans acquired *a lot* of land without paying anyone for it. White
Americans used unpaid labor to cultivate that stolen land for centuries. Only
in the last fifty years has it become illegal to bar non-white people from owning certain tracts of real estate.

When you put distance between yourself and those suffering stories, you
put distance between you and the people telling them. When we start nitpicking about who exactly did what, who benefited, who deserves, who should be
included or excluded in the repentance story, we miss the point, and we miss
the chance to be part of the healing story that follows. We choose individual
distance when community kinship, as explained by Krawec and others, is an
option. We choose an "us vs. them" when solidarity is available. These communities have not been shy about the amends they would like to see. Have
a look at the NDN Collective or the Land Back campaign, which seeks to
restore public lands to Indigenous ownership. The place where I write—on
the land of the Tap Pilam Coahuiltecan Nation, a consortium of Indigenous
groups colonized by Spanish missionaries through the San Antonio Missions—has a thorough list of initiatives and priorities our city and citizens
can support. Your community probably has something similar. Listen to them.
Listen to the Black teachers in your city, to the Black and Brown candidates
running for local office on police reform agendas. When our Indigenous hosts
or Black neighbors tell us what needs to be done, we have two choices: closeness or distance.

In the nitpicking about who counts as privileged, I see something akin to
the "expert in the law" who approached Jesus in Luke 10, "seeking to justify
himself." The expert engages in what Kwon and Thompson identify as "casu-

istry"—trying to find clever, specific exemptions to moral rules. When the expert correctly summarizes the law as loving his neighbor, he quickly follows up with "Who is my neighbor?" prompting the story of the good Samaritan.

I love the story of the good Samaritan, because it's a blatant redirection as an answer to the question. The expert asks, "Who is my neighbor?" He wants to know the limits of his obligation, to justify the distance and disregard he feels for some people and their suffering stories. If Jesus were just trying to point out that everyone is our neighbor, it would have made sense to tell the story with the Samaritan being the victim of robbery and the Jewish passerby realizing that, even though they are cultural enemies, this is, indeed, his neighbor, and then helping him. That heartwarming version of the story keeps our ethnic and cultural differences at the center. But the gospel tells the story inside out. Jesus makes the Samaritan the hero, the one demonstrating neighbor love. The Jews gathered to listen to Jesus were being told that there's no "us" and "them," only acts of the close-up, linked-arm love that makes us neighbors, that makes us kin.

HEALING OUR RACIAL NARRATIVE

We need to have so many conversations, and it would be so much easier if we would all just agree to have them. We need to talk about material reparation, we need to talk about how we teach kids history, we need to talk about how we are going to address the suffering in the myriad ways it shows up. That's difficult to do with half the country unwilling to even agree to the basic premise that the conversation needs to be had. But if we could agree to a healing narrative like the one shared by Kwon, Thompson, Stevenson, and Krawec, I think we could start.

Context: A healing narrative must live in the context of truth. We have to be ready to accept uncomfortable truths and allow the suffering of others to change our perception of what we thought we knew, relying on love, not perfectionism or power, to keep us safe.

Judgments: For there to be society-wide healing, we must collectively decide that racialized suffering—suffering created by the sorting of people into races with different statuses in society—is unjust and deserving of alleviation. We must judge that whatever advantage or prosperity has been built on injustice will need to be re-evaluated.

Trade-offs: The trade-offs of amends-making will be many, but even as we lay the narrative foundation for those further conversations, we face an initial trade-off, a primer on pain. We must die to the flattering or comforting lies that allow us to leave suffering unaddressed. But if we make that trade-off, we gain hope in return.

Us vs. them: As we become "kin," we become a single "us." This does not, as many of us good white liberals think, mean disavowing our ancestors. To live as kin means taking responsibility for one another, out of love for ancestor and racialized neighbors alike, naming and making repairs.

Distance and compassion: When we stop trying to distance ourselves from the sins of our fathers, and instead understand and repair the damage, we can close the distance between us and our neighbors and work toward a future of mutual thriving.

Chapter 7

ABORTION–THE HISTORICAL FICTION

"We'll make our fortune, boys."

—WYATT EARP, in the predictably problematic
1993 movie everyone loves to quote, *Tombstone*

Sitting in Kendra Joseph's living room, I was flooded by the fixtures of a "happy home." I was surrounded by seasonal Halloween decor, dogs were licking my feet, and a kindergartner in a tutu was offering me juice. Kendra was doing the hostess thing, preparing to tell me her story, but I could already see the suffering in her husband Eric's face. Polite, but intense, he kept a wary eye on Kendra, possibly wondering if telling their story to a journalist was indeed a good idea.

Texas had recently passed a law prohibiting almost all abortions, and the *Texas Tribune* was looking for stories about the less-obvious effects of that bill. The lobbying, marching, press-releasing voices had gotten a lot of play in the run-up to the new law, resulting in two narratives: "bans off our bodies" vs. "life begins at conception." The *Trib* wanted to expand the conversation, to look for the ripple effects of the bill beyond the spotlight.

It was my own birth doula who introduced me to the Josephs. Kendra had, the previous year, terminated a pregnancy in the second trimester when she found out that the baby she very much wanted was suffering from painful, life-limiting birth defects. Her own health puts her in a high-risk category, so carrying any pregnancy to term could be her last. She and Eric sat down and considered a balance of suffering. Should they wait out a probable miscarriage and almost certain death within hours of delivery, to the devastation of their then-preschool daughter, and possible preemption of future pregnancies? Or should they end the life of the unborn baby to minimize the suffering, both his and theirs?

81

She chose to have an abortion in 2019. Several miscarriages later, in 2021, with Texas's new law and a high risk of other complications, Kendra and Eric were worried about trying again. Their eyes welled with tears while they told their story. Eric's face flushed with frustration from time to time, talking about the counternarratives other had proposed, seeking to undermine their confidence that the decision they were making was necessary. My chest grew tight with sorrow for the baby they wanted, and the fear they felt. But even sitting at that table, our voices wobbly with emotion, I could already hear the rebuttals on social media. Like Eric, I knew the counternarrative, and how Kendra's suffering did nothing to unsettle it.

The counternarrative had been my upbringing. I knew it better than I knew every line of my favorite movie in high school, *Tombstone*, a historical fiction based on figures that had grown larger than life and achieved legendary status well beyond their actual historical significance. And that's not completely un-like the abortion conflict, which has made single-issue voters out of so many Americans, mostly because it became an easily dramatized icon for a clash of cultures. Fictionalized versions of Wyatt Earp and Doc Holiday uphold and whitewash the taming narrative of the 1880s Wild West. Abortion exemplifies and oversimplifies the 1980s battle for the soul of America. And like gunsling-ing hero stories do for the settling of the West, the iconic status of the abortion conflict overshadowed the real human suffering involved. In a movie moment harrowingly accurate to both 1880 and 1980, a dashingly squinty Kurt Russell surveys the dusty stagecoach town waiting to be monopolized and says to the other Earps, "We'll make our fortune, boys."

WOMEN OR CHILDREN FIRST?

Abortion-the-issue is a caricature of the actual situations and medical con-siderations of abortion procedures, and way more simplistic than the ethics involved. Abortion is also very common. As a result, ordinary people have a broad range of opinions on the circumstances in which abortion should be provided. Nevertheless, the issue is often framed as a debate, implying two clear sides that disagree on the basis of logic and evidence. The debate framing—the judiciary emphasis on black-and-white "rights," the language of "life" and "bodily autonomy," and the coalition-building role abortion has played in campaign politics since *Roe v. Wade*—has led Americans, with their broad range of opinions based on mimetic stories of people they know, to treat abortion as a political issue, sorting stories into narrow thematic categories of "pro-life" and "pro-choice."

When a journalist calls a pro-choice or pro-life political activist, they will be given a simple absolute judgment: either abortion is the taking of an innocent life and murder is never justified, or a person should never be forced to endure a pregnancy against their will. Surveys show that most Americans hold more nuanced views of the parameters of "never," but people don't get into activism based on their love of moderation.

While *Roe v. Wade* was the law of the land, most of the suffering stories were told by those seeking to overturn it, primarily the Religious Right. Occasionally we would get a glimpse of the medical complexities at play during state-level debates about which trimester could be off-limits, which medical situations constituted an "emergency," or various burdens added to the process of obtaining an abortion. But those nuances were largely drowned out by more absolute narratives, shouted by those who see every tiny decision as a step toward one of the poles. Bodily autonomy is being either preserved or reduced. Lives are being either saved or lost.

It wasn't until the country had a Supreme Court favorable to overturning *Roe* that the generation born after 1970 started to hear suffering stories from people who needed abortions. As Mississippi and Texas passed laws designed to bring down *Roe*, we in the press started getting previews of suffering that had been alleviated by legal access to abortion—women on the verge of sepsis during miscarriage, children who had been raped, people trapped in violent partnerships, and women like Kendra carrying children doomed to short lives of constant pain.

But many of our listeners and readers had already been primed to tolerate that suffering. And those accustomed to having the law on their side, as they mourned the overthrow of *Roe*, continued to fight in terms of rights and autonomy. They quickly turned to a rhetorical strategy that made the childbearer the only human life involved. The actual debate about abortion didn't originate in politics, it originated in medicine and ethics, but because we have been told for forty years that the state must make a trade-off between the life of the adult or the life of the baby, we have an increased tolerance for the suffering of whichever we are not defending. The manufactured political context has made us numb to the suffering of one or the other, and we have given up imagining a world compassionate to the suffering of both.

WHEN DID THIS BECOME AN ISSUE?

The burden placed on childbearing women has been the subject of discussion since literally "in the beginning." Or at least two chapters later when Eve was told that having babies would be painful. Painful is only the half of it though. Having children is dangerous. You know that book *What to Expect When You're Expecting*? Well, if it had been written anytime before the 1920s it probably would have been just a single page: "Expect to die, because you might. If you don't, call your mom and ask her what to do. Unless she died in childbirth, which she might have."

I want to make a quick note that up until now, I've tried to be careful to use gender-neutral terms for pregnancy, because trans men and nonbinary and intersex people do get pregnant, and they do seek abortions. As we are talking about the historical context of abortion, however, I am going to use *women* and feminine pronouns more often, because that has been the predominant context of the history of birth and abortion. The vast majority of birthing people are women, and thus the status of women in patriarchal systems is germane to the birth and to abortion as a social issue.

Even now, when the risk of dying is much, much lower, it does still happen, in damning racial disproportion, as do catastrophic injuries. People get diabetes while pregnant. Preeclampsia, frequently fatal in previous generations, can damage the liver and kidneys. Some are violently ill for the entire nine months of pregnancy, to the point of needing intravenous fluids. Even those of us with "normal" deliveries were often millimeters away from life-altering complications. Had it not been for the top-notch surgeon on call the night I had my son, I would have had to catheterize myself in order to pee *for the rest of my life*. Then there are the statistics on increased poverty for single mothers and intimate partner homicide. Being pregnant, having a baby, and raising a child are not always the blessed events we'd like them to be.

In the mid-1800s many states had antiabortion laws on the books. But, as Marvin Olasky reported for *Christianity Today*, such laws were rarely enforced.[1] Olasky chalks this up to nineteenth-century America already embracing a culture of death, but I see it as a sign that judges and juries knew that pregnancy was socially, ethically, and economically complicated, to say nothing of the physical dangers. It was highly likely that judges and juries in the nineteenth century had seen those dangers play out close to home. In a world where pregnancy had a mortality rate between five hundred and a thousand of every hundred thousand, there would have to be reasonable debate about whether or not a woman could end a pregnancy. And for a long time, even as medicine advanced, there was such reasonable debate.

This was a lively, multifaceted conversation, because there were also multiple viewpoints on fetal development. Reform Jews believed that life begins at breath. Catholics believed it begins at conception. Protestants were sort of all over the map before the 1970s, and most considered various factors when weighing in on abortion and whether it was ethical in specific cases. As genetic testing has advanced alongside lifesaving medical procedures, there's another conversation society needs to have about unborn children with severe disabilities, life-limiting conditions, and chromosomal mutations. We need to have clear-eyed, ongoing ethical guidance on which kinds of interventions are compassionate and which are based on a particular opinion about quality of life. Speaking of quality of life, we need to talk about whether something other than a heartbeat (either the mother's or the child's) should be taken into consideration. Lots of people who do not support abortion also want to support pregnant women, so we need a nonpartisan debate about what actually is and is not helpful. We need to talk about a lot of things, but that conversation is really hard to have when activists and politicians want to define words that were medical and ethical long before they were political. Abortion itself is a medical term for a miscarriage. I'll never forget the shock of looking at the paperwork from the obstetrician's office after I'd had a miscarriage and seeing "spontaneous abortion" listed as the reason for my visit. For a woman who'd been raised on pro-life rhetoric, it was a weird moment.

Our ability to discuss and debate the medical ethics of childbirth changed when abortion became a powerful coalition-building issue for the Moral Majority, a moment Dartmouth historian Randall Balmer documents in his book *Bad Faith: Race and the Rise of the Religious Right*.[2] Since the Catholics weren't wholly on board with segregation and women weren't super activated by hawkishness in the Cold War, conservatives needed a moral rallying point to deliver votes.

In the Religious Right, politicians found a vote-producing dairy cow, and abortion was the ring in its nose. They could guide her wherever they wanted to go, to any primary or gubernatorial race for a politician to fill up his vote bucket with those creamy pro-life votes. But for the ring to stay relevant, it has to work post-*Roe*. So now that *Dobbs v. Jackson Women's Health Organization* has replaced *Roe*, making abortion a state-by-state issue, red-state politicians are in a race to the right to establish themselves as the most pro-life.

Courts have long taken up investigations into miscarriage and stillbirth, suspecting that women purposefully induce them, and those watching conservative state legislatures expect such investigations will increase. As doctors struggle to figure out where they can and cannot legally intervene, imminent death has become the only reliable measure of a "health risk." It's a chaotic time to have an impregnable uterus. Or to have a uterus that is difficult to impregnate, for that matter—many of these laws will restrict certain procedures commonly used during in vitro fertilization.

The goal in this race to the extreme is not to find the right balance, or a consistent ethic of life, but to find the most antiabortion stance out there, to claim the prize for "most pro-life" either because they themselves were raised on the rhetoric or to get that pro-life voter milk.

In response to the deepening of the antiabortion trenches, those who want to expand abortion access have also entrenched, and that has left very little room for pro-life Democrats. Supporting abortion as a legal right is all but essential to be a viable candidate in the Democratic Party. As part of their ethic of life, socially minded Catholics and evangelicals are against the death penalty and for strengthening social safety nets, immigration reform, and gun control. But they are outliers in the Democratic Party, because they include the unborn in that life-affirming ethic. Even socially progressive people who are not necessarily politically affiliated are, post-*Dobbs*, being explicit about supporting "a woman's right to choose." Being anything less than shout-your-abortion enthusiastic will leave you politically homeless in this hyperpolarized conflict.

"There is no issue over which Americans are divided more starkly and passionately than abortion," writes legal scholar Jamal Greene in his pre-*Dobbs* book *How Rights Went Wrong*. "Partisans in the debate over abortion rights seem to agree on nothing, indeed seem to hold views that are literally irreconcilable. They seem, moreover, to hate each other."[3]

ALL ABOUT EVE

We just skimmed a whole history about how religious people turned to politics to advance their values and politicians turned to religious people to deliver votes. But before they became indistinguishable, married till death do them part, what was it that made abortion a thing for the church? What was behind religion's meet-cute with the Right? We touched on segregation and war, but there's another "us vs. them," and while you won't hear a lot of preachers these days speaking out against racial integration, and there's an increasing ambivalence about war, complementarian theology is still something pastors and theologians proudly proclaim.

The rising threat of feminism in the twentieth century was a real concern to the church; it busied women not with free volunteer hours but with paid work. It challenged the denominations where men enjoyed uncontested authority. Feminism gave women control over their budgets and their bodies—things men had rather enjoyed controlling.

Feminism challenges the Christian patriarchy from the very first page—maybe the second or third page, depending on the size of the print in your Bible. In the creation story, after Adam and Eve fall from grace, God curses them, and in Genesis 3:16 God says to the woman, "I will make your pains in childbearing very severe; with painful labor you will give birth to children." In the hands of complementarian teaching, this curse is expanded beyond just the pain of labor to explain the ravages of raising children in a world determined not to help. It creates the self-sacrificial mom who gives up her body, her time, and her mental health for her kids and chuckles with long-suffering affection when they forget her birthday, interrupt her conversations, and wake her up at all hours of the night. But wait, it gets better. The curse goes on to say, "Your desire will be for your husband, and he will rule over you." Complementarian teaching interprets this to mean that women, who were designed to be subject to men, will fight against that design and wish to be over men, and men will be domineering and awful. The complementarian premise—that women were designed to be ruled by men—makes the curse so slippery. Under this interpretation, the fight against subjugation is not the starting place for her liberation journey, it's the source of her suffering. So the complementarian interpretation of the curse basically says women will hate being dominated by men, but trying to do anything about it will only make it worse.

The curse is an immutable part of women's lives because, as belligerent patriarch John MacArthur put it in a June 2000 sermon on Genesis 3:16, "God wants to remind you all the time how terrible sin is and what it's done."[4]

The complementarian curse—that both raising kids and being married is going to be a source of suffering—is used to reverse engineer the nature of

women. Because God cursed those two activities, they must have been her entire purpose. "That's what God wants out of the woman. Forget the briefcase,
forget the road show, forget the career, love your husband, love your children.
Stay in that category where the curse has fallen and by the power of God
and the work of the Spirit you can transform it into something of paradise
regained," MacArthur said.[5]

Wait, though. Men's curse is specific to work; does that mean he's supposed
to stay out of the home? No, because, according to the complementarians, he's
very much needed at home to rule over his miserable, accursed wife. So . . .
what then? It's almost as if the Genesis story wasn't written as a prescriptive
theology on gender, but rather by an ancient civilization trying to explain
things they didn't understand. Like where all this stuff came from and why
shit is so difficult.

Whatever your belief about the historical accuracy and divine inspiration
of the creation narrative, much suffering has come from the doctrine that
women's only sanctioned place is in the home. It has blocked women from
education, economic independence, and voting rights and kept many in dangerous situations—including pregnancy. When feminism came along and told
women there was an option other than misery, it messed with that dynamic. It
gave women standing to improve their situation just like men had been doing
forever (I don't see MacArthur digging for his own potatoes), and that meant
control over if and when they had children. Tied into nearly every antiabortion
sermon I have heard is a little detour into the lies of the sexual revolution and
feminism. Unwanted pregnancies wouldn't happen without sexual immorality
and women wouldn't mind having more and more children if they weren't
trying to advance their careers. Blaming feminism for abortion is rooted in a
theology that sees women's desire for bodily autonomy as a curse.

Lost are the Kendra Josephs. Lost are the women being exploited and
abused. Lost are the women who need chemotherapy and other lifesaving
treatments incompatible with pregnancy. When we tell women that abstinence
and life as a stay-at-home mom are what will save them from the pain of unwanted pregnancy, we ignore the fact that, globally, women are often not the
ones who get to decide when they have sex, and pregnancy can be dangerous
and detrimental to stay-at-home moms too.

We don't have a clear picture of the diversity of abortion experiences,
because we don't have a clear picture of pregnancy and what it means to be a

woman in the United States. But it's not just religion fighting to override the mimetic stories of real women with a thematic story about Eve's curse. Political word choice keeps our vision blurry and maintains the distance between the thematic stories we tell about abortion and the mimetic stories of people whose lives don't fit.

PUTTING BABY IN A CORNER

The well-trained reader will notice that I have not referred to the unborn as fetuses or embryos, even though that is what they are scientifically called until birth. However, in today's debates, I think we have traded honest wrestling for rhetorical analgesics.

The proabortion analgesic erases the suffering of the infant through depersonalized language—insisting on *fetus* instead of *baby* and *cardiac activity* instead of *heartbeat*. It also erases the suffering of the woman by insisting that she revel in her rights. But that's a caricature of what it means to support women's healthcare. It's a disservice to the range of reasons and situations that have led women to end pregnancies. It does not allow us to alleviate suffering, because it insists that suffering doesn't exist. I know many women who have had abortions, and some referred to their aborted fetuses as "babies." Others did not. When I told their stories, I used the language they used, because that brings us closer to the heart of the issue and forces us to reckon with the actual suffering story, not the story where an abortion is a happily-ever-after.

But neither would I use the favorite analgesic of the Right, which is to suggest that it is selfishness, not suffering, that leads people to have abortions: the selfishness of the pregnant woman. The selfishness of society. The selfishness of feminism and "free love" (I truly do snicker when people, usually older pastors, throw this term into the mix. "The Age of Aquarius" always plays in my mind.) We need to "help" these women, they might admit, but that help usually comes with a pretty heavy dose of getting your life on the right track, because at the heart of this view of suffering is a belief that suffering is the result of immorality.

Moral language creates easier binaries (right vs. wrong), which makes it easier to establish distance. I think that's why we prefer to talk about abortion as a moral issue, not an ethical or medical one. But with the overthrow of *Roe*, an interesting thing started to happen. Because *abortion* is a medical term that applies to all sorts of methods and causes for ending a pregnancy, laws prohibiting abortion quickly ran into sticky situations. Having committed to the "abortion is evil" party line, lawmakers tried to argue that certain abortions were in fact not abortions. One pro-life activist, speaking before Congress, said that a ten-year-old having an abortion after being raped would not really be an abortion—which is incorrect. It's not even true to say that abortion always means the death of an unborn child. When I had my "spontaneous abortion," there was nothing inside the pregnancy sac. It was what is called an *anembryonic pregnancy* or, if you prefer your medical conditions to sound like you lived in the Victorian era, "blighted ovum." No baby. No human life, other than mine.

I'm not saying that there are no selfish reasons for abortions, or that there are no happily-ever-after abortion stories. However, when we insist on those two narratives, we will always see abortion as a political issue, and we will have no compassion for those who suffer inside of it.

THE BROKEN BONES OF OUR ABORTION STORIES

We've gotten ourselves in quite a pickle on abortion. In this case we have two dueling narratives that in some ways refuse to honor the suffering or death of another human being.

Context: We know that elective abortion is a multifaceted decision, en-compassing the social, medical, and spiritual realities of parent and child. But we talk about it in high-conflict political, legal language that does not allow for those complexities, and over time such language has made us think (or not think) about abortion as something more simplistic than it is. We told everyone that an octopus was a sock and then tried to prove it by cramming the octopus into a shoe.

Judgments: Since this is a useful political issue, campaigns and legislative showboating have morphed abortion into an issue of moral absolutes. The law must grant all or nothing. While ordinary Americans poll closer to the middle on abortion, the people making the decisions and the primary voters who elect them push further and further toward those poles.

Trade-offs: Our two primary suffering narratives on abortion force a trade-off: either we must always allow abortion to alleviate the suffering of any unwanted pregnancy or we must intervene with the law to prevent the death of the unborn child.

Us vs. them: The political potency of abortion is fueled by more fundamental "us vs. them" divisions: religion and gender—in particular, that intersection of religion and gender where sin and women get blamed for stuff.

Distance and blame: Maintaining the distance is essential to the political power of abortion, and it's done through character selection and the language used to describe those characters. We use words such as *fetus*, *zygote*, and *embryo* to create distance that *baby* doesn't allow. Blaming the human parents suffering among us for the circumstances of their pregnancy helps anesthetize our heartstrings.

Chapter 8

AN ABORTION LAMENT

"Sadness . . . Mom and Dad, the team. They came to help . . . because of Sadness."

—JOY, in Pixar's *Inside Out*, upon realizing
the purpose of Sadness, whom she spent
the entire movie working to suppress

The stories of Jesus's healing ministry are fascinating to me. They provoke almost as many questions as his parables. Why heal one guy at the pool of Bethesda and not the rest (John 5:1–14)? Why did the woman have to touch him to stop bleeding (Luke 8:40–47)? Why did he cry if he knew he was going to raise Lazarus (John 11:1–43)?

In addition to the questions they raise, all three of those examples speak to the deep emotional ministry of Jesus that accompanied his healing work. The loneliness of the man at Bethesda who had heretofore missed out on healing because he had no one to help him. The desperation of the bleeding woman who was willing to risk rebuke to be made well. The grief over the death of Lazarus, even though relief was imminent. In a world full of superstition, sanctimony, and rules, the gospels present stories. People's stories often include suffering, and I believe Jesus honored that as part of the journey. Particularly in the case of Lazarus, but also in his own crucifixion, Jesus didn't skip the lament before he brought the joy. Jewish Jesus would have been raised in a tradition with an understanding of lament; it was something the ancient Hebrews did well. The laments in the psalms are narratives of complicated feelings, hope and sorrow that sound like anger, resignation, and even petulance to American ears.

Lament admits that sorrow is part of life and that there is pain we cannot, of our own power, alleviate. It's an important part of humility as we navigate a world that is not fully redeemed. We are not God. We cannot fix it. But lament is also a plea for relief. It is a hopeful cry, like a child who holds their tears until they are within sight of their parents. Or like when Joy, in Pixar's therapy-in-film-format *Inside Out*, realizes that the point of Sadness is to cue those around to come and help. The child cries in hope that the parent will offer comfort. Lament is so foreign to our narratives that many of us cannot imagine allowing grief and sorrow to mingle with hope or relief. We cannot imagine our pain coexisting with the abundance of life Jesus promised. We are not humble children but masters of our experience.

The power of lament is mostly lost on triumphal Americans, especially white Americans, who like our winning with a side of ice cream, not bitter herbs. Technology, medicine, and entertainment have alleviated and soothed our pain to the point that we sometimes forget that not all pain can be alleviated or soothed. It's not that I think we should be suffering for suffering's sake or to keep ourselves in touch with some bygone emotional tradition. I'm all for technology, medicine, and entertainment. I'm the nest urchin who has a book, a podcast, a bottle of Advil, and a stash of almonds with her at all times so that she doesn't have to feel bored, achy, or hungry even for a moment. But I do think that we modern folks have to work extra hard to remember that pain is part of life, and sometimes it is unavoidable. I find myself lacking the words and practices to meet the pain, unable to practice radical acceptance, because lament is like the language I learned in school but never used. I know it exists in theory, but I am not fluent. I'm not even conversational in the language of lament. I know very few people who are.

Lament forces winning out of the center of our stories and invites us to consider how we can make our society more supportive and accommodating for those whose situations don't conform to the All-Holy Plan for Your Life. I borrow this idea from the disability community—though I have modified it, because suffering and disability are not synonymous. I am also treading very carefully, because abortion and disability is like one of those intersections where seven roads come together and there's no stop signs.

The "social model" of disability maintains that the way we build our communities determines which abilities are necessary to participate. For example, if we refuse to add ramps, we make the ability to go up stairs an essential part of participation in community. In this model we don't "cure" hearing loss or cerebral palsy; we "heal" the broken parts of society that exclude those people.

If our response to suffering includes the possibility of lament, the acceptance that there is struggle, there is loss, and there are situations without a win-win outcome, it would change the way we talk about abortion and how we regulate it. It's possible that if we knew how to lament for the suffering inherent in an untenable pregnancy—if we felt abortion as a loss of life and simultaneously acknowledged how pregnancy can also be incompatible with life—we would be more serious about the care and community offered to people in need of abortions. We would also consider which of our policies make more pregnancies untenable. We do not support pregnancy, birth, or new parents well at all in this country. We do not make it easy to raise a child with special needs. If we saw untenable pregnancy as something socially created as much as it is medical or personal, we would ensure that our laws, healthcare system, and spiritual support were like ramps, not stairs. Having a baby and having an abortion would both be accommodated. In Jesus's inside-out paradigm, we do not have to choose either a parent or the unborn child to place at the center of the "us vs. them" debate but rather honor the dignity of both lives.

ROOM TO FEEL

The most common emotion women report after abortion is relief. For some, it is that simple. They, with scientific support, view the zygote or embryo as "a clump of cells," or they do not feel connected to the fetus on a human level. However, for many, grief and relief make up a complicated ambivalence, however supportive they might be of the general right to end a pregnancy. Ending the pregnancy might be grievous, just less grievous than the situation that makes it necessary.

Laura Molinar's nonprofit collective Sueños Sin Fronteras de Tejas works with undocumented people in need of reproductive healthcare—often after being raped or exploited on their immigration journey. When I interviewed her for a news story, she pointed out that telling these women "your body, your choice" was almost never effective.[1] Not only had their control over their bodies already been taken from them but elective abortion was often against their religious beliefs. If they were going to pursue an abortion at all, it would be an issue of survival, because that was the mode they were in. Molinar knew this, because that's how it had been when she had an abortion to escape an abusive relationship. Not every woman who has an abortion does so thinking she is exercising her rights, making a choice, undergoing a simple medical procedure. If the child is born, they will live on the edge of death. They and their unborn child are drowning, and only one life is savable. They grieve, but they live.

In our combative context, admitting any kind of relief—again, the feeling most women report after an abortion—makes their decision suspect. "Aha! So abortion *is* selfish!" At the same time, acknowledging the unique grief of taking a conscious role in the death of another being opens parents up to the "abortion hurts women" narrative. Rev. Katey Zeh leads the fifty-year-old faith-based abortion-support ministry Religious Coalition for Reproductive Choice, and she accompanies women for spiritual support during abortions. She compiled a series of stories about the complicated emotions many people feel when ending pregnancies. Her book, *A Complicated Choice: Making Space for Grief and Healing in the Pro-Choice Movement*, makes the case that "abortion is a blessing," while giving the people who had abortions the space to share the sad parts. "We can honor the full spectrum of abortion experiences and provide sacred spaces for anyone who needs supportive spiritual care along the way," she writes.[2]

Zeh encourages churches to actively and explicitly welcome people to tell their reproductive stories. The Religious Coalition for Reproductive Choice worked with Faith in Women, a Mississippi-based group, to create Abortions Welcome, a repository of prayers, blessings, and ritual liturgies from across a multitude of faiths. "We wanted to have something in place for people who might not have a supportive faith community," Zeh told me when I interviewed her for a *Sojourners* story.[3]

Honoring requires proximity. We distance ourselves through simplistic language, but when we let seemingly contradictory terms live together in one story—such as grief and relief—we are drawn closer, into the specifics of each mimetic story. The tension makes us think harder and resist easy categorization. Our thematic stories of blame or choice or empowerment or selfishness may have a hard time making room for the realities of many, many pregnancies.

The very existence of abortion doulas, people who assist parents in the physical and emotional processes of ending a pregnancy, testifies to the complexity. Speaking on the podcast *Abortion, with Love*, Zachi Brewster, an abortion doula and founder of the abortion-support group Dopo, explained the range of needs individuals and families have as they consider ending an emotionally, socially, or medically complex pregnancy. "It is a spectrum of emotion," she said, but often those emotions are not welcome on one side of the debate or the other. Grief counseling often comes from an antiabortion agenda that does not want to acknowledge the relief. Support and affirmation of the decision often comes from abortion advocates who are hesitant to allow for regret, grief, or wondering what might have been. "The art of holding multiple truths . . . that is the experience of abortion often . . . how does this fit, especially with the narratives we have around it," Brewster said.[4]

I don't know if Jesus would have supported any or all or certain abortion procedures, but I know that the story of his life is filled with complex emotions. A Jesus who sweated blood, a Jesus who cried for the man he was about to raise from the dead, a Jesus whose compassion defied social stigma—this Jesus embraced the fullness of life and death. "I came so that they may have life, and may have it abundantly," he said (John 10:10 NET). And then the gospels show us what abundant life looks like: reconciliation, resurrection, and restoration, a constant rhythm of dying and rising, all of it blessed by God. The Jesus of the gospels does not say, "I came that they may have a heartbeat and figure it out from there."

MORE GERMANS

Broadening our view of life creates the context of a healing story, but abundance doesn't mean we never have to give anything up, never have to stop saying "more" or "mine." The abundant life that Jesus offers always comes by way of a cross.

If we lament suffering rather than explaining it away, we lose the power granted to us by black-and-white thinking and absolutes. We lose the power to ignore the suffering of others, to ease our spirits by judging their decisions. We are called to broken hearts, to weep with those who weep, even if they made a decision we would not have made. There's also political power to be willingly sacrificed. Black-and-white, hardline stances are great for our current politics. People aren't mobilized by nuance, and coalitions fall apart as people choose different issues to champion. If we become a society that allows compassion to muddy the waters, we lose the power generated by crystal-clear moral certitude. Suffering, disagreeing, wandering together through a wilderness of shitty options—that is the cross we are asked to bear.

Right now, we look to language to spare us from those muddy waters.

When he wrote the majority opinion for *Roe v. Wade*, United States Supreme Court Associate Justice Harry Blackmun wrote that acknowledging the humanity of a fetal human made abortion untenable. Blackmun used medical terminology to circumvent the question of fetal rights, making abortion a medical decision between a person and their doctor, a private issue in which the government should not interfere. This is why so much opposition to abortion in the United States hinges on the personhood of the unborn. If that fetus is a baby, a person, and a citizen of the United States, pro-life people argue that it has a right to life regardless of the effect on the carrying parent.

But fetal personhood and abortion are not actually mutually exclusive, argues legal scholar Jamal Greene in *How Rights Went Wrong*. He compares the US abortion debate to West Germany, where a court refused to say that the unborn are outside the protection of the law.[5] The German courts kicked the issue back to elected representatives, forcing them to hash it out in accordance with public opinion. There was no winner and loser with a summary verdict, just good old rotten compromise.

I want to pause here to say that I am not advocating for the German approach, nor am I or Greene pointing to Germany as an exemplar. I just want us to acknowledge that there are other ways to have a conversation, because the American version is going terribly. Could not be going more poorly.

What emerged in Germany, Greene explains, was a discourse not on *choice* nor *privacy* nor *bodily autonomy*—all terms used to advocate for abortion in the United States. Germans instead speak in terms of *protection*. Both the unborn life and the life carrying it are protected under German law. How those conflicting protections are reconciled is the result of ongoing debate and, like any good legislation, leaves everyone a little unhappy.[6]

The resulting laws are anathema to pro-choice activists in the United States—abortion is illegal in Germany. Germans are not entitled to abortion. But they are entitled to life, with a much broader definition than what Americans are promised under the law—the German constitution promises every German the freedom to "develop his personality." Economic and social life—not just physical health—are serious considerations when doctors consider whether the mother's life is at risk. In the United States, we have made a quantifiable, medically verifiable, beating heart sacrosanct, but that's about it. Since the fall of *Roe* in the United States, women have experienced nightmare scenarios where slow miscarriages left them dangerously ill while they waited for the fetal heartbeat to stop so that fearful doctors could perform a lifesaving procedure. We can barely conceive of a post-*Roe* scenario in which a woman could obtain an abortion by saying, "I can't afford to have this baby. It is a threat to the economic conditions necessary for my life." Yet in Germany, where abortion is illegal after twelve weeks, they can, and they do.

Germans are legally entitled to a quality of life that could be endangered by pregnancy and parenthood. Thus the law sounds like something straight out of an antiabortion manual, but the reality is the opposite—Germans have a far easier time obtaining abortions than residents in Republican-governed states right now.

There's another interesting debate that then stems from the German arrangement. When politicians want to reduce the number of abortions in Germany, they are tasked with adding social support, ways to make pregnancy and parenthood less of a burden. In a society where women can get abortions because having a baby is too expensive, increasing social support and extending parental leave are abortion-reduction measures. While she is wholly in favor of legal abortion, this debate reminded me of Zeh's vision that "every positive pregnancy test would be cause for celebration." Zeh imagines what kind of world it would take for many of the reasons women seek abortion—finances, mental health, partner violence—to be nonissues. In the United States a segment of pro-life people has been making a similar argument for decades: pro-life cannot end at birth. We have to take care of kids if we want people to keep having them.

But even in the ideal social context, some of the pain caused by carrying a child is unavoidable. If you are someone who struggled with postpartum mental health, gestational diabetes, or hypertension, or any of the myriad struggles of birthing and raising children, then you might also know how flimsy your moral absolutes can become when your period is late. For those cases in Germany, the law provides for a medical or "social indication" to allow the abortion to go forward.

Greene allows that things are not perfect in Germany; he's not even advocating for the particulars of the German laws. People in Germany would like to get abortions without having to first obtain a certificate of necessity, a *Beratungsschein*, and they argue against the three-day reflection period required before the procedure. For Americans, whose only frame of reference for abortion is in terms of rights and moral absolutes, those are intolerable hurdles. Or, conversely, insufficient deterrents.

Greene isn't valorizing the German laws; he is simply showing that calling an unborn human a person doesn't make abortion untenable. It simply means we have to honor the life that ends when abortion is necessary. I would argue that treating the unborn as a human life helps us name the grief that often accompanies abortion, as well as the relief that so often accompanies a death that ends suffering. It allows us to make sober and honest decisions. It helps us value the life of the parents more, not less, because saving their lives—their abundant lives—is no small thing. It is a grave measure, but it is worthwhile.

We could find ways to be even more compassionate, even more life-affirming toward both parent and child. We could tell a beautiful healing story, but there's one more thing in our way. For an abortion healing story to ever move forward in the United States, I think we need to talk about the endless suffering we will tolerate for people we deem immoral.

SAINTS AND SINNERS

At the heart of our argument about abortion is an argument about gender and uprightness, about morals and good, clean living. This is by design, Greene explains. "The overt political strategy to help Republicans regain power moving into the 1980s was to use abortion and the human life amendment to create a permanent home in the Republican Party for Catholics and evangelical Protestants, aligning them with white southerners who associate Black civil rights with moral degradation. . . . Phyllis Schlafly led the charge against the ERA [Equal Rights Amendment] by arguing that the word 'choice' was code for both abortion and homosexual lifestyles."[7] In this rhetoric, abortion was (is?) inseparable from feminism and sexual revolution, the overturning of the traditional family and its values. Seeing it listed alongside Black civil rights and homosexuality paints a telling picture of what "traditional family values" really means, but for people inclined to agree, abortion moved from medical ethics and into religious absolutes.

In a moral debate, it is easy to justify that immorality begets suffering, and that we are not obligated to ease suffering brought about by people's own bad choices or sins. Even though we're locating this discussion under the abortion debate, it really may be one of the most foundational discussions in this book. It also may be heretical. Buckle up.

Advocates regularly speak about the frustration of finding a sympathetic victim. People fighting to end the death penalty are pressured to focus on the wrongly convicted. Marriage rights for LGBTQ people came through a gay white couple desiring legal sanction for their stable, loving home. When I was covering family separations at the Texas-Mexico border in 2018, I was invited to sit in on an interview with a mother searching for her HIV-positive, queer teenager. She was terrified that her child would not have access to their medication and would face additional persecution and violence because of their sexuality. The interview was heartbreaking, but the other journalist in the room admitted that he would likely not be able to use it in his coverage, because his producers wanted a more sympathetic case. Americans didn't want a queer teen bringing HIV into the United States, not only because it was a health concern but also because it was not the moral vibe we are trying to cultivate here.

Abortion advocates face the same challenge, because teenage premarital sex is still considered a sin by many Americans. Irresponsibility runs afoul of our "every man for himself" brand of individualism. Poverty is even seen as an indication of some sort of vice, such as laziness or a lack of self-control. So they have to look for the rape victim, or the middle-class, heterosexual white couple whose unborn child is suffering from a painful abnormality.

We play into this perfectionism when we try to paint abortion-seekers—like immigrants—as deserving of compassion based on their moral uprightness. But the thing about perfectionism is that it never stops; we buy into the idea that good people deserve relief, then *only* good people deserve relief, and then the very act of seeking relief means that you are not good. Abortion isn't just a relief withheld from sinners. Now abortion itself is the sin. Wanting one, feeling that you need one, is evidence of sin, if not illicit sex, then some selfishness or weakness or lack of trust in God. It's heavily gendered, because women are supposed to want a never-ending parade of children and not supposed to be interested in sex for any other reason. Public assistance works this way too. The logic of the New Deal was that good people needed relief. But then you have a bunch of rules attached to public benefits to make sure that the poor receiving them are the deserving poor. And in places where they just really don't want to expand Medicare or some other program, you start to see the logic that if you really are industrious and virtuous in America, you won't need public benefits, and so the very act of seeking them carries a stigma.

The inside-out stories of Jesus simply do not support this equation. The story of his life ends with the world's only sinless person taking on all the suffering so that people who have sinned—every single person ever—can have their spiritual suffering alleviated. "I came that they may have life, and have it abundantly" (John 10:10, again). In the gospels, Jesus specifically breaks the religious link between sin and suffering by healing the blind and paralyzed without implying that it was their sin or their parents' sin that caused the malady. But unfortunately the gospels do not say, "There's no such thing as sin." I wish they had. Instead, the Jesus of the gospels forgave sins. He told people not to sin anymore. His response to sin was compassion. There was table flipping too, but that appears to be reserved for a specific kind of corruption.

Like everyone mauled by evangelicalism, I get queasy using the word *sin*. I'm used to the 1980s, Moral Majority version of sin, combined with a Reformed tradition that really loved to talk about original sin. Sin was both a judgy scold at a pride parade and a deep, gnawing sense of unworthiness. But when I opened my heart to the idea that sin was something other than "badness" or "not-good-enough-ness," that it was an incompleteness, wounding, or scarcity, that changed. Jesus's compassion made so much more sense, as did Paul's and the prophets'. Even the Torah reads differently when God offers wholeness and sin is state of fracture.

In the creation story, sin is described as death entering the world. No longer would all the needs be met. There would be scarcity—a limit to the resources that sustain life. As theologian L. Ann Jervis writes, summarizing Paul's discussion of sin in Romans, "Sin's agenda is to put out the life and light of God."[8] However, in Romans Paul also talks about all of creation groaning because of "sin." Surely the trees are not jealous. The rivers don't lust. But they decay. They suffer from drought and hurricanes. They suffer from scarcity. And that's why we need to know how to lament.

So this is where I'm going to dabble in a little heresy, maybe. And I'm not a theologian, so disregard if you want to. This is not my lane, but I'm going to swerve here for a minute:

Sin isn't the bad thing we do. It isn't the bad thing we are. Sin is the part of us that is trapped in a world where bad things happen, and sometimes we respond to that by making it worse. Sometimes there are only shitty options, but we have to choose one. Sin is why we need lament. We fight against that need by trying to make sin something we do or don't do. We try to make it about our wickedness, but it's not; it's about our woundedness. It's the fact that we are all dying, and our every instinct says to fight against it, to push the suffering away and onto someone else, or to hoard resources so that we stay safe. Sometimes the scarcity nurtures a power hunger in us that makes us cruel. Sometimes it blurs our vision of the dignity of those around us. Sometimes we do everything right, and the cancer still grows. It's the same looming death haunting us all, so there's no space to judge. To see another person suffering because they live in a groaning world should elicit compassion—even if they are not handling it the way you think they should. Whether that suffering manifests as an unwanted pregnancy or a nonviable pregnancy or an abusive partner or a rape, our response should be as an "us" who looks at both parent and unborn as fellow travelers on a brutal road and offers our compassion for whatever comes next. To make their journey as much "on earth as it is in heaven" is to give comfort, welcome, healthcare, ritual, relief, and companionship to mitigate whatever parts of the suffering cannot be alleviated. Death bears down and we brace our backs to help shoulder the load.

The gospels' whole, radical thing in response to scarcity is the resurrection. Life isn't scarce in the end. It is abundant. We can accept the suffering inherent in loving and sharing and hospitality and compassion because we don't see death and scarcity as the most powerful forces. We see abundant life as the thing that prevails—the comfort that outlasts the struggle. It's more than just alleviation, Scottish disability theologian John Swinton argues. Christians in particular practice what he calls "practical theodicy" when we respond to suffering in ways that heal—when we reconnect the sufferer to the source of life, reaffirming "God's commitment to be with the world in its struggles, as it awaits transformation and redemption."[9]

But "awaits" is a key word there. We're not experiencing abundance yet, and the need for abortion as relief from suffering is a stark reminder of that. Lament and compassion are the snacks and matchbooks we have to sustain us as we await transformation and redemption.

HEALING OUR ABORTION STORIES

We are never going to agree, universally, on the morality of abortion. We do not agree on the personhood of the unborn or our obligations to them. But that doesn't have to stop us from acknowledging the complicated suffering that leads to complicated decisions around pregnancy and childbirth, and supporting the people making those decisions. We need a narrative that does not pit the suffering of parent and child against each other but honors both.

Context: A healing narrative requires a context that allows for complex emotions, each met with love and compassion. It requires us to back away from black-and-white thinking on an issue with a long history of ethical gray area and to think of life as more than a heartbeat.

Judgments: A person's failure to or choice not to adhere to our moral standards should not be grounds for their suffering. Nor should a choice be invalidated if it involves suffering.

Trade-offs: If we will trade our politically expedient binary positions on abortion, we might make our way to a definition of life that results not in political wins but in more compassion for the suffering inherent in living. We have to die to a system that can alleviate the suffering of one only by denying the suffering of the other, and rise to a community that supports the wide range of life-giving choices a person may need to make.

Us vs. them: For the individuals caught between the sides of this debate, the most difficult decision of their lives becomes fraught with social suffering on top of everything else. If birthing people knew that we would not weaponize their suffering or grief, then we could act as a community that truly supports life.

Distance and compassion: The pregnant body and the unborn body are as close in proximity as two can possibly be. We have to honor that closeness, knowing that we can never be closer to parent or child than they are to each other. Whatever suffering must be addressed between them, we can draw close with compassion, making a sacred space for both lament and relief.

"That's just part of what it means to be divinely created. We're connected that way," Zeh said during our interview. The call of faith is to care for each other in that intimate, mutual way. "We've really missed the mark on what it means to live out our faith."[10]

Chapter 9

CLIMATE CHANGE–THE SPECULATIVE DYSTOPIAN THRILLER SERIES

"God is change, and in the end, God does prevail. But we have something to say about the whens and the whys of that end."

—Protagonist LAUREN OLAMINA in Octavia Butler's
frighteningly familiar dystopian novel *Parable of the Sower*

I was driving down Highway 99 in California on a Sunday morning, looking for a tiny evangelical church that served farm workers in the San Joaquin Valley, America's salad bowl. But all the salad seemed to be on one side of the road. To my left, leafy orchards stretched for acres. To my right, dust. Wherever someone wasn't hauling in water to irrigate neat rows of peach trees or almond groves, the land became dust in the wind.

I was there to report a story about pastors ministering to field workers. Woven into the story were issues of labor rights, immigration, and food chain economics. But it was the highway running between literal feast and famine that had me shaken. It didn't help that it was the summer of 2020, and the COVID-19 pandemic was still new and mysterious. Or that just days after I left, smoke from wildfires would descend on the area like a heavy blanket.

It felt like the opening scenes in a movie about an apocalyptic disaster. Like at any moment a murder of crows would overtake my car, followed by a zombie army.

Nothing so cinematic happened, of course. The apocalypse I was seeing so starkly in Central California has been unfolding gradually across the globe, but it's picking up speed—the extreme weather events, the wildfires, the water shortages. Climate change is a series of suffering stories, and the core disagreement seems to be whether it is indeed a big, connected narrative or hundreds of small coincidences. I'd been home from America's wilting salad bowl for about seven months when Winter Storm Uri left me and 4.5 million other Texans without power for days. A year later, historically huge Hurricane Ian leveled beach towns in Florida. And those are just the headliner disasters in the United States. The global story is far more harrowing. Scientists warn that in between these catastrophic events, melting ice cover is the long-term disaster that will continue to make our weather and resources less predictable and could even unleash long-frozen viruses to which the global population has no immune resistance. When you line the research papers and news reports up next to each other, you come to the inevitable conclusion that zombies may actually be preferable.

Speculative fiction writers Octavia Butler and Margaret Atwood can keep me up well past my bedtime, partly because their characters and world creation are spectacular. But also because what they write is far more terrifying than any thriller. Both authors claim to have based some of their work on what they saw in the news. Suzanne Collins, who wrote the *Hunger Games* books, wildly popular dystopian thrillers for young adults, has also said she got her ideas from watching news coverage juxtaposed with reality television. These writers simply asked, "What if?" What if this idea caught on? What if that politician won, or that hurricane landed just a little further north, or that virus broke free? What if those things happened all at once, or in a different order? Speculative fiction imagines a different outcome of this vicious decoupage of climate, extremism, and inequality.

The fiction writers and the scientists aren't the only ones with stories to tell. In fact, climate change wouldn't be a hot-button issue if it weren't for the counternarrative: the narrative that climates always change, and humans have nothing to do with it.

Climate change is a little bit trickier than the other topics in the book. The elements of suffering stories are there, but they work together differently than in other stories. We are not talking about two distinct groups fighting over whose suffering matters, or what kind of sacrifice is merited to end obvious suffering. There are climate change deniers and activists, sure, but the vast majority of those who bemoan climate change are also contributing to it. We have a hard time getting worked up enough to take action, because the problems feel big, unsolvable, or far off. The vast majority of the world isn't in the coastal town when the hurricane hits. The news-consuming United States is far away from the sinking Maldives and starving Somalia. Eventually, climate scientists explain, the blanching coral and melting glaciers will lead to more universal suffering, but as long as those consequences remain in the future, all but the most anxious of us will continue to feel distant from them. The climate change narrative doesn't feel like our other suffering narratives, so we continue to careen toward global disaster as fast as fossil fuels will carry us.

WHATABOUTISM

I want to put aside full climate change denial for a second and speak first to the things that complicate the suffering story for people who do want to prevent the ominous future predicted by climate science. Psychologists can tell us how difficult it is to make present sacrifices for a future benefit. Even personal improvements such as diets and savings plans can be difficult. So even though we know what actions will mitigate or reduce the effects of climate change, small though many of them are, those reusable bags, lower emissions, and reforestation efforts are often pitted against a future that doesn't hurt yet—at least for most of the people reading this book.

Even for those of us inclined to see climate change as an urgent matter—because we do see the hurricanes, sea level rise, droughts, wildfires, and blizzards as present threats—climate change stories are frequently drowned out by the chaos of politics, poverty, and violence. It feels more effective to pay attention to the things we can fix through money and elections, not a situation measured in decades and tenths of degrees. We allow ourselves to think of climate solutions as a trade against other forms of human suffering. Putting bleached coral reefs side-by-side with hungry children diminishes the threat of declining biodiversity and makes it less likely that we will feel the urgency we would need to feel to make the small but real sacrifices we would need to make in our daily lives.

Some of this is unintentional overload, but it makes room for deliberate bad faith arguments as well. Some religiously motivated climate change deniers claim that a concern for the poor is at the heart of their resistance to climate change mitigation strategies, such as a reduced dependence on oil and gas. The pro-fossil-fuel Cornwall Alliance for the Stewardship of Creation has an entire declaration outlining how moving away from fossil fuels will harm the poor in rich countries by increasing the price of energy and harm poor countries by forcing people to rely on unnamed "dirty, inefficient cooking and heating fuels" that will cause disease and birth defects.[1] Economists have raised similar concerns as they look at the energy needs of developing nations, but those not shilling for fossil fuels usually conclude that subsidizing green energy technology in developing nations is a more favorable solution than continuing on with coal for the whole world.

The fact that the slow science of climate change has been championed by scholars and scientists has also made room for those who don't like their conclusions to characterize the issue as a "white liberal" issue—something for Patagonia-wearing, leisure-time-having granola-eaters to worry about because they don't have anything more dire at their doorstep. When I was growing up, my conservative evangelical parents claimed that movies like *FernGully* were made by people who believed that trees were more important than people.

So without real human suffering to trade, the judgment reflected in our policies and economics suggests that we have deemed the costs and inconveniences of a world without fossil fuels to be intolerable.

So is it just that? Is it just the product of a bunch of overstimulated people descending into the plot of *WALL-E* with no human symptoms until the day climate change hits us in one giant apocalyptic event?

No, because, of course, real humans are already suffering. Real humans are losing their homes and livelihoods in hurricanes and droughts that are outpacing our considerable technological advances and mitigation efforts. The climate justice movement points out that those people, the ones most affected by the increasingly severe weather events, will be the poor—not only the poor in coastal cities who cannot afford to move uphill or fortify their homes, but the global poor. Laborers whose livelihoods are not part of the weightless economy, the metaverse, or the financial industry but who are tied to the land and its resources. The future is here for those the West typically shoves aside—Africa, Southeast Asia, and Latin America. It is here for arctic cultures and creatures. It is here for reefs and rainforests. It is here for those who lose their homes in the increasingly wild weather events.

The timeline of climate catastrophe—scientists place a lot of the big-ticket items between 2030 and 2050—is paced so that our policymaking, economy-building grandparents in the global West would not live to see our drought-fleeing, resource-rationing grandchildren. We, the adults of today, are the only ones who know them both. And not everyone is doing nothing about it. Freaking Greta Thunberg is sailing around leading packs of teenagers to get the attention of lawmakers. People are biking naked through London and throwing soup on paintings to protest oil dependence. Less confrontationally, at the desk next to me, my architect husband is strategizing with colleagues to design more energy-efficient buildings. Engineers are working hard on alternative energy and conscientious investors are divesting from oil. Publications such as *The Narwhal* in Canada are reporting not just on the problems but on the solutions, giving people stories and information, if they are willing to hear them.

But the distances and contexts of the suffering stories have been an ongoing challenge for climate scientists and reporters. They know that by the time we really are paying exorbitant rates for water in Los Angeles, unable to go outside in the summer in New Orleans, or pumping water out of the streets of New York City, island nations will be submerged, species extinct, and humans displaced across the globe. The scenarios that might spark fear for ourselves, the great motivator for political action, are a few decades behind scenarios that could spark compassion for others.

There's an "us vs. them" inherent to our slowness to move on behalf of people far away, poor people, and future generations. While teenagers and young adults are marching on behalf of their future, and we look into the still-chubby, innocent faces of children whose entire adult lives could be spent fighting this battle, we have to acknowledge that we are treating them as "them" if we can't be bothered to leave them any clean air.

That's all difficult enough, and we'll get more into it in the chapter about healing narratives in climate change, but first we need to address the concerted effort to undermine climate suffering stories, because we're not even yet to the point where we can all agree it's our fault the air's so dirty.

THE CROWN OF CREATION

Whether climate change stories incite compassion or fear, those who do not want to see reduced dependence on fossil fuels have come up with a steady stream of narratives to contradict science. In the American Sociological Association's magazine *Footnotes*, sociologist Jeremiah Bohr wrote about the cultural elements of climate change denial. He noted that by refusing to submit to data, the climate-change-is-not-a-concern spin doctors could use political messaging to shape the narrative, which allowed them to opportunistically expand and contract the distance between data and the suffering it portends. "While arguing against scientific consensus will always present an uphill battle," Bohr wrote, "the organizers of climate change denial repeatedly prove their ability to strategically adapt to their political environment, shifting between narratives of 'climate change is not happening,' 'climate change is happening but humans are not driving it,' and 'climate change is happening but it is nothing to worry about.'"[2]

Journalists are trained to follow the money, and that's obviously part of this. Fossil fuels are big money. But money isn't the only thing that motivates people to resist planet-saving policies. Following the climate change debate is, ironically, like drilling through strata of incentives. On the surface, the conflict appears scientific, then economic, and finally, under all of that, we find the cultural "us vs. them."

Climate science is highly specific, and it focuses on key indicators and data points, such as the amount of carbon in the atmosphere or ocean temperatures. Rebuttals from the various energy corporations and the think tanks they fund often use scientific language, provided by the individual scientists hired to contradict the growing consensus. Following the money, Bohr explains, makes these findings suspect. They serve a clear financial agenda. But the people who stand to gain the most from continued dependence on fossil fuels need the support of those who stand to lose a lot if food supply chains collapse and plagues emerge from a melting permafrost. The financial interests need to resonate with the common man and resonate deeply.

Bohr writes about attending a conference organized by the Heartland Institute, where he witnessed the parallel between climate change denial culture and the cultural hallmarks of right-wing populism more generally, including chants about "locking up" their opponents. "This parallel illustrates a political culture undergirding the denial movement, premised not on good-faith disagreements about the proper role of government, but a visceral hatred directed at anyone identified as the enemy. In this case, enemies include most climate scientists, but also anyone perceived as an opponent to the lifestyle made possible by access to cheap fossil fuel. While I understand the motives of corporate actors as a desire to protect profits, I would characterize many of the rank-and-file activists I encountered at this conference (who were almost all white men) as motivated by threats to their 'industrial masculinity.'"[3]

Industrial masculinity could be called the animating spirit of the entire twentieth century, from the Industrial Revolution to the space race, to the Cold War, to Silicon Valley. Words such as *titan*—not *maiden* or *damsel*—were used to describe the power of those who went further and faster, fueled by the earth's own resources. It's the same spirit of conquest and colonization, but now with physical science as the frontier. For the five or six of you who saw Disney's *Strange World*, it was the grandfather, Jaeger Clade, giving way to the son, Searcher Clade.

The masculine resistance seems to imply a gendered "us vs. them," but I think that masculine face of the resistance to climate science is a religious "us vs. them."

For the conflict to become intractable, it has to get into our core. The "us" worried about future disasters and catastrophic changes to our ecosystems has a pretty strong motivation: survival. Doesn't get much closer to the core than that. But the opposition did not bring a garden hose to a tsunami fight. Their counternarrative to our future demise as a species is based not on our survival but on our status. Humans are not one among many species whose fate is bound up with the health of the earth; humans are the crown of creation.

So in this "us vs. them," one side is made up of defenders of God's created order, and the other is godless scientists who would debase man by making him one of the animals and plunging the world into moral disorder. That sounds like I'm hyperbolically satirizing the debate, but I'm more likely accidentally plagiarizing a sermon from an evangelical pulpit in the 1990s.

Like most teaching developed to serve economic and political agendas, this position is full of holes and can get downright ridiculous—like Illinois Congressman John Shimkus's 2010 assertion that God's promise to Noah never to flood the earth again precludes rising sea levels. We can chuckle at that, but there are two more fundamental teachings, also based in Genesis, that have given the religious opposition to climate change more credible mileage: dominion and *imago Dei*.

The doctrine that man was given dominion over creation—and not *man* as in all humankind, but *man* as in the gender—has been used to suggest that the earth was put here specifically for him to explore, extract, and convert all plant and animal life into whatever is good for him. Fossil fuels, I have heard it explicitly argued, are a gift from God, and therefore no bad can come of using them. There are backflips required, of course, because these same people will teach that sex, food, and alcohol are all gifts from God that can absolutely be misused.

The idea that humans alone are made in the image of God (*imago Dei*), and thus should not have to set aside our interests in order to preserve the rest of creation, serves not so much climate change denial as environmental apathy. The image of God comes up whenever someone is trying to eliminate plastic straws to save sea turtles, or activists camp out in trees to prevent them from being cut down. As long as the argument seems to be pitting humans against the rest of nature, human suffering will always be intolerable—even if the human "suffering" is actually just inconvenience.

We will get more into a healing narrative based on the stories of Jesus later in the book, but for now, I would simply say that those very same doctrines could lead to a different position on climate if we take them seriously. For instance, looking at the person of Jesus, we know that the most accurate image of God is inherently sacrificial and deeply concerned with the flourishing of all creatures. Any dominion or ruling would have to be marked by sacrificial caretaking and preservation.

I have always been baffled by religious bases for climate change denial, because the same people who insisted that the crown of creation could not possibly misuse creation were often the same people who believed in the doctrine of original sin! I myself have moved away from the belief that we're born evil. But obviously every human being has the capacity for evil. Whether it is woundedness, scarcity, or alienation from God that causes it, we all do bad stuff. Status prevents nothing. Being a parent doesn't mean you don't hurt kids. Being a priest doesn't mean you don't harm parishioners. Being a doctor doesn't mean you don't run over people with your car. These two doctrines—*imago Dei* and dominion—only make the case against climate change if we do not believe that humans can and do cause suffering. No one believes that in good faith. But I think we're seeing a trend here: not all counternarratives are based on good faith, and that makes it even harder to respond to our neighbors when there really are legitimate and opposing suffering stories, as was true during the COVID-19 pandemic, which we'll chew through a couple of chapters from now.

THE BROKEN BONES OF OUR CLIMATE STORY

Nothing shows the power of narrative like climate change. All the data and science point in one direction, and humankind barrels in the other, ambivalent about our own suffering. We accept arguments that are made in bad faith or, like Esau in the Bible, trade our future for some immediate comfort. The suffering is increasing, and it will continue to, scientists tell us, but it remains unclear what it will take for us to adjust our stories accordingly.

Context: We've made ourselves dependent on an economy our planet cannot sustain, and the felt need for "more" and the existential peril of "more" have placed us in high conflict, as we have built narratives to support whatever we see as the greater threat.

Judgments: Climate change can be judged to be a privileged concern, or misplaced priority—one that ignores more suffering than it acknowledges. Questioning the sustainability of our current way of life disrupts debates about market solutions to poverty and macroeconomic theories, which allow some room for the idea that the rich can continue to get richer and this will somehow benefit the poor.

Trade-offs: There are several trade-offs happening in the climate change debate. Fundamentally, the trade-off is our present for our future suffering. Globally. All of us. And that delayed gratification trade-off is already a challenge. The benefits I can feel now—the ease of hopping in my car and driving somewhere, the joy of air conditioning—are pitted against the incremental, invisible benefits of the personal sacrifices I'm being asked to make. At a macro-level, consider the need to reallocate our resources and attention and the disruption that will bring to the economy, and you see the appeal of just kicking the can down the road. If you're in the position to make those big decisions, then the current economy is probably working well for you.

Us vs. them: There is a short-term "us vs. them" due to climate change. People are getting wealthy, and others are starving. Humans continue to pursue their own comfort while other species go extinct, and the imbalance has started to affect humans as well. The longer-term "us vs. them" of climate change is not between those who suffer and those who benefit—because we are all going to suffer—but between those who are willing to sacrifice to alleviate global suffering and those who are not.

Distance and blame: Both geography and time create distance between the United States and the most devastating effects of climate change, but of course that window is closing. There's plenty of blame to go around, but our survival demands that we spend less time assigning blame and more time accepting responsibility for the world we share. We may not like it, but our fates are linked.

Chapter 10

A CLIMATE CHANGE SURVIVAL EPIC

"After a thousand years of darkness, he will come, clad in blue and surrounded by fields of gold to restore mankind's connection to the Earth that was destroyed."

—OBABA the wise seer in the environmental survival epic
Nausicaä of the Valley of the Wind

I've read the Bible cover to cover a handful of times, and minored in biblical studies in college, but I don't have every verse memorized. So I'll occasionally turn to Google to help me search for something topical. I have consulted everything from "50 Great Verses About Joy" to "Ten Prophetic Visions in the Old Testament" to "All the Foods Mentioned in the Bible" to kick-start research at various times. But when I typed in "Jesus and nature" to see if my own list had missed anything, I was disappointed. My first search resulted in pages and pages of debate about the hypostatic union, which, while fun to debate, is not what I meant by "nature." I tinkered with my search terms and eventually got to the lists I usually find so helpful. Except that these lists were not helpful at all.

While the Old Testament lists were extensive, full of poetic imagery, creation narrative, and wilderness landscape, the New Testament was limited to Jesus's exhortation not to be anxious, because God takes care of the grass and the flowers and the birds.

Then I turned to my trusty Thompson Chain Reference Bible, which is like if your search engine took three thousand times longer and you could tear the pages. Again, however, when the editors of that search tool thought of *nature*, they limited their search to metaphors. Jesus uses lots of nature metaphors—mustard seeds, vines, soil quality. I think his extensive use of nature metaphor is telling of both his and the general population's relationship to the land, but this wasn't what I was looking for.

I was already thinking of Jesus calming the wind and the waves, saying the rocks would cry out, and cursing the fig tree. I was thinking about Paul saying that creation groans in his letter to the Roman church. It suits our head-centric faith practices to think of nature as a trove of lessons and metaphors applicable to our all-important orthodoxy, but Jesus clearly had a relationship with nature itself. When Jesus calms the wind and the waves, he says to them, "Peace! Be still." We tend to focus on the power of the miracle, skipping right over the relationship.

I imagine Jesus speaking to the wind and waves in his dad voice, the way my husband talks to our kids when their trampoline wrestling match is getting out of hand—we've crossed from "ninja training" to escalating retaliatory strikes. The parent swoops in, and while the kids may act annoyed, you can see the relief on their faces that someone intervened. My children know that while their sibling might keep fighting until someone loses a tooth, Dad's demand for peace and stillness is protective. They know that if they obey and stop fighting, he's not going to let their sibling keep pummeling them. He's not going to sacrifice one for the other. Most parents, I hope, envision a household where all their children thrive. The wind and the waves went still for Jesus without a fight, because they knew and trusted that voice.

By contrast, the wind and the waves we see now, in the ever-increasing natural disasters caused by rising sea levels and temperatures, are a response to our one-sided, self-centered exploitation. We do not have all of creation's best interest in mind, and the wind and waves cannot trust us the way they trusted Jesus in the gospels.

"When we abandon our posts as God's good stewards of any area of the Kingdom of God, including territory that formerly welcomed God, we block His needed hand of protection," writes Maori evangelist and chemist Winkie Pratney.[1] Indigenous theologian Randy Woodley quotes Pratney in his book *Shalom and the Community of Creation* and then himself concludes, "Mother Earth is now trying to rebalance the overuse through random 'acts of nature.'"[2]

I'm not comfortable saying that natural disasters are God's way of punishing us for specific wrongdoing—the hurricane doesn't target the home of the town gossip or the guy with the closet full of porn—but I do believe increasingly violent weather is a demonstrable consequence of a broken relationship. We have exploited the earth, and now the earth's imbalance is freezing pedestrians in Buffalo and drowning motorists in California and flooding homes in Florida. The flattened homes and raging storm surges are collateral damage in what Woodley compares to a messy divorce between humankind and the earth.

Anishinaabe-Ukrainian writer Patty Krawec urges readers to see the connection between abuse of the land, abuse of its people, and the emotional responses of each on behalf of the other. "The land mourns and wastes away not only because of the things humanity has done, but because of the things it has not done, such as our lack of care for those who suffer. The land has absorbed the blood of that suffering, and it mourns."[3]

Paul's observation that creation is groaning under the curse of sin reinforces my hunch that those closest to Jesus's teaching shared an awareness of nature's connection to God. If we think of sin as an exploitative lust for power over others based on scarcity, we quickly see that sin's first victim is always nature. It's our desire to possess and exploit the land that leads, repeatedly, to our exploitation of the people who live on it and work it.

The gospels don't get into God's relationship with the earth—maybe because it's beyond what we have language to understand. Maybe Jesus did talk about it, but nobody repeated it because it didn't seem relevant. (Do you ever think about that? How many "red letters" are missing from the Bible? Who was Jesus when he was chatting about innovations in carpentry or how he liked his fish cooked?) We do have Jesus on record saying that God's care for the birds and the flowers should reassure us that God won't let us go naked or hungry, but the bulk of the gospels focus on humankind. Still, as Woodley points out, in the agrarian Jewish world, the flourishing of nature and humankind would not have been far apart. Furthermore, he writes, as the Roman empire introduced broader commercial trade, connection to the land and social class would both have been in flux.[4] Individuals, society, and nature were renegotiating their relationship, which opens up room for conflict and hunger for power. The Jesus Way articulated in the Sermon on the Mount, Jesus's parables, and his various interactions with people, is the expanded version of "Peace! Be still." The gospels show us how to pursue *shalom*—the restoration of harmony and equilibrium and wholeness where our scarcity-driven lifestyles have caused harm and chaos among society, relationships, and ecosystems—and how to turn our will to survive inside out.

Jesus's Way teaches us to take our anxious hoarding out of the center and replace it with a universal shalom. This forces us to submit to limits on our consumption, comfort, and convenience. It opens the door to gnarly dilemmas that cannot be solved by sacrificing the poor and the earth for the benefit of wealth, as we usually do. It's messier than simply building a bunker to wait out the apocalypse in comfort.

A universal survival story might have a lot in common with the complex plot of Hayao Miyazaki's movie *Nausicaä of the Valley of the Wind*, in which a princess must convince fearful, warring nations to live peacefully at the edge of a "toxic forest" that is trying to heal itself, guarded by terrifying giant insects. The tribes don't like the limits the forest places on them or living under the constant threat posed by the insects, and so they begin a supernatural arms race to bring humans under one leader and wage war on the forest. Only Princess Nausicaä—one of the best Christ figures in modern cinema—sees the wisdom in humbly maintaining balance, living without certainty or excess while the forest's redemption work goes on.

I usually hate survival stories, but I loved that one, because it was a healing story. The happy ending didn't involve walking into some secret valley or new planet of endless resources. The people of Nausicaä's world have to figure out how to manage with the world they have. They have to humbly cooperate and maintain the balance, even if it means they cannot have the excesses they once had. We can dream of some miracle cure that will calm our winds and waves and bring rain and frost in predictable patterns. We dream of some innovation that will allow us to carry on as we are, fueling our ever-growing needs. But it's more likely that we are the ones who need to hear the voice of Jesus say, "Peace! Be still."

NO PRIVATE ISLANDS ON MOTHER EARTH

Indigenous peoples' connection to land defies the limits of colonial imagination. Our capitalist formation teaches us to think of the land as a resource we can claim, not as the source from which we are formed. Calling it "Mother Earth" may make modern Christians uncomfortable, because we have been raised to both fear and ridicule Indigenous spirituality and animism, but as Woodley and others point out, we are made of the same molecules, minerals, and genetic code as much of creation. The Christian creation story even refers to the formation of man from the dirt. Just like a growing fetus draws from the material of the parent's body to grow, we survive by absorbing the stuff of creation, and it survives by absorbing from us, in kind. "Whether one believes that these relationships are from an evolutionary connection or that the Creator used much of the same materials in our construction, or both, we cannot escape the fact that we are all somehow related," Woodley writes.[5]

Indigenous cultures, Woodley explains, usually ascribe to an ethic or way of life that prioritizes this balance not only between humans and nature but, from that balance, a peace between humans themselves. Woodley's Cherokee people call this the *Harmony Way*, and he compares it with the ancient Hebrew understanding of shalom. Shalom and the Harmony Way are not so much sets of beliefs as ways of living, actions that accomplish balance. Rather than a specific list of dos and don'ts for the purpose of purity or righteousness and thus blessing (moralism), these lived principles are what Greeks would call a *telos*, the purpose embedded in our actions. We make decisions and take action with the flourishing of all as our guiding goal. If something appears to be good for me and bad for you, then it's not actually good for me. If my desire for "more" leads to an overgrazed field or a destroyed habitat, then my desire is out of balance.

These ideas show up in Indigenous theology throughout the world, as well as in philosophies such as Buddhism and Stoicism. People who have made peace their goal—instead of conquest—have reached a lot of the same conclusions: wanting peace precludes some other desires. In our industrialized world it's easy to focus on interpersonal peace, or even inner-personal peace, but the stuff of real life—food, air, water, shade, wind, climate—has always been included in shalom. As Woodley points out, the ancient Semitic cultures were among those embodied, earthy systems that include the literal source of life in their spiritual understanding.

As I have tried to learn to see the world this way—not as a big shopping cart full of things God gave me to consume but as a life-sustaining community with sacred purpose—I also think about Richard Rohr's teaching on *panentheism*, the belief that God is in all things. For me, thinking of a God who (note the personal pronoun) is interwoven with things we consider inanimate or lacking a soul brings science and spirit into harmony. You don't have to believe that to want to take care of the earth, but it helped me.

Because they have been fighting for power and control for as long as it's been offered to them, the Christian church has historically opposed scientific discovery that contradicted their interpretation of God's relationship to the world. Instead of greeting scientific discovery as an exciting new insight into a world filled with God, they viewed science as a threat to their authority, their position as the "this is how it is" guys. The power of premodern deities came from their inscrutability, and the fear that they could wipe us out without warning or reason. Sun gods were common because the sun is a mysterious life source until you have a telescope and astrophysicists explaining what it's made of and how it works. Fertility gods have been replaced by fertility doctors and agricultural science. Monotheism, if it depends on a lack of explanation or understanding, is a sitting duck. It's so vulnerable. But if God is not separate from what's under the microscope or beyond the telescope, then explanation and understanding become worship. We will have a reverence for all those molecules when we see that the God who "holds all creation together" (Col. 1:17 NLT) cares about the molecule's role in keeping the whole thing from falling apart. If you can read the Bible and make yourself interpret words such as *shalom* and *creation* not from the perspective of a post-Enlightenment brain-on-legs but as an embedded, earthy person whose source of knowledge about God and God's provision begins with the land, the whole of Scripture starts to sound more like the Harmony Way.

An emphasis on our place—the earth we share over the generations—should also give us pause as we listen to the voices of young activists. We are obsessed with progress and growth, but often without the telos of harmony. We want more for the sake of more, but we have not considered that all these progressing generations are tied to one place: the earth.

In the hands of people who have amassed billions of dollars and get richer every day, words like *progress, future,* and even *optimism* have a dark history, says technology theorist Douglas Rushkoff. "Usually these are just euphemisms for conquest, colonization, domination, and extraction. They describe ends-justifies-the-means campaigns to change the landscape and achieve monopoly."[6]

Think about the railroad titans, the European colonial empires, and every terrifying sci-fi disaster movie you've ever seen. The narrative of progress almost always glazes over a suffering story.

Rushkoff has gotten up close to the conquistadors of our dystopian future. He was once summoned to a private island retreat by a bunch of super rich Silicon Valley types to discuss the issue keeping them up at night: surviving the "Event," a.k.a. extinction-level disasters brought on by climate change. In his subsequent book, *Survival of the Richest: Escape Fantasies of the Tech Billionaires*, he explains that the tech bros have basically given up on the survival of the planet and are thinking more about *when*, not *if*, they need to abandon the rest of us and become the next evolution of mankind through some sort of technological advance. There may be some wisdom in accepting that mitigation is more valuable than prevention at this point, as the wheels of catastrophic climate change are already turning. The future is indeed here. But with the combined billions in the room where Rushkoff was sitting as a survival consultant, a lot could be done to slow, offset, or lessen the impact of climate change. Billions of dollars is at least seed funding for innovations to offset the effects of rising sea levels and drought, for taking big swings at reforestation and renewable energy. Instead, Rushkoff had been invited to offer insight on the future of humanity as disembodied technology. They wanted him to offer some practical advice on what those in Silicon Valley call "the Mindset." "Ultimately, according to the technosolutions orthodoxy, the human future climaxes by uploading our consciousness to a computer, or, perhaps better, accepting technology itself as our evolutionary successor," he writes.[7]

But the Mindset is a lie, Rushkoff argues in his searing conclusion. We are biologically, neurologically—and I would say spiritually—connected to each other and to this place.

"To the extent that we have any goals at all, we should not strive for the Mindset's individual achievements, discrete wins, or profitable exits, but rather seek more incremental progress toward collective coherence," Rushkoff concludes.[8] There is no alternative survival story—no man is a private island. Our survival story has to include everyone, or it is simply the same old story of suffering.

FRAGILE JUBILEE

Early in my journalism career, I decided to focus on equity in all my reporting and on solutions to pernicious problems as much as possible. I joined a scrappy team for a short-lived project dedicated solely to covering inequality and people working to change it in San Antonio. In pursuit of a story on environmental justice, I asked an older reporter, a Black man, if he knew of any local climate activists who were engaging communities of color. It was tough, he said, because a lot of environmental messaging targets white, liberal, college-educated audiences. Activists talk a lot about preserving our beautiful world so that we can continue to enjoy it. (Woodley calls this a utilitarian argument.[9]) But when your community is barred in various ways from enjoying it already, it's a hard sell, he explained. Marginalized groups are distanced by the utilitarian arguments for climate action.

But the idea of mutual thriving brings economic and environmental justice together. It suggests we have enough, and that "enough"—not "more"—when correctly distributed, is the true meaning of abundance. In the Old Testament, Hebrew farmers are told to leave the edges of their crops for the poor (Lev. 23:22). The underlying idea is abundance—there's enough for everyone if it is distributed correctly. The Year of Jubilee (Lev. 25) reminded Israel that they would be okay if there was a year of economic reset. Their security didn't come from amassing generational wealth at the expense of others or overusing the land. In fact, in that year they could eat only what grew naturally. They had to remember how to live off what the land gives willingly, to forage. They had to take a step back from the Neolithic agricultural revolution—the basis of class society.

The Year of Jubilee reminded Israel that humans don't need to endlessly extract from the earth or from each other to have enough. As long as there's balance, they will be okay. They weren't dependent on debts being repaid or amassing more land. They had enough, and if they ever lacked, their neighbors would have enough to share. An individual might experience scarcity on their own, but they are connected to the abundance of the community, and that abundance can only be accessed through an abundance of spirit, what we call *generosity*.

In the New Testament, Jesus provided abundant food for the crowds gathered to hear him teach, but as Christian climate activist Vanessa Nakate told *Sojourners* magazine in an interview, he also told them to gather up the extra, presumably to do something good with it. "God is not a God of waste," Nakate said.[10]

As a Ugandan, Nakate is familiar with the exclusion of marginalized people from the global community conversation—she herself was clipped out of an Associated Press photo at a Davos protest where she was standing with four white, high-profile European climate celebrities. It motivated her to speak up more, to make the world see that climate activism is neither impractical nor a "white" interest. In East Africa the effects of climate change are immediate and tangible. It isn't just the destructive power of a hurricane or a fire—real though they are—but the economic devastation of drought and flood. The people most harmed in economic crises are the poor who don't have a backup plan, who depend on the land for their food and their income. When communities must uproot because their crops are gone, it is poor women and children who lose their security first, she told *Sojourners*. They don't have a private island to flee to, and they can't upload to the metaverse.[11]

The Harmony Way, Woodley explains, is measured by the margins. We have to be attentive to the suffering stories of those most affected by natural and economic imbalance, because they offer unique insight on the global survival story. If any species is going extinct, we cannot celebrate a healthy ecosystem. If poverty and oppression are widespread, we cannot claim that our progress and innovations have brought peace. These are signs of the imbalance, but those most harmed are rarely those to blame. There's a reason so many activists show up to protest at Davos, where the billionaires gather to discuss the state of things. Knowing how many of them are cynically looking for an escape raft, the protesters outside represent those whose destiny is tied to the ship. Theirs are the stories we need to hear, and that's where the solutions will come from—from the people whose lives are jeopardized by our current race to Ragnarök.

"Climate change is more than statistics," Nakate said in her interview with *Sojourners*. "We need to look at what actually happens to the people, what happens to the women, what happens to the girls, what happens to communities when these disasters happen. When we bring in the conversation of the people, then comes in gender equality, there comes in poverty, education for all—so it's really a place of knowing that it's not just a fight for one thing, but it's a fight for many things."[12]

Taking up our climate cross means dying to the idea of abundance as "more for me" and rising to the idea of abundance as "enough for all." Our imagination has to change. When someone says "abundance," we should not picture throwing dollar bills in the air and rolling around in them, or dancing in a spewing oil well, or having food flown in from exotic locales to suit our Tuesday-night whims.

We also have to stop thinking of abundance as having the most well-stocked bunker just in case this Jubilee idea doesn't work out. I, for one, took notes on what happened when Israel had to look to Egypt for help during the big famine in Genesis! If Joseph hadn't had the wisdom to plan ahead, Israel would have been sunk. If Israel had thought to stash some rainy-day grain, they wouldn't have ended up as Egyptian slaves. But that's the rub: in times of scarcity, we fear being the one who has to trade freedom for survival. Not everybody is going to play by Jubilee rules, so we want to protect ourselves. Some degree of planning ahead is obviously wise, but it might not hurt us to consider how much of that is too much. Whether our abundance is crops or cash or some other capital, we have to maintain a balance personally, communally, but also globally. There's an aspect of shalom you can't control, but if we respond to that lack of control by trying to hoard resources or arm ourselves—we adopt an "us vs. them" view of our neighbors as competitors for resources—we tip the balance faster.

Of course, this brings up a real dilemma: the gospels describe a way of abundance, but it's really still in a tug of war with the scarcity and death described in the story of the fall of man in Genesis 3. Plants have to die for us to live. Animals have to die for carnivores to eat. Our bodies break down. The earth still groans. We do still have to face the reality that if I live the way Jesus described, there might come a time when I don't have what I want, maybe even what I need. I might choose to consume less and share more, only to die in the end, while some tech bro laughs at me from the metaverse. I am convinced that this sort of fear and cynicism keeps a lot of people from joining humanity's quest for survival. The apostle Paul, who was apparently plagued by the persistence of death in the world, saw the temptation of this logic. If there is no hope, if death gets us all in the end, he writes to the Corinthian church, then, "Let us eat and drink, for tomorrow we die" (1 Cor. 15:32).

Death and scarcity together are the big fear, and when we avoid them *at all cost*, we end up losing our balance. The logical thing in the face of scarcity is to hoard. It does make sense to make sure I get mine. But note the full context of Paul's hedonistic words to the Corinthians: "*If the dead are not raised*, 'Let us eat and drink, for tomorrow we die.'" Ah, but we know that Paul does believe the dead will be raised. He does believe that beyond death, the ultimate scarcity, there is life, the ultimate abundance.

If we do not fear death because life is on the other side—however that might look—we can live without fear in a world where at some point, to maintain the balance, it will be our turn to go without, and eventually our turn to die. Maybe that will be at a peaceful old age with a full belly, and our bodies will be able to put nutrients back into the earth. Maybe we will die because we shared our emergency supply of beans with someone else during the apocalypse. But speaking of beans, the beans were alive once too. Something always has to die, but if we treat it as sacred, the way we want our own life treated, that death is not inconsequential. It's not without meaning. We pray over our food to give thanks to God, the God who is everywhere, and thus was within the living things that died to give us life, and we don't take more than we need.

HEALING OUR CLIMATE STORY

To alleviate the suffering of climate change will require action and ingenuity. It will also require cooperation, which is why we need a new guiding story, one that allows us to hear Jesus say, "Peace, be still." The mythology and stories of capitalist competition have driven us to use earth's resources in a "bigger, faster, further" way—often conflating wealth, comfort, and convenience with need. It will require a different imagination to make us better global neighbors.

Context: If we see the earth as our home and our source, without alternative, we know that when it suffers extinctions and imbalance, humanity will suffer with it. If we relate to our home with love and understanding—and extend that to our fellow earth dwellers as well—our conversations have to change from responsible extraction to sacred investment.

Judgments: Keeping the earth in a life-sustaining balance should be prerequisite to all human activity, a guiding criterion. This will create limits on industry and economics, but those limits should be judged to be appropriate. Limits on "more" are tolerable suffering for the people and planet exploited by a culture of ravenous extraction.

Trade-offs: Nowhere is it clearer that we must die to the quest for "more for me" and rise to the idea that "enough for all" is the true abundance. For some of us this means having less than we have now, which does feel like suffering, but if we have harmony and balance as our goals, the suffering will be tolerable.

Us vs. them: We have to stop imagining ourselves among the lucky few uploaded to the future or hiding in the secret bunker. First of all, it's assholery. Second, there's no guarantee that the end of all this is anything short of global extinction. We share a planet. We are all earthlings; we are all children of God.

Distance and compassion: Being still allows us to see how close we are, how limited we are by our humanity and our dependence on the earth. We can panic about that reality—I do, regularly—or we can keep that inner stillness as we listen to the people telling us what we need to do next to ensure that our global neighbors and our children's children have enough.

Chapter 11

COVID-19–THE LOST PLOT

"*I shall kill them all!*"

—ABRAHAM LINCOLN, in the 2012 movie about his side
hustle, *Abraham Lincoln: Vampire Hunter*

I f you're tempted to skip this COVID-19 chapter, know that I was tempted
to skip writing it. We're all overstuffed on pandemic analysis. I get it.

In May 2020 I took a contract gig with *The 74 Million* to cover what we
thought would be a three-month school shutdown. We imagined an eight- or
nine-month timeline, from shutdown to full recovery. I was to focus on the
local impacts in San Antonio, where I live.

Two years later, I wrote what I vowed would be my last education story
about San Antonio, my last education-and-COVID story, and started considering an end to education reporting altogether. I told people I was tired
of shitting where I slept, that I was tired of reporting about the schools my
kids attend, tired of running into sources at the grocery store or coffee shop
where they would be telling me their conspiracy theories and then, when I
asked for evidence, reply, "Well, I'm not going to do your job for you. You're
the journalist."

Really, though, what had burned me out was the shrill, combative, often
unhinged tone of pandemic discourse, and the fact that many of my friends
and sources in San Antonio had become people I no longer recognized, con-
sumed by anger and anxiety, because they felt they were living in a world—be
it Democratic San Antonio, Republican Texas, bureaucratic school district, or
chaotic country—unmoved by their suffering.

Honestly, I sympathized with most of them. I was worn out from being
worried, from wondering if every camping trip, every birthday celebration,

every family dinner was going to be derailed by the little sniffle I'd overheard from my kids' bedroom. Summer in a mask in Texas was miserable, and so were the endless days of sameness without playdates and activities and vacations. And all of that, for me, paled in comparison to the social anxiety and the fear that I was doing COVID wrong. I score pretty high on scrupulosity, and there was *no end* of trying to prove your pandemic righteousness by how isolated, how masked, how careful you could be, and how many family members you cut out of your life because they were less so.

But then I was working on a piece for *The Grade*, an education journalism analysis column, and I talked to Alec McGillis, who was sitting in a parking lot in the Texas panhandle, trying to recover from some recent reporting he'd been doing for *ProPublica*. McGillis was an early voice foretelling the second pandemic, the children's mental health crisis, heading our way. He wrote about a young man he mentored who was falling through the cracks of distance learning in Baltimore, and then he wrote about Hobbs, New Mexico, which had kept schools closed well into 2021 when I spoke with him.

Teens in Hobbs were watching their peers just thirty minutes and a state line away in Texas, where schools were open and the football season was underway. The Hobbs teens were losing hope, and a spate of suicides had rocked the small town. McGillis was livid. Reading the story when it came out, I was overwhelmed. I pivoted my reporting away from mask battles and on to solutions for the youth mental health crisis, as much as possible. If I wanted to stay in journalism, I was going to have to tap out of the national screaming match and start a more subtle, kid-by-kid search for the answer to suffering. I stayed in the game, but I've watched superintendents, pastors, and other leaders retire in droves after the pandemic, and I understand why.

The pandemic's jarring, meandering, disjointed plot is still unfolding as I write this in 2023. The 2019 edition of SARS-CoV-2 is still very much with us. People are still dying. Much has returned to normal—you can even go on cruises, which I thought for sure would be a dead industry—but we have not even begun to address the tatters of our social and emotional health. The anger and alienation are still there, the anxiety is there, the distrust. The pandemic was made of global suffering stories. Stories of lost loved ones and wrecked livelihoods. But there's a dynamic to the suffering stories in the United States that is unique, and it's not coincidental that we've seen a higher death rate than any other wealthy nation. We were, in many ways, structurally set up to fail.

THE MIDDLE CHILDREN OF GOVERNANCE

When schools closed in March 2020, a lot of people, my husband included, wondered if this would be our generation's World War II. If we would unite, ration butter, light candles, manufacture rivets, etc., but with viral health protocols. And for a while, the briefest of moments, we did. For the briefest of moments, we were delivering groceries to elderly family members, sewing masks, and meeting up with friends on Zoom for virtual tours through art museums.

And then we apparently remembered that we were Americans and all this unity was ruining our vibe. The pandemic became less like our World War II moment and more like our Civil War moment. Instead of *Saving Private Ryan*, we were living in the plot—if you want to call it that—of *Abraham Lincoln: Vampire Hunter*: a transmissible condition, a country coming apart, and what would have been a massive conspiracy cover-up if the conspiracy were not fictional.

Despite what the name may suggest, the United States is not built for a united response. We have fifty states, all of which have some degree of sovereignty. The Constitution outlines the powers of the federal government while all other issues are, in theory, left to the states. But things were a lot simpler in the 1780s when the Constitution was written and ratified, and today we spend a lot of time debating whose jurisdiction applies when and where. Education, abortion, healthcare—essentially every conflict in this book is also a conflict over state and federal power, which means at some point the Supreme Court has had to referee the fight. During the pandemic we saw a lot of what legal scholar Jamal Greene calls *rightsism*, the prioritizing of certain rights as absolute, even to the point of negating other rights. "Americans are more than a little bit rightsist. They discriminate firmly between those rights that count—and which judges must apply vigorously against public officials—and those that don't count—which the government must therefore ignore."[1] Living in a Title I school district in a Democratic city in a Republican state under a federal government, I experienced pandemic rightsism as the daily monitoring of various court cases to figure out if my children's classmates would be wearing masks or not.

I live in Texas, which has made state sovereignty its whole personality, and where the state attorney general does little more than intervene in public high school religious liberty cases and sue the federal government (though as I write this, he is being impeached, so perhaps he had been doing other, less legal things).

I know I said I wasn't going to talk about partisan politics as the basis of "us vs. them," and I'm going to try to avoid oversimplifying it. As you'll see later, the "us vs. them" of the pandemic is not blindly partisan but a sort of primal, threat-sensitive partisanship. It is sadly ironic that the most politically agnostic source of suffering in this book—a virus that did not care who you voted for—elicited the most irrationally partisan response. It was an unforced error. It didn't have to be a chapter in this book! I don't have chapters on cancer, shark attacks, or car accidents. Those sources of suffering don't divide our society, but this one did. Politics—particularly partisanship and the structure of government—are essential pieces of context for pandemic suffering stories and have shaped the entire narrative and counternarrative.

The squabbling over pandemic protocols was not based on political principle. It was not about relegating decisions to the government closest to the people *or* about efficient disaster response. State governments' antipathy for city governments predates the pandemic by at least two hundred years. In the *Texas Law Review*, Richard Schragger argues that anti-urbanism is the result of a federal system that places a layer of governance between the national and local governments. The Constitution sets us up to constantly wonder who is really in charge here. Like any middle child, the state-level governments resent the larger and pick on the lower, trying to not let too much power seep out of their jurisdiction. Sensitive to the concerns of rural states—those middle children without a hefty population to boost their influence—the framers of the Constitution saw to it that the way the states are represented at the federal level privileges rural areas through the Senate and the Electoral College—which each, in their own way, discount the population density that would otherwise tip the federal government toward urban priorities.

Cities tend to be more liberal and regulated—I love my queer neighbors and don't want them to lose local contracts based on their sexuality, so I support the nondiscrimination ordinance. I also don't want them to run a twenty-four-hour auto body shop right under my bedroom window, so I might sign a petition against a rezoning request. Conservative state governments often punish cities by passing laws that preempt local nondiscrimination ordinances or tree preservation efforts or plastic bag bans. But then, Democratic state governments and their cities also bicker over who can impose what or who can distribute which money.

Preemption is bipartisan, but partisan politics obviously influence the federal-state-local relationship. Overlapping state and federal districts are often gerrymandered to carve up cities into strangely shaped parcels of people who feel the same way about abortion and income tax, instead of, say, people who have to share a waste management service or major thoroughfare. Partisan *bona fides* then become incredibly important for state legislatures and the US House of Representatives. A tiny fraction of primary voters determines who gets nominated to a sure victory in a general election where the "R" or the "D" by a name is the only thing that matters. Thanks to gerrymandering, 75 percent of Americans live under *trifecta* state governments, where the governorship and both houses of the state legislature are controlled by the same party. They then appoint judges who share their interpretations of the law. After a while, there's a lot less balancing that needs to be done between the branches of state government, and instead the state acts as a counterbalance to local and federal governments. The dominant party indicates what kind of counterbalance they will be. North Carolina's infamous 2016 "bathroom bill" was actually a Republican trifecta state preemption of an inclusive facilities ordinance in Charlotte. New York, which was essentially a trifecta state in 2017 despite some funny business in the state senate, preempted local short-term rental ordinances, to the great displeasure of the booming New York City Airbnb market.

Into this highly contested landscape of governance, with local, state, federal, and partisan interests vying for control, we introduce the pandemic, a quick moving, evolving, deadly virus that would require sacrifice to avoid suffering. An individual could not protect themselves against the virus without the cooperation of others. Plus, the emergency funds needed to be allocated, flowing through overlapping governmental bodies.

To make matters so, so, so much worse, one of the most intense battle grounds of the pandemic would be schools, where state and local governments collide regularly, the federal government funds little and requires lots, and yet another layer of government also gets to make rules: school districts. It's also where we stash our kids, whose well-being really gets us riled up. It's *also* where millions of American children get most of their food and the only way that millions of American parents can hold the jobs that put food on their tables at home.

The suffering from the pandemic increased as our precarious systems, already built with political feasibility rather than efficacy and equity in mind, collapsed in unique ways for every family. For those in the service industry, income evaporated instantly. For those who could work from home, they had to figure out how to do that while overseeing virtual learning. The immuno-compromised had to fight the loneliness of isolation, and frontline workers had to figure out how to protect themselves and their families from inevitable and repeated exposure. We ran out of hospital beds and respirators. Vaccines were developed quickly, which was nice, but then the rollout was chaotic, complicated by conspiracy theories, mandates, and opposition to mandates. As our systems and lives collapsed, Americans channeled our collective anxiety into two primary narratives: either our rights or our safety was being violated, and half the country was to blame.

LIBERTY VS. SAFETY

Pitting the rights of the individual against the safety of the community was a recipe for disaster, because no prosocial person would ever want to sacrifice either of those things. At the extremes, both are intolerable. But we were told, explicitly, that these were our choices.

Early in the pandemic, two things sent shivers down my spine. The first was in spring of 2020, mere weeks after the shutdowns, when Texas Lt. Governor Dan Patrick went on national television and said that Texas should reopen businesses because older Texans would gladly risk their health for a stable economy. The reaction was swift, claiming that he was suggesting our grandparents sacrifice themselves for Wall Street. Now listen, that very well may have been what he was suggesting, but a collapsing economy is nothing to shrug off. Patrick may or may not have had working-class Texans in mind, but I was reporting on the conditions for children of working-class Texans, and the reality was grim. We all saw the now iconic photo of cars lined up at the San Antonio Food Bank. I do think most grandparents would risk their health to spare their grandchildren from chronic food insecurity.

What scared me about Patrick's statement was how cavalier he was about allowing *that* to be the choice. We can have a stable economy, but only as the trade-off for letting our grandparents die.

The other ominous piece of news analysis came out in *Politico* under the headline "Wearing a Mask Is for Smug Liberals. Refusing to Is for Reckless Republicans." The article rightly described the landscape, even before mask mandates were widespread and hotly debated. Kids weren't back at school yet. Businesses were still shut down. No one was flying. Masks, a reasonable barrier between us and a deadly virus, were suddenly equivalent to putting one of those "In this house we believe . . ." signs in your front yard.

The *Politico* article summarized well: "For progressives, masks have become a sign that you take the pandemic seriously and are willing to make a personal sacrifice to save lives. Prominent people who don't wear them are shamed and dragged on Twitter by lefty accounts. On the right, where the mask is often seen as the symbol of a purported overreaction to the coronavirus, mask promotion is a target of ridicule, a sign that in a deeply polarized America almost anything can be politicized and turned into a token of tribal affiliation."[2]

It went on to analyze some of the pandemic-downplaying groundwork laid by Fox News and others who warned that manufacturing an emergency would legitimize increases in power by power-hungry entities like, you know, the Centers for Disease Control. Masks were a reminder that we were in unprecedented times, they implied, and unprecedented times would end with us all wearing gray government-issue work suits, marrying and procreating based on government assignment, and sending 95 percent of our income back to Big Brother.

Pandemic downplay, of course, reached its nadir in the conspiracy theories and pseudoscience from sources such as QAnon and vitamin salesman Joseph Mercola. Mercola and others spun narratives to allow ordinary people to fight Big Government overreach without feeling like they were indifferent to the suffering of their neighbors, the gullible idiots who had been deceived by Anthony Fauci. The narratives let them off the hook for their lack of compassion. They couldn't be indifferent toward suffering that didn't exist! Or maybe COVID was real, but it was just a bad cold. Or maybe the only people dying from COVID were weak and needed to be weeded out anyway. Actually, that last position, which I heard spoken into my own living ears, isn't so much trying to walk the line between compassion and politics. That's eugenics.

Linguist Amanda Montell explains the connection between tribalism, conspiracy theory, and our weak and fractured American social systems in her book *Cultish: The Language of Fanaticism*. The United States has historically been not only more religious than other well-off countries but also exceptionally cult-prone, she writes, because it is socially chaotic.[3] I would add that the aforementioned federalist structure also facilitates this chaos. There's no assurance that the government will protect or provide, and so Americans feel "all on their own." They are looking for a tribe, and groups such as QAnon can, through insider language and mantra-like slogans, generate an almost religious loyalty, no matter how bonkers their claims. The slogan "Make America Great Again" became almost creedal as it created the Cult of Trump and gave the science denial of the pandemic a religious tone.

The Trump era already felt like a constant fight, and it was intensifying as 2020 careened toward the November election. Nothing, not even the suffering of billions, could escape the framing of high-conflict politics. In fact, the suffering of the pandemic sort of put some proof to the bones of the argument that half the country was indifferent to your suffering. Or at least that they were ready to tolerate it for the sake of their concept of the nation.

Liberty and safety were the trade-offs offered to us in the early pandemic, and I will be very honest and say that I don't have a lot of tolerance for pandemic downplay. I think it was crafted in bad faith, because we were in an election year and domestic economic crises are bad for the incumbent. Plenty of people adopted pandemic downplay narratives as they tired of social distancing and masks, but the narrative's source was political.

But the pandemic wore on, and our entrenched positions on liberty and safety prevented us from considering different kinds of suffering, and in this pandemic safety diehards were just as culpable. It should have been obvious after the spring shutdowns that keeping schools closed would do lasting harm to children—not just academically, but emotionally. While we were all focused on making sure their test scores could recover, kids were sliding into a developmental fugue state, some racking up what child development experts call "adverse childhood experiences" that could have lifetime impacts at least as detrimental as the effects of COVID-19.

But by the time we started seeing youth mental health data, we were committed to the initial trade-off of liberty vs. safety, and both deemed that children's suffering was tolerable in some way. Because the "open schools" crowd was so synonymous with the anti-mask, anti-mandate crowd, many kids in Democrat-controlled states languished in virtual learning longer than they had to. Their suffering was deemed tolerable. Kids in Republican-controlled states returned to schools, but, in the name of liberty, mask mandates and mitigation strategies disappeared prematurely and outbreaks followed. Their suffering was also deemed tolerable.

Again, we had options. We could have been meticulous. We could have prioritized getting the kids back to school at the expense of other things. We could have rallied around them as a society, sacrificing other liberties to keep our kids safe and connected to their peers and teachers. What little nuance I saw during the pandemic did come from school districts, the governing body most closely connected to the people it serves. There were smart reopening plans, well-done virtual hybrid options. There were long-standing mask mandates and teacher vaccination requirements that allowed kids to continue getting the meals, social worker visits, and other necessary services provided by schools.

But that was not the case everywhere. In many places and cases, we had our early pandemic positions and stuck with them. These were our choices, but we could not make them in isolation, either. The "us vs. them" of the pandemic was reiterated every time we left our houses.

VECTORS VS. NEIGHBORS

The person-to-person transmission of the virus reiterated how closely we live together, how connected we really are. Unfortunately, that closeness often felt like blame more than compassion, because the trade-off forced by our pandemic responses made others into threats. People became vectors of disease rather than those who might help us stay safe or aid us when we fell ill. Should you slip up on a protocol, you would imagine others sneering at you from behind their N-95s. In one important sense, the pandemic made the whole world feel like "them" despite our best intentions to be "all in this together."

The isolation, the exhaustion, the perfectionism—it was all alienating, and I think that's an under-addressed issue we need to confront as a country. We have to find our way back to each other not as the imagined community of the nation but as the actual community of people who bump into each other every day. Because while viral contagion underscored how closely connected we are, being forced to distance from each other reminded us how much we need that connection.

In the place of closeness and connection, we settled for "people who vote like I do" as "us." We looked to the coercive power of the state to take care of us because we felt we had lost the compassion of our neighbors. While we started alone in our homes, we ended at ballot boxes, boardrooms, and statehouses. The suffering of the pandemic felt ubiquitous and intolerable—whether it was mask fatigue or virtual learning failure or succumbing to the actual virus—and we demanded a "them" to blame.

The "us vs. them" of the pandemic divided Americans into one nation committed to life and another nation committed to liberty, bound together by a federalist system ostensibly committed to both. It was a chaotic, jarring mess of plotlines, and we all suffered as a result.

THE BROKEN BONES OF OUR COVID-19 STORY

Really, this story couldn't have gone more off the rails.

Context: Fighting a contagious virus requires cooperation and efficiency, but the United States was not built for cooperation and efficiency. The context of overlapping governments and high-conflict partisanship made the country a hospitable landscape for the virus to spread.

Judgments: During the pandemic, the public had to judge whether losing some degree of liberty or safety was preferable, and most of us made that judgment based on what our political tribe told us was more important.

Trade-offs: The absolute nature of the judgment forced an impossible trade-off that ultimately led to more suffering. A few months into the pandemic, adherence or nonadherence to safety protocols was being used to signal a moral code, and political messaging began to discourage compromise and balance. We were unable to adjust our stance to accommodate the real suffering in front of us as it evolved—whether it was the lethal effects of the virus or the languishing of a generation of school children.

Us vs. them: As much as I have avoided letting politics be the ultimate "us vs. them" of each story, that's really what was going on with COVID-19. The pandemic deepened the already tectonic Right vs. Left divide in our country. Anyone who argued for nuance or balance was placing themselves in the no-man's-land between the trenches, taking fire from both sides.

Distance and blame: The pandemic underscored the need for connection, but also the inherent danger of connection. In our isolation, we blamed each other for all the suffering.

Chapter 12

AN ALTERNATIVE PANDEMIC MYTHOLOGY

"We finally have a common struggle now. Think about that. For once,
all the people who've been begging and, I mean, literally begging for
you to feel how hard any given day is, now, you know. How did it
feel to be helpless? If you can remember what it was like to be helpless
and face a force so powerful, it could erase half the planet . . ."

—SAM WILSON, in his very first outing as
Captain America, in the Marvel series
The Falcon and the Winter Soldier

Every now and then, some beleaguered pastor on Twitter feels the need to say, "If you're too liberal for conservatives and too conservative for liberals, you're probably thinking like Jesus." Or something like that. It's chum in the water for the Twitter sharks who rightly react against the arrogance of twenty-first-century Americans doing cheap apples-to-figs comparisons of our current politics and the summarized teachings of a scantily documented rebel mystic. I rarely join in the feeding frenzy, because Twitter sharks bite indiscriminately, but if I did I would probably say something about the compulsive need to plot everybody on an American-based political spectrum, the inconsistency of most pastors' grab bag of political opinions, and the hubris of seeing that tons of people disagree with you and concluding, "I must be right."

"So, what, McNeel, let me guess, Jesus was a socialist?"

I have no idea. Which is why I'm not Tweeting about it. The historical record suggests Jesus of Nazareth never governed anything. The gospels are deliberately vague about the particulars of Jesus's politics. We see this in Matthew 22 when the Pharisees and Herodians try to get him to either advocate rebellion against Rome or legitimize the exploitation of the Roman empire by asking whether he thought Jews should pay taxes to Rome. There's quite a tone in his reply: "You hypocrites, why are you trying to trap me?" (Matt. 22:18).

Those opposed to his message of liberation from both the spiritualized tyranny of the religious authorities and the exploitation of the Roman empire would have tried to discredit him using irrelevant political mudslinging. Honestly, that sounds about right, historically. Before you martyr him, at least try to expose him as a fraud. In the gospels, then, Jesus replies skillfully, neither refusing to weigh in on taxes nor acknowledging Caesar as God. "Give back to Caesar what is Caesar's and to God what is God's" (v. 21). Slow claps, all around.

At the same time, Jesus, the guy who was politically executed, would probably have angered modern congregants for being too political. He would have received some sternly worded emails on Monday morning.

When Jesus announced his ministry in Luke 4 as the "year of the Lord's favor," he was reading from a scroll that corresponds to what we know as Isaiah 61. In it, the prophet inaugurates "the year of the Lord's favor" which scholars explain as a reference to the Year of Jubilee—the big reset year of rest, liberation, and debt relief. There are loads of other prophecies to choose from. He could have talked about being the heel that would crush the serpent's head (Gen. 3:16); he could have talked about being the promised offspring of Abraham in whom all the nations would be blessed (Gen. 22:18). Instead, he inaugurated the Jubilee, linking spiritual and material liberation, calling up all kinds of political and economic narratives for Israel and its Roman occupiers.

Can you see the email in your mind? "Why do you have to get so political, Jesus? Just stick to the gospel." Jesus got a sternly worded message from his hometown audience too: they tried to drive him off a cliff.

The gospels refuse to define Jesus's ministry in terms of the politics of the day—we don't see him joining up with Zealots, Romans, or Pharisees—while at the same time deeply involving him in what would be seen as political issues—because politics affect lives. We can learn from that. We need to learn from that, because we live in a suffering world that needs healing, and right now healing stories are hard to find unless your suffering meets the right political criteria.

Our approach to COVID-19 was completely derailed by the politicization of science and medicine. Different opinions on the social contract—the exchange of total, anarchic personal freedom for the security of governance—

influenced the compassion we were willing to show to our neighbors. Reporting on COVID-19 was the most I have ever hated journalism, because it was sometimes impossible to balance what Jim Phelan the narratologist called the ethics of telling and the ethics of toll. I had to tell the truth about the second pandemic of children's mental health. I also had to consider how it would be used as fodder for people who dangerously minimized the health risks of the coronavirus pandemic.

The recovery stories are just as fraught. Not only do we have widespread pandemic fatigue, but the virus, as of my writing this in 2023, is still circulating. Some of us feel obligated to act more cautious than we feel, while others are living with regrets about caution not taken. Some of us have ongoing health anxiety, while others have ongoing health effects from the virus. Some lost family members to the virus, while others lost family members to conflict over the virus. When a particularly nasty round of flu and RSV filled children's hospitals to capacity in 2022, some of my friends wondered if their child had weakened immunity from years of social distancing. Others wondered if their child's weakened immunity was from contracting COVID-19, which, at the time, they'd compared to a bad cold. But they whispered their concerns, because usually their community, like that of most people in the United States, was politically homogeneous, and expressing doubt about your side's accepted COVID-19 beliefs is still viewed as treasonous. If I admit that my anxiety spikes any time I put a fun event on the calendar, am I condemning the protocols that led me to cancel so many fun events over the past three years? If you decided to get vaccinated in late 2022, would you be scolded by those who feel you are too late to the game? Or would you be ridiculed by those who feel you gave in to the propaganda? If your four-year-old is still struggling with speech development, can you admit that you wonder whether masks played a role?

We learned a lot from the pandemic, but until we break the habit of politicizing suffering narratives, we are no more well-suited to take on the next crisis, or to do what needs to be done to heal from this one. The casualties are not just from our war against the virus but from the rhetorical civil war as well. The former demands a healing story, but it is the latter that keeps us from telling it. We have a hard time admitting that there were costs to the choices we made, because doing so sounds like we are giving up ground.

Jesus cut through the political noise and stuck to his healing and liberation story like a man with nothing to lose. Like Sam Wilson in his first big moment as Captain America in the Marvel Cinematic Universe series *The Falcon and the Winter Soldier*. The series picks up after the successful battle in *Avengers: Endgame* brings back all the people who had disappeared for five years in the "blip." The sudden return of half the earth's population is causing political mayhem. Their jobs are gone, their homes are occupied, and no government wants to claim them. A band of displaced people goes on a violent quest to take back their lives. Avenger Sam Wilson, who inherits the Captain America mantle, chooses not to accept the political "them" framing foisted upon people who had been displaced. He averts a violent disaster but then confronts the powers that be, who want him to agree that the displaced people are the enemy. He urges the politicians and world leaders to find a more universal response. He urges them to heed the suffering stories of the displaced people.

Look, I know Marvel metaphors don't stretch very far, because superheroes use physical dominance to subdue their enemies. It's absurd on its face. But superheroes are not real, and the scapegoating, tribal political tactics Sam Wilson confronts are real. Like the Jesus of the gospels (and a little like the new Captain America), we can say things that will cause political upset but refuse to let our agenda be linked to a political quest for domination. Like Jesus (and a little like the new Captain America) we can die to political tribalism and rise to a healing and liberation story. We can reject the mythology in which safety and freedom cannot coexist and embrace a mythology in which what is sacrificed for the good of others is ultimately restored. It won't make us "too conservative and too liberal"—a redemptive, cruciform approach to suffering refuses to let political labels define acts of love and service, which undermines the efforts of people trying to use politics to gain control of people. Such a subversive way of living in the United States will likely feel like being alone in the wilderness. But you're in great company, because guess where Jesus was in Luke 4 before he announced his ministry to set the captives free? He was in the wilderness, being tempted by the devil to assert dominance. Luke's Gospel suggests a direct link between our resistance to the desire to dominate and the healing stories we are able to tell.

NEW PLAYBOOKS

I don't think there's much to be said about the federal model that made such a mess of our pandemic response. The United States may decide to reorganize itself one day, but no one is asking me how to do that, nor should they.

However, as part of the corps of journalists writing the first draft of pandemic history, I do have some thoughts on some other things that could change.

The same forces that dragged our national pandemic response into political morass are still with us, largely for lack of an alternative. In his challenging book *To Change the World: The Irony, Tragedy, and Possibility of Christianity in the Late Modern Age*, University of Virginia sociologist James Davison Hunter considers the possibility of an alternative. Our world is defined by politics, he writes, because the state is our only strong institution. It is the only authority we recognize, the only source of protection or identity. Evidence of this is in our language, Hunter writes, noting that we define all things as liberal or conservative. Churches, universities, and even communities are defined by their political ideology.[1] With no alternative constitution to claim them, politics gobbles up all the concerns of life—medicine, science, marriage, family life, curriculum, and all the other topics we've covered in this book—and puts a stamp on them. If you want to be part of public life, you're getting politics all over you.

The idea of a government by the people, for the people lulls us into believing that the state is the proper place for all this power. But ultimately, the state's power lies in what it can coerce us to do, mostly by threat of punishment. The rule of law can stop the marauding hordes, but it also keeps the peasants from revolting and rarely applies without bias. A society defined by politics, as we have seen during COVID-19, does not equip us to unite and care for one another. It is only designed to allocate resources and enforce mandates and restrictions. It's a necessary role, but I think we can all agree it's inadequate for inspiring the kind of cooperation needed to face down a pandemic, let alone foster the kind of healing we need to do.

So, suggests Hunter, what would it take for the church, meaning Christians in society, to be the alternative influence? His book asks what role Christianity has to play in public life. I would ask it this way: What would it take for the church to offer hope and healing on public issues without simply becoming a shill for a political solution?

Hunter considers three approaches Christians have taken in society— dominate, accommodate, and withdraw. None offers a compelling benefit to the world we are called to love, he suggests. Christianity's only path toward being a "good" in the world—a foreshadow of the peaceable kingdom Christ will one day bring to fullness—is to reject the temptations of politics and economics and devote itself to, again, *shalom*.

Sometimes that shalom will look like care for the poor, care for creation, and binding the wounds of the suffering. Sometimes it will take the form of a "community of resistance," Hunter writes. "As a natural expression of its passion to honor God in all things and love our neighbor as ourselves, the church and its people will challenge structures that dishonor God, dehumanize people, or do harm to creation."[2]

He suggests that the church devote itself to being a "faithful presence" in the world with a very different relationship to power—that we be able to engage public issues without looking to a political playbook. Hunter points to Jesus as an example of a very different kind of power. Not a power *over* but an ability to bring about goodness. Efficacy. In addition to being completely aligned to God's purposes and non-status-seeking, Jesus's power was bound up with compassion and used on behalf of all. It was the opposite of "us vs. them" playing to win. "In contrast to the kingdoms of this world, his kingdom manifests in the power to bless, unburden, serve, heal, mend, restore, and liberate," Hunter writes.[3] He goes on to suggest the Christian church find ways to be such a presence in society.

So I am wondering, what might such a context open up in terms of a healing story for a world traumatized and devastated by a pandemic?

INCONVENIENT SUFFERING

Following the Way of Jesus in the political wilderness means we do not expect a triumphant exchange of righteousness and blessing meted out in public policy. We cannot insist that the "right" policies and decisions are those that come with no price tag. The cost—be it rationing, taxing, regulating, or restricting—would not negate the policy, but we would not ignore the cost of policies we support. The church would be there with food, financial aid, childcare, and ministries of presence to help the community endure what had to be done. We would offer masked gatherings beyond the end of the mandates, and we would have found safe ways to keep our kids and teenagers together. We would lament and support while we and our neighbors give to Caesar what is Caesar's.

Political narratives downplay the cost of "our" policies and vilify or ignore those who suffer as a result. Counternarratives develop, and those counternarratives demand that the offending policy be changed to alleviate the suffering of a different "us"—a political remedy for a political problem.

When COVID-19 landed during the 2020 election season, no politician wanted to tell people that they would have to suffer—least of all their wealthy donors who lost money when we feebly attempted a lockdown for a couple of months that spring. (We in the United States did not technically lock down. There were no police with hoses like in South Africa or squads of police enforcement as in China.) When the counternarrative emerged in the form of angry parents refusing to wear masks or demanding that schools be opened, the narrative that allowed them to do so denied the seriousness of COVID-19. It was a way to downplay the suffering that would come from their proposed policies.

We were driven apart by the judgment that suffering was avoidable. We bridged the distance between us with blame. Reckless Republicans caused unnecessary deaths. Overbearing Democrats caused unnecessary damage.

The incredible suffering of the pandemic—the freezer trucks full of bodies, the overflowing hospitals, the 250,000 US children who lost at least one parent—demanded a response. But that response was painful—it was a line of 10,000 cars at a food bank in San Antonio. It was children who, teachers tell me every day, are still, after a year of in-person schooling, not quite the same.

A church in the wilderness can hold both truths in a way that politics cannot. It can hold both the suffering of a pandemic and the suffering of pandemic response with compassion, because it doesn't need to win a debate about what was not enough and what was too much. It doesn't need the suffering of one side to disappear to validate the suffering of the other. It draws us close to one another as a wounded people, all longing for and receiving compassion.

OUT OF CONTROL

Trying to spin the suffering stories of others—from underselling to lying outright—is an effort to control people's political and economic behavior. Wounded people drawing near to one another in compassion, listening to each other's suffering stories with compassion, are not going to be as politically useful. They will be less fearful, less angry, less convinced that getting their guy into office is the only way to prosper. They will be more difficult to control, because their compassion will flow in more than one direction. Rather than flowing toward a center, toward "my team," it will run from the inside out, in all sorts of politically inconvenient directions.

Acknowledging politically inconvenient suffering, we affirm that people often have good reason to be upset with people in power—including the leaders and elected officials we voted for and support. People have good reasons not to set aside their concerns for the sake of choosing someone "electable." A wilderness church would not have a desired political outcome in the back of their mind as they try to reason with the suffering person. We would stop trying to get people to set aside their concerns and support our agenda, because our first agenda includes their well-being. We would respect the agency of those who come to us for compassion, knowing that they alone can decide whether their suffering is tolerable or intolerable and what to do about that. They may choose to vote for the candidate we hate. They may choose to violate an ordinance we support. They may choose not to attend an event we planned. They may need financial assistance longer than they would have if they were willing to take bigger risks. They may choose to go to a different school or church. They may move away from our city or state. Giving up that persuasive, even coercive control is the cross we are asked to take up. It is the trade-off we are asked to make: dying to control so that we can rise to compassion.

This is different from how the state operates. The state must, for the sake of "stopping the spread," or preventing violence, or running out of water, make tough rules sometimes. It must, at times, demand compliance through mandates, taxes, and laws. Our relationship to the state might compel us to protest or to engage in civil disobedience. Our consciences sometimes compel us beyond the requirements of the law, like kids who sit in full car seats until they are ten years old, or people who bring three forms of voter ID. Whether resisting or going above and beyond, we relate to the state as a coercive power, something a wilderness church should not be.

We need a compassionate COVID-19 narrative for two reasons. First, we've got a lot of healing to do. I don't believe that we can find that "We're All in This Together" early-pandemic-yard-sign unity unless we take compassion seriously. The political framing we continue to allow is only making the world feel hostile, and it's really hard to be less anxious when you low-key hate half the people you encounter on a given day. Or at least you suspect you'd hate them if you knew how they voted.

The second reason we need to learn how to move toward one another in compassion is this: COVID-19 is not the last pandemic, disaster, or crisis we're going to face. We have got to get better at this. Those in charge will always make decisions based on some weird mix of science and politics. We will have to render to Caesar what is Caesar's. We need another place in the public sphere where we can, in showing deep compassion to all, render to God what is God's.

HEALING OUR PANDEMIC RESPONSE STORY

There's still time to get this right, because suffering is still with us—suffering caused by the pandemic and other suffering made worse by politicized responses to it. A healing story will take our compassion into places our politics cannot go.

Context: Instead of capitulating to a political context that shapes how we respond to suffering, Jesus's story offers a shalom-seeking context. Instead of letting our politics tell us how best to dole out compassion, we begin with the desire to see God's peace and love extended to humankind. With that goal in mind, some policies will look right. Others will look wrong. None will look perfect, and people of shalom can be prophetic voices—rather than shills—speaking truth to any political party, but not looking to that political party for permission to help, feed, fund, shelter, accommodate, or march with our neighbors.

Judgments: A healing narrative judges that suffering is suffering, even if it was necessary. When we see suffering, we should respond to it as suffering, without first asking if it undermines a policy or position we support.

Trade-offs: Allowing the suffering of the world to direct our attention, not a political agenda, we lose the confidence and moral superiority of perfectionism and the momentum that perfectionism affords us. If we move forward knowing that our positions cause suffering, we cannot barrel through, pushing our agendas without pause. We have to listen for the consequences. We die to expediency and rise to an uncertainty that allows us to hear each other.

Us vs. them: When we trade control for compassion, people will do things we wish they wouldn't. We will disagree. We will, at times, vote differently. But if we see our political foe as part of "us" with agency given to them by God, we will continue to approach them with a desire to understand and heal, not simply try to convince them or force them to do what we want.

Distance and compassion: We draw close in compassion not just to those whose suffering makes the case for our preferred policy but to those who suffer as a result of the policy we have to support.

Chapter 13

MASS SHOOTINGS—THE MURDER MYSTERY

A loss like this was a progression of miseries, like stepping stones. Until they reached the other side. The new continent. Where the terrible reality lived, and the sun never fully came out again.

—LOUISE PENNY, *A World of Curiosities*

In my childhood mind, Luby's Cafeteria was a dangerous place. It wasn't because the regional restaurant chain specialized in dishes like liver and onions and carrot slaw. It wasn't because their dinner hours were something like 4 p.m. to 8 p.m. It was because you might get shot at Luby's.

I was six years old in 1991 when the Luby's massacre happened in Killeen, Texas, a military town an hour north of Austin. My family ate Sunday lunches at a different Luby's—in New Braunfels, a tourism town an hour south of Austin—and I remember sitting terrified through lunch after lunch, plotting my escape route.

It was the deadliest mass shooting in the United States at the time and would remain so until the Virginia Tech shooting in 2007. Since then, the number has been topped again and again. Luby's now ranks sixth on the list, and Virginia Tech number three. Of the top ten, four are within a couple hours of my home: the University of Texas (1966), Luby's (1991), Sutherland Springs (2017), and Uvalde (2022). You have to be specific when you talk about the Luby's massacre. You can't say only "Killeen," like you usually would to identify a mass shooting in a town that size—like "Parkland" or even "Las Vegas." You have to be specific, because there have been two other high-profile mass shootings in Killeen since then, in 2009 and 2014.

I remember sitting in a car dealership watching the first reports coming out of Robb Elementary in Uvalde, watching the death count tick up. Thinking,

"No, no, no, not that many. Not little kids." As we know now, the total came to nineteen fourth graders and their two teachers. I would spend the next six months driving back and forth along a drought-parched US Highway 90, meeting people who had harrowing stories to tell about that day. I wrote an op-ed about sending my own children to school the next day and about deciding what to tell them. When to tell them. How to tell them. I've been writing about Uvalde ever since.

As I wrote the first draft of this chapter, in fact, I had to stop several times to take care of some edits on a story about Sylvia Uriegas, who ferried injured children to the hospital in her school bus because the city and county did not send enough ambulances to the school.

The suffering has been palpable. Whether at protests or board meetings or church services, the entire town seemed raw for months, and still feels heavy. Obviously they are angry too. They were angry in the way so many Texans are, as we watch our state government continue its saccharine relationship with the gun lobby, giving a Mad Libs version of thoughts and prayers and a paint-by-number portrait of Wild West cowboys, the alleged good guys with guns.

No one will deny the suffering of bereaved parents who lost their children, but as time went on in Uvalde, and parents and neighbors began to demand answers and action—as they pointed at specific gun laws and politicians—the compassion for their suffering cooled. They were no longer victims but opponents, and the politicians had a story ready, a dismissive hand to wave them away: their suffering was now tolerable, because they had chosen the wrong narrative. They were asking for the wrong kind of response.

From where I sit at my computer, with about ten thousand words on Uvalde's suffering transformed into stories and news articles, I think I understand the problem. The families demanding change are breaking the rule that says we must continue to be mystified by gun violence. Unlike a murder mystery novel, the question is rarely "Who?"; we usually know. But we still, like detectives, try to understand the two important components of any murder inquiry: motive and opportunity. Without motive and opportunity, you have no murder.

After a mass shooting, politicians often focus on the motive for such a "senseless act of violence." They reference "evil" like it is a fickle wind, blowing through our communities, brooding without explanation, unless that explanation fits a certain political paradigm, which it rarely does, because the shooters are so often the same gender and race as the politicians, sometimes even touting similar rhetoric about invasion of immigrants (as in El Paso) or the travesties of feminism (as at Luby's). They focus on nebulous evil, because there's not a lot you can do about nebulous things.

For those who do want to understand the motives, especially when they indicate something we might be able to change in our society, the hero of my favorite murder mysteries, Louise Penny's Chief Inspector Armand Gamache, has a helpful axiom: murder begins in the past. It is one tiny thing that has festered and grown into something that we might describe as "senseless." Which leads Gamache to conclude, "Murder was deeply human, the murdered and the murderer. To describe the murderer as a monstrosity, a grotesque, was to give him an unfair advantage. No. Murderers were human, and at the root of each murder was an emotion. Warped, no doubt. Twisted and ugly. But an emotion. And one so powerful it had driven a man to make a ghost."[1]

Murder has been around forever, and those who want to are going to find a way. Rocks. Fists. We absolutely need to deal with the mental health and social health issues that lead to murder. But the motives we know about in mass murders are also myriad. One guy didn't get the job he wanted. Another was bullied. Another couldn't get a girl to like him. Another hated Black people. Another believed Brown immigrants were replacing white people. But motive alone doesn't make a mass murder. There also must be opportunity and means. The opportunity appears to be simply a normal function of society: we gather together. Wherever there are people gathered in public, there's an opportunity. Especially for these shooters who seem to know that death is a likely outcome for themselves. Police and "good guys with guns" aren't much of a deterrent for someone ready to die or spend life in prison. For those who have lost loved ones in a massacre, the shooter's motive and opportunity don't matter nearly as much as his means. Taking away the means to kill indiscriminately is what's driving survivors' and families' demands for relief. If people who want to kill don't have access to efficient killing machines, they will be able to kill fewer people. That's the conclusion that will get you kicked off Texas Governor Greg Abbott's guest list.

Data from around the world says the survivors are correct. Preventing murder requires intervention on several levels. Preventing mass murder largely comes down to weapons regulation. But there's a reason this narrative is still anathema in places like Texas.

Gamache's insight on motive also applies, in the case of mass shootings, to means. There are deeply human reasons why shooters are able to obtain guns with a killing capacity unimagined in a world without light bulbs or combustion engines. It's not a mechanical function of the Constitution. It's an emotion, a desire, a fear, cultivated over centuries. The person pulling the trigger has a reason. They have a very human motive, even if we don't want to see it. That motive is not totally separate from the narrative that continues to provide them with the means.

Many families and survivors of mass shootings have, in the wake of tragedy, tried to change gun laws and culture in the United States, only to get an up-close view of how entrenched those things are, and how the laws and the culture feed off the pain and isolation of people in the United States. Once they have gone a few rounds with politicians and Second Amendment activists, the killing is not senseless—it is the logical result of a system built to privilege guns as the way people care for themselves, to ease the suffering of both real and perceived danger.

This is the suffering story at the heart of our national murder mystery: people living in isolated fear passing bullet by bullet into isolated grief.

WHEN A BULLET IS A HURRICANE

The trickiest part of the suffering wrought by mass shootings is that there is so much *agreement* about it. We rightly judge that this suffering is not necessary or deserved. In a sense it is the easiest of judgments: mass murder is wrong and bad. It should not have happened.

But we part ways on how to prevent it from happening again. Those who stay close to the suffering typically look for concrete changes to keep it from happening to anyone else. Those who operate at a distance make peace with a shapeless fear and consider what they might do to prepare for it, the way we might prepare for a hurricane we cannot prevent. But instead of boarding up windows, we install metal detectors. Instead of stockpiling water, we stockpile guns of our own.

The distance is created by the way we tell the stories, heightening the sensational, extraordinary details of the event. It is created by political interests throwing up their tried-and-true arguments, predictable pundits and nonprofits taking to the airwaves to recycle messages. We see images of nameless people hugging and crying by a memorial, we spotlight parents living a nightmare most of us will never have to live. Distance grows when politicians tell us to stop politicizing the tragedy, making it sound as if any response other than "How sad!" is shamelessly opportunistic.

The distance we feel from those unlucky victims and their families increases as we memorialize, always looking back at the event as a singular tragedy instead of looking forward to prevention or changes. We talk about their pain, originating at a point in the past, but we are far less fascinated with the legal and social mechanics of how to keep others from joining their unhappy club. To be clear, we need to do both. We need to honor the mimetic suffering stories of families and survivors, but so far what I'm hearing those families and survivors say is exactly this: look forward, put an end to the thematic story.

We treat the suffering as Russian roulette: a hazard we can prepare for, but not avoid. That's why, in the wake of the 2017 Santa Fe High School shooting, the Texas legislature allocated $100 million per biennium for school safety. It's usually spent on "hardening" measures like metal detectors for schools. Proposals for school hardening measures also regularly include arming teachers or deputizing people in the community to be armed defenders of the schools. The world is big and scary, the discourse implies; we must arm ourselves against it. Arming oneself—whether as a military, a household, or a school system—is also enticingly profitable. *The Washington Post* did the math and found that gun manufacturers would stand to make as much as $360 million by training and arming just one-fifth of America's teachers, creating an armed force just slightly smaller than the US Navy and Army combined. That force would need to be trained (cha-ching) and would most likely need to be expanded when school shootings continue to happen (cha-ching).[2]

The message to kids is clear: gunmen bursting into your school is just a thing that happens, like a fire or a tornado. You need to be ready. That's why they do drills. While I was on site for a story in 2021, the school called a lockdown drill, and I stood in a hiding spot with twenty teenagers who for thirty-five minutes did not giggle, whisper, check phones, or even cough. It was unnerving for me, but for them it was routine. When I told my own kids about Uvalde, they were sad but quickly reassured themselves that their school was prepared. They knew how to stay safe when, not if, it happened there.

As their mom, I was glad that they had that safeguard against fear, but I know it is not a safeguard against the reality of school massacres. It will help a little, maybe shrink the shooter's opportunity a little, but maybe not enough. People who have been through the particularly gruesome reality of a school shooting—in Newtown, Parkland, Santa Fe, Oxford, Uvalde—regularly call for changes to gun laws, not better drills. They are calling bullshit on our preparedness and demanding we get serious about prevention. And that's just schools. How are we supposed to be prepared in our churches, movie theaters, grocery stores, and parades? The opportunity for a mass shooting is simply for a mass of people to be gathered. The means is easy to obtain and have on hand. We've set it up so that all we need for a mass shooting is for the motive to strike.

Standing on the steps of the Texas Capitol, the adopted father of one of the victims urged Texans to stand with the families of the Uvalde victims, calling for gun reform and voting against politicians who resisted it. Fight for change now, before it happens to you, Brett Cross urged. "Because you don't want to be fighting from this side, with a hole in your heart."[3]

He also said that anyone not with them was against them. Anyone not trying to change the status quo was reinforcing it.

The victims, Cross was saying, had passed to the other side of that chasm, to the place where bad things happened. They cannot explain away the evil as unlikely or statistically improbable, nor consider how their good decisions and precautions might protect them. They are living on the other side of that luxury. Over and over, people in Uvalde told me they had been shaken out of complacency. Once the suffering was in their community, in their homes, in their schools, it was not a foggy far-off one-in-a-million chance dispensed by an arbitrary, reasonless bingo caller in the sky. It was a real person with a real grievance, who bought real guns in compliance with real laws, and real ammunition from a real local sporting goods store, and drove to a real elementary school, and killed twenty-one real people.

Once it became real and present, the blame was easy to see. Not just the bungled local response, which is, yes, undoubtedly something that needs to be accounted for, but the various systems that put the gun in the young man's hands.

That kind of clarity leads people to seek change. It's why getting too close to the grief, letting it be as real as our neighbors, our children, feels so dangerous. A lot of people I know, people in my family, simply refuse to do it. There is certainly wisdom in moderating how much we empathize—there can be a level of over-identification that makes us self-centered and unable to help—but if we don't enter into it, we will not see as clearly as we need to.

I will be personal here, because as a reporter, this is what I do. It is my job to both keep and communicate a proper distance. I reached a point in the Uvalde reporting when I had to take a break. I couldn't look at my own kids' photos without picturing them in the newspaper. My empathy had taken me as far as it could, productively.

I was not, however, retreating back to my happy place. Because with the suffering, which we all agree is terrible and unjustified, I was seeing the context and the teams forming on either side. Maybe this is just my personality, but where empathy stopped, something else started. When I think about the families and the loss, I feel sad, compelled to help them, compelled to protect my own kids. When I think about the context, about what the survivors are up against as they try to seek remedies and prevent the next tragedy, I feel white-hot, clear-eyed rage. And that makes the storytellers—the politicians and certain segments of the press—uncomfortable. In a teary blur, we can all be on the same side. But when we see the situation clearly, we see that the seeds of suffering were sown long ago, before there was a nation, before there was a constitution, before there were Democrats and Republicans, and to alleviate the suffering will require us to get into the roots of who we think we are as individuals and as a people.

SCOTS WITH GUNS

Having grown up in Texas, I'm more than familiar with gun culture. I know about hobbyists and hunters and self-defense. I grew up in a house full of guns, none of them properly secured. For most of my life it didn't occur to me to question where gun culture came from, and when I finally did it was easy enough to chalk it up to money from the NRA and gun manufacturers influencing Washington and Austin.

That's not untrue, but there are enormous popular issues with guns as well; private Americans own more than three hundred million guns. In the book *Loaded: A Disarming History of the Second Amendment*, Roxanne Dunbar-Ortiz traces the development of gun culture in the United States alongside all the other parts of our history the nation tends to gloss over: slavery, the removal and genocide of Indigenous people, and some of our less-glorious foreign wars. In all the places the United States needs to wrestle with its racial and ethnic supremacy issues, there's an element of gun culture, the idea that private citizens should be armed for their own protection. The question is and must be, Protection from whom? Private families "civilizing" the frontier needed to be armed against the invading "savages." Private slavers had the right and responsibility to patrol the countryside, armed to subdue Black people escaping to freedom. This, Dunbar-Ortiz argues, is the origin of our military and police culture, respectively, as well as the justification for an individual right to "bear arms," as enshrined in the Second Amendment.[4]

In modern law, castle doctrine—the right to defend your dwelling—and "stand your ground" laws continue this legacy of arming the public for their own defense. While those laws do not target people of color the way that Indian Wars and slave patrols did, the outcome is similar. When George Zimmerman killed Trayvon Martin, he was acquitted by a Florida law based on castle doctrine. Study after study shows that a white population will nearly always feel fear when encountering people of color in uncertain situations, increasing the likelihood that they will feel the need to use deadly force to defend their "castle." Just like prisons and police violence disproportionately punish people of color, it's reasonable to expect that private citizens executing justice will follow the same trend.

While pro-Constitution gun reform efforts try to frame the right to bear arms as an establishment of the National Guard or the need for hunting rifles or even protection against a totalitarian government takeover, Dunbar-Ortiz argues that veneration for the Constitution will almost always lead to the same place, back to the values of its authors, many of whom enslaved people and supported the ongoing dispossession of Indigenous people. "The Constitution is the sacred text of the civic religion that is U.S. nationalism, and that nationalism is inexorably tied to white supremacy."[5]

The national "us vs. them" undergirding gun culture is not only inherently racial but in this case is also tied to a specific idea about how the nation works, particularly those within the nation who operate according to *honor culture*—a system wherein the individual is responsible for their own prosperity and safety and maintains it through a rigorously cultivated reputation for toughness. Touch my truck and die.

Private property was a major perk in the newborn United States as a rare land without a monarch. But if the land is yours, so is the responsibility to defend it. We do a lot of fighting in the United States about the rights and responsibilities of the individual and the government. The places where you're most likely to see a slogan like "Trust God, not Government" emblazoned on the back of a tractor trailer are the places most likely colonized by a group of people who saw possession of land as their individual birthright from God. These rough-and-tumble folks, the Ulster-Scots, were accustomed to protecting themselves. Their forefathers were the tough, tribal Calvinists of the Scottish Lowlands who were dispatched by King James to subdue recalcitrant Catholic Ulster (in Northern Ireland, in case you're wondering how that went). Having never known a government proximate enough to defend their interests, they had lived generations in relative lawlessness, with only their reputation for avenging their own honor to keep them safe. Touch my sheep and die.

After the Ulster debacle, a new generation of tough cookies made their way to the American colonies as frontiersmen in the South and Midwest, where the native people were proving to be firmly attached to their land.

Sociologist Ryan Brown has researched honor culture across the United States (it's spread around quite a bit) and found that in places where it is strongest—mostly places settled by Ulster-Scots—rates of everything from bar fights to domestic violence to accidental death were higher than in the rest of the country.[6] Gun ownership is high in honor cultures, which makes sense. A reputation for toughness only lasts if you can back it up. Gender roles are typically strong in these regions as well, so there's a lot of rooster-crowing about masculinity and possessiveness of women, which leads to more fights. Touch my woman and die.

And therein you see the connection to a man who must shoot up a cafeteria diner because he felt his masculinity was diminished by "bitches" who refused to be wooed. Or kids who were bullied and so plot their revenge on their classmates. Boys who feel they must display power by using a powerful weapon, made accessible to them by a culture built on the idea that we need to do exactly that.

The fact that honor culture in the United States is so closely tied to Ulster-Scot settlement also tells an important story about isolation. Honor culture develops where the rule of law is weak—as it was in the Scottish Lowlands where the Ulster-Scots originated—and eventually competes with it. Calling the cops when you can handle a problem yourself? Sissy stuff. That's why it's typically white women, not men, being caught on cell phones calling the police to enforce their will. Police are used as proxies for their honor-defending men.

Brown doesn't get into this as much in his book, but there's another reason, I think, that honor culture has leaked beyond those of us with Scottish surnames. I think that the United States has recreated the conditions necessary for honor culture to develop independently. We see it in areas of our cities where gangs or personalities, not formal institutions, establish order. It's not that the rule of law is weak in these areas as much as the social fabric has been weakened by disinvestment and mass incarceration. When law enforcement doesn't work for a neighborhood, but against it, it disrupts community support systems and leaves too many to fend for themselves.

On the other side of town, politicians scare up votes by telling us about the encroaching danger. Look how the incumbent has failed! You're in danger! We are told constantly that we are in crisis, and if you keep hearing "Everything sucks!" no matter how many times you vote, eventually you get the message that there's actually very little society can do, so you should probably be prepared to protect yourself.

We also have a news media that has developed under the maxim "If it bleeds, it leads." We are constantly told how the bad guys are winning, the systems are failing, and there are increasingly few safeguards left. This is why I personally love solutions journalism, but it's still very much in the minority.

But things get tricky when honor culture becomes romanticized and marketed.

Rather than lock our doors and hide out for the rest of our lives, we create heroes. We make music and movies to valorize the fight we've been left to fight. We celebrate survival against the evil we've been left to manage on our own. The inherent drama of honor culture captured the imaginations of Hollywood directors and novelists, more people became enamored with the John Wayne of it all. Religious fundamentalism also thrived in honor cultures, and so a lot of evangelical culture in the United States is steeped in it, and churches can create little pockets of honor culture in geographically unlikely areas.[7]

It's sort of beautiful that we can summon that will to thrive, but we can also become so enamored of this idea of the strong man that we miss how sad it is. We are so smitten with cowboys, kingpins, and Liam Neeson characters that we miss how utterly destructive this is to ensouled beings. Our souls are our connection to a common God and common Spirit, and when our material life is fragmented and our well-being placed in opposition to our neighbor's, we do bear a spiritual wound. A wound that manifests, sometimes, with the right ingredients, as violence.

Rather than mental healthcare, spiritual community, and a functional justice system helping us find peace and a sense of agency within a system of democratically determined laws—we've got the ingredients!—we are left to struggle through a world that feels big and hostile and out of control. And to protect ourselves against that hostile world, we're told that only a gun will do.

KILL OR BE KILLED? IS THERE, LIKE, A THIRD OPTION?

It is true that in Sutherland Springs a gun-enthusiast was the one who stopped the killing spree inside First Baptist Church. It is true that neighbor Stephen Willeford shot and injured the shooter, forcing him to flee, but not before the shooter killed twenty-six people. What if Willeford hadn't been there? The shooter's opportunity would have been greater, and more would have died, that is true. But what if the shooter hadn't been there at all? Or what if he had been there—because he felt disrespected by his in-laws and wanted revenge—but he didn't have access to a gun? In those last two scenarios, the body count is way lower.

Everyone would prevent the next mass shooting if they could, but both solutions offered—arm the good guys or disarm the bad guys—have spiraling implications. Ultimately we are either in an arms race against our neighbors, tolerating nineteen thousand homicides per year, or we are committing to rigorous control of deadly weapons, and I must tolerate the fear that if I don't have an AR-15 I might not be scarier than those who wish me harm. Only one solution has data on its side—where it has been enacted, gun control has kept epidemic-level gun violence at bay. We should absolutely take whatever steps are available to reduce the numbers that can be killed in mere minutes of opportunity. But violence will continue to plague the United States in some form or fashion until we change our idea of what it means to be an individual, to have rights, to function as a society. We will have to lean heavily into our care for one another rather than our fear of one another. And the gun industry would obviously lose some money, so don't expect them to go quietly.

We should take any steps we can on gun control, because every life saved is worth saving, but our gun problems are so much deeper than just a few words on parchment, and they are going to haunt us until we make a revolutionary change of direction.

As a reporter, there is a cynicism deep in my bones, born of watching suffering explained away, ignored, or justified rather than treated with compassion. I'm not your girl for "this compromise law changes everything" or "hope and change" in our current configurations. If we are going to be saved from our deepest suffering, the suffering we have chosen for each other, then it is going to require a radical reorientation. Radical in our roots and exhaustive in our reach. We are going to have to turn the system inside out.

THE BROKEN BONES OF OUR MASS SHOOTING STORY

I've spent a long time being stymied (read: blindingly enraged) by our country's repeated mass shootings, particularly in schools. It's a suffering that seems impossible to tolerate. But as I dug deeper into gun culture, it became clear that the narrative behind our ongoing gun violence epidemic is a lot like the other narratives that have us tangled up in conflict.

Context: In the context of settler-colonialism, the United States left it up to private individuals to defend their private property from racial others. The most effective frontiersmen, the Ulster-Scots, brought with them an honor culture that requires us to be personally intimidating to stay physically and socially safe. We have, through drama and politics, turned honor culture into something sexy, and we relish the high conflict of pitting the survival of good guys and bad guys against one another.

Judgments: While no one judges mass shootings to be morally tolerable, our unwillingness to consider a country without unfettered access to guns leads us to *act* as if this suffering were natural or inevitable. Few will say that, but it is how we behave, as we turn schools into fortresses and consider arming more and more "good guys," meanwhile ignoring the suffering in areas where we deem violence to be due to some sort of communal decay, rather than the result of societal disinvestment.

Trade-offs: In a world armed to the teeth, whoever lays down their gun first is the one standing there without a gun, opening themselves up to suffering. There's also the trade-off of Second Amendment rights as such, but I really have a hard time dignifying that when the trade-off is the lives of elementary school children.

Us vs. them: In the narrative that upholds gun fanaticism in the face of this much suffering, the "us" shrinks impossibly small. We become totally isolated, and "they" are anyone who may wish us harm. Literally any other human being could be "them." Additionally, "they" are also the people who regulate guns—infringing on "our" rights and leaving "us" defenseless.

Distance and blame: The distance we put between ourselves and the suffering stories makes the gun debate look like political opportunism, or victims searching for reason in the midst of the unexplainable. If we shrink that distance, or when that distance is erased by a bullet, we often find a lot of clarity about who and what is to blame.

Chapter 14

AN ODE TO NONVIOLENCE

> *No man is an island entire of itself; every man*
> *is a piece of the continent, a part of the main;*
> *if a clod be washed away by the sea, Europe*
> *is the less, as well as if a promontory were, as*
> *well as any manner of thy friends or of thine*
> *own were; any man's death diminishes me,*
> *because I am involved in mankind.*
> *And therefore never send to know for whom*
> *the bell tolls; it tolls for thee.*

—JOHN DONNE

One of the sexiest scenes in all of movie history has to be the scene in *Mr. and Mrs. Smith* when the title characters take out a room full of assassins while executing a pas de deux to "Mondo Bongo" by the Mescaleros. If that movie gives you the creeps because of the whole Brangelina debacle, think about Kylo Ren and Rey taking out the Praetorian Guards in *Star Wars: The Last Jedi*. Few things capture our imagination like a good standoff. I just watched *Wakanda Forever*, and the climactic moment involves the Wakandan champions in tight formation, weapons facing outward as the Talokan army closes in. Or think about when Butch Cassidy and the Sundance Kid shoot their way out of the hideout in Bolivia. Many of us, especially those who grew up in honor cultures, have fantasized about being the good guy with the gun. Or lightsaber. Or Vibranium blade rings. If we lived in the Roman-occupied Near East, we would fantasize about drawing a sword in defense of our people or place.

We can almost feel the inner monologue of the apostle Peter in the Garden of Gethsemane as he prepares to take on the armed crowd sent by the religious leaders to arrest Jesus in Matthew 26. The more I learn about honor culture, the more I envision Peter as the patron saint of honor cultures like the Ulster-Scots and the American South. Ready to react, ready to prove himself, ready to take matters into his own hands. Peter's narrative puts the bad guys on the other end of the sword. But Jesus, in a quick, one-line story, reverses that. "All who draw the sword will die by the sword," Jesus says (Matt. 26:52).

From the conspicuous absence of fight scenes in the gospels, we derive modern movements like nonviolent resistance and pacifism. Leaders like Shane Claiborne lead active antideath campaigns to urge both state and citizens to lay down their weapons. I also think there's a second dimension, and it explains something about Jesus's nonviolent MO in the gospels.

In the garden, Jesus puts Peter on the other end of his own sword. It's not the first time we've heard this narrative from Jesus, and he says it in the middle of the climactic week of his life story. In fact, I like to imagine Jesus looking at Peter and thinking, "Have you listened to a damn thing I've said?"

The gospels place Jesus—and those who have union with him—on the receiving end of violence. He told us to turn the other cheek, to bless those who curse us, and then he went and showed us how literally he meant that when he was humiliated and beaten before being publicly executed. Unlike the Old Testament, we are offered no instructions for when to use violence, how to determine who deserved it, or what our rights were in exercising it. Jesus didn't, as far as we know, go on any long diatribes about just war or capital punishment and how to get it right as the executioner. Whenever he spoke of violence, he spoke from the perspective of the victim. I think this is important, because Jesus was acknowledging the existence of violence—his kingdom was not dependent on ideal circumstances—and thus leaving no room for exceptions.

Healing stories always require us to reorient or turn away from other narratives, but none is as radical as this change of paradigm from violence to nonviolence, or from "us vs. them" to oneness. Oneness in the face of death was on the mind of poet John Donne when he penned the famous poem we all memorize in high school, "No Man Is an Island" (quoted in full at the beginning of this chapter). The poem was published in 1624 and has been quoted in all kinds of stories as a reminder to rugged individualists, usually men, to reach out and ask for help. But the meaning of the poem is less of a nudge to establish human connections and more about inherent human connectedness in the costliest of circumstances. Connectedness hurts.

When I got married, I was a paranoid mess. I was certain Lewis, my heart on a bicycle, was going to die during his work commute. When I gave birth to Moira, those fears doubled. When I had Asa, my heart walked around in three vulnerable pieces outside my body. Those are easy connections to feel because I love those urchins deeply, but Donne is pointing to a humanity-wide connectedness in spite of the fact that many of us do not feel it.

Look, passing commonsense gun laws does not require a radical change of paradigm. We don't have to feel a transpersonal kinship with all humanity. Gun reform would not require us to embrace nonviolence as individuals, and certainly not as a state. There are countries with tight gun laws and large militaries. A valid legal debate, community organizing, and political muscle can incrementally drag the United States forward on this topic. But gun culture is just one part of a larger, more pernicious culture of violence in this country. With the strongest military in the world and our condemnable company among the world's minority of countries still practicing the death penalty, the high rate of gun ownership is a branch of the tree, not the root.

Violence is the United States. We were founded in genocide and war. The violence of chattel slavery ended only with the violence of the Civil War. We hear the suffering stories of gun violence, and we greet them with narratives of protective violence. But that has not stopped the suffering. It has not healed anyone. If we want to stop dying by the sword, we have to stop living by the sword. We have to trade our narrative of good guys with guns—even sexy Hollywood versions—for a narrative of everybody making it out alive.

WAR AND PEACE

Even before everybody had a gun, the great philosophies of civilization have been at odds with the great realities of civilization. The emergence of a unified Chinese state was, in many ways, a triumph of warriors over nonviolent Confucian philosophers. The idea of noble, restrained, nonviolent leaders was appealing, but no match for the warlike Qin, the dynasty that first brought the various states under one emperor and ended the violent Warring States period (475ish–221 BCE).

Christianity and Islam also have long histories of tension between peaceful religious observance and the violent realities of statehood. The separation of church and state was unheard of in the earliest days of both religions; the will of the king and the will of God and the will of the people keep getting murky.

It's worth noting that in ancient civilizations, nonviolence was preached most comprehensively by philosophers from the lower classes. Mozi and Jesus were not noblemen trying to decide how to hold on to their power against those who would take it. Siddhartha Gautama was said to have been born noble, but he renounced nobility to live as a wandering ascetic. The power of money and the power of the state were always, historically, associated with violence, if not against human life, then against livelihoods.

But nonviolence in the face of oppression definitely isn't a given. It's difficult to argue that those being violently subjugated shouldn't have recourse to respond in whatever way is necessary to ensure their freedom. The violence of colonialism regularly elicited violent resistance from Indigenous and enslaved people. "Not a single era of U.S. political history has gone by without violence employed to maintain the status quo," writes Africana scholar Kellie Carter Jackson. "For Black Americans, a worthy response to such violence is required: not one that is based on vengeance, but protection and justice."[1] Her work on the use of force in the antebellum abolitionist movement, particularly among Black abolitionists, examines the limited choices available to those trying to resist oppression in a culture of violence. To stop the violence of slavery, she argues, enslaved people had to use force. She argues that every system-level step toward equality has required coercive power, and most of that was brought about by Black people's demonstration that they were willing to use force. She points out that even famously nonviolent Martin Luther King Jr. had an arsenal of weapons at home because his life was under constant threat, a threat that proved tragically valid.[2]

Like King, most people who take nonviolence seriously do not have their heads in the clouds or the sand. Most know it's not enough to be piously nonviolent, to let people die so that they don't have to sully their consciences. Mennonites like J. Lawrence Burkholder had to consider what their pacifist tradition had to say about the necessity of stopping the Holocaust and stopping it quickly. Christian ethicist Reinhold Niebuhr revised his pacifist position in the lead-up to the United States' entry into World War II.[3]

What unites those committed to nonviolence is not the extreme ends of their "what if" scenarios but their imaginations—where they focus their attention and how they pursue their goals, argues philosophy professor Aaron James.[4] They might have different answers to whether a nonviolent person can join the military, or what they would do if someone broke into their house, but their goals are to end war and cultivate a culture of peace. It's not impractical, James writes, if you look at the life of King as an example: "This suggests that the best argument for nonviolence may be nonviolent lives animated by nonviolent vision."[5]

Our imagination fuels the stories we tell, and how we respond to the suffering stories we hear. When my kids come home from school saying their teacher treated them unfairly, my imagination about my ideal role in their life will inform my response. If I have fed the mama bear imagination, I'll be up at the school in a heartbeat, demanding a resignation. If I have, instead, imagined my kids as resilient, independent, and able to handle conflict, I'll probably help them think through some options for how they might address this with their teacher themselves before I get involved.

While some have followed Augustine and Aquinas into just war theory, others like Mae Elise Cannon expand Christian calling beyond reacting to violence and highlight our call to be peacemakers, not peacekeepers or enforcers. We have to seriously address the violence already happening around us and seek to end it. Peacemaking movements have sought to eliminate the conditions that lead to war, and Latin American Liberation Theology differentiates nonviolence from nonresistance, in that it actively seeks to end exploitation, demand justice, and stop things that are harming people. It confronts violence in active, but nonviolent, ways. Being radically anti-fascist and anti-imperialist and yet not joining guerrilla groups or taking up militia-like roles, figures like Óscar Romero remind us that the gospels do not espouse a political movement. They do something more radical.

We should argue about the particulars of how nonviolence looks. We should be wary of reinventing our ethics to fit every situation, but we should also be wary of ethics designed to privilege purity of thought over bringing shalom to real life. We should go into each unique situation trying to discern the demands of love and justice. Do we need to stand between Nazis and Jews? Do we hide them like pacifist pastor André Trocmé, or do we take a more active role like Dietrich Bonhoeffer? Do we march on Washington? Boycott bus systems? Walk out of schools? If we have an imagination, an orientation toward nonviolence, we won't have itchy trigger fingers on any action, and we will be highly sensitive to the work of anger, vengeance, power, and fear in our hearts. We resist the violence outside, but also the violence inside us, which is why so many in the nonviolence movement, including Howard Thurman who preached that desegregating schools was a powerful tool of nonviolence, believe that inward renewal is essential for nonviolent action, and that nonviolent action necessarily flows from a spiritual awakening, particularly a life devoted to following Jesus's Way.

Whatever we do, nonviolent theologians remind us that we must be aware of the temptations to turn resistance into a bid for power—which is one reason so many are wary of military force. There's just too much financial and imperial incentive to use the military for more than a mandate to protect the vulnerable. We use the term *interests* to describe our reasons for military involvement in various international regions and conflicts, and the scope of those interests has proved hard to pin down. Gun culture in the United States is fueled by the protection of our private interests: our property and rights. Like oil in the Middle East and bananas in Honduras, private interests are also hard to define and regulate, as assault rifle sales numbers will tell you.

These are murky waters, and we have a world in bondage to scarcity to thank for that. But we can check that our imagination is leading us in the right direction, as Cannon reminds us, by considering the potential costs of peace: "May we each, when presented with the opportunities to diligently pursue peace and advocate for justice, be willing to pay the ultimate sacrifice for the sake of the gospel of Christ," Cannon writes.[6]

Sometimes it will mean putting our bodies between the bully and their target. Sometimes it will mean a long walk to work when we can't take the bus. Sometimes it will mean lots of angry emails, public embarrassment, and rejection. It's worth mentioning that Jesus himself, while calling us to nonviolence, also calls us into conflict. That verse that anti-pacifists use to insist that Jesus condones, even approves of violence—"Do not suppose that I have come to bring peace to the earth. I did not come to bring peace, but a sword" (Matt. 10:34)—is situated in the middle of a paragraph about interpersonal conflict and the cost of following Jesus. It's more contextually plausible that Jesus was talking about how poorly people are going to respond to his disciples' newfound nonviolent inside-out kingdom. Remember that Jesus, Romero, and King were all assassinated by the very violence they were resisting. Yet, because love does transcend death, as Jesus showed us, their legacies did not die by the sword.

I don't think that a healing narrative on guns in the United States requires every last one of us to embrace radical nonviolence, but as we stand here with our guns drawn, ready for the shootout, I do think it will take a radical change in our tolerance for the suffering of others. I'm not going to say, like Henri Nouwen, that this is possible only for those who have been changed by becoming one with Christ. But I am inclined to believe, with Thurman and King, that an ego-shattering conversion would lead us to a oneness with all humankind—and that *is* necessary to our new narrative. I don't think it's a coincidence that the stunning violence of the world we live in has not just pastors but actors, activists, and a growing community of psychologists and neuroscientists calling for a spiritual revival. Not the kind with snake handlers, but an awakening to our connectedness (to God and each other) that would bring about the changes that policy and protest simply cannot.

WHICH END OF THE GUN?

When I was growing up, the men and boys in my family hunted deer, turkey, doves, and hogs, and they talked about a recurrent nightmare they all had. They would be stalking a deer, and finally they would shoot it. When they went to collect the carcass in the dream, they reached for it to find it transforming into someone they love.

These dreams haunted me as a young person, even though I never had one myself. I was afraid of having one. The only explanation offered to me at the time was that the human mind is weird, and our subconscious is fearful. The boys were obviously afraid they were going to accidentally shoot each other. Maybe that's it, but now I wonder if the dreams speak to the deep connectedness of nature, and our awareness that any gun we fire is aiming at a piece of ourselves. I don't think killing a deer is the same as murdering a schoolroom full of children, or that the two are karmically linked. Nothing like that. But I do see those dreams as the ancient voices in my family's DNA choosing a quiet moment to remind the hunters of what their spirits know: every death is my death; every life is my life.

In the chapter on climate change we listened to Indigenous theologians, writers, and scientists explain how we are connected to the earth. We are made from the same minerals and molecules, by the same Creator who has joined our fates together as creation. That, combined with rich traditions of Christian nonviolence, leads us to the kind of radical solidarity—a shared root system—we need to confront something as confounding as our nation's tolerance for massacre.

We know what ends gun violence at the scale we experience in the United States: regulation. The data is abundant and undeniable. But what counters the population-level data is the fear put out there by those who profit off guns: but what about *you*? What are *you* going to do when the bad guys come for *you*? As long as we see ourselves as islands, we won't be able to put down our guns. But if every bullet has our name on it, as part of the whole, maybe we could get somewhere.

The judgment, trade-off, context, distance, and "us vs. them" of a healing story when it comes to our nation's tolerance for violent death is radical solidarity with the dying. Until we see no difference between it happening to you or happening to me, we do not have the compassion we need to confront the narrative that we must have guns drawn to stay safe. Obviously we have to follow (and block) the money. Obviously we have to confront politics. But I don't believe we will do that until we, like Jesus, place ourselves in the victim's position, not the shooter's.

We will become intolerant of our country's love affair with guns when we are always victims, never heroes, when the only thing a gun can do is kill me, never save my life. In a way, the healing narrative on the issue of guns is the most extreme and idealistic, but if we can tell this healing story, we can tell all the others described in this book.

THE CROSS AT THE CORE OF IT ALL

The premise of this book has largely rested on the idea that healing narratives require us to tolerate personal suffering and sacrifice in our pursuit of shalom, as Jesus did in the gospels. This cannot be forced on us; we must decide for ourselves. We do not tolerate injustice in the name of "taking up our cross," but we are able to identify it and address it without perpetuating it. We know the difference between injustice and not getting my way. We know Mahatma Gandhi was right that "an eye for an eye makes the whole world blind." The only way we can do this is by taking ourselves out of the center of the story and judging our collective achievement of "prosperity," "justice," and "flourish-ing" by the well-being of those with the least economic, political, and social power. This is the heart of womanist theology, postcolonial feminist theol-ogy, and liberation theology. It's also the heart of solutions journalism and solidarity movements.

Consider for a moment Carter Jackson's conclusion on violence in pursuit of Black liberation. Violence—not necessarily bloodshed, but force—will always be necessary for Black liberation while white people hold on to the violent system that is white supremacy. The only way to stop the cycle is to get to the vi-olent spirit that drives it. "In overthrowing the spirit of slavery, it is not violence that is required, but sacrifice. Advantage and inequality cannot share the same space. Likewise, one cannot end inequality without sacrifice. . . . It is impossible to bring about change and transformation without the forfeiture of power."[7]

I think this is applicable even beyond racial violence, to all the suffering stories we have addressed in this book. The spirit of patriarchy, nationalism, and religious imperialism all have at their heart a clutching at power.

It's been healing to my own imagination to consider an immigration story that honors newcomers, a story that allows us to teach history and civics in schools in ways that link repair and hope, an abortion story that holds the ten-sion of sacred life in a wounded world, a climate story that literally saves our lives, and a COVID-19 story that frees us from the grip of politicization.

However, in this chapter, I have been tasked with imagining a healing story for our current divides over mass murder. Our nation's tolerance of the mass slaughter of children inside their classrooms is damning. It's hard to imagine a healing story for a rot that deep. It's hard to imagine what would heal a nation that refuses to do everything it can to prevent the next tragedy.

I've looked at the suffering stories I've published throughout a decade in journalism and considered what would be required for those stories to be met with compassion instead of blame and indifference. In each chapter I've suggested what it might mean to take up our cross in that particular debate or divide. We must take up our crosses and die to self-righteousness and self-protection from unjust policies, to racial advantage and national myths, to easy answers and triumphalism, to "more for me" attitudes, to the need to win an argument.

But there is no cross you can take up with a sword in your hand. If you live by the sword, you die by the sword, not the cross. This is the radical thing the gospels present to us: A world where violence is never in your favor, and so you have no reason to draw your sword. Not your political sword, economic sword, or the sword of the laws you wrote to your own advantage. In the Jesus Way, the incentive to end oppression and violence is high, because there's no benefit in oppression and violence, only risk. If we're really following the Jesus Way, unwilling to exercise power over our neighbors, then we are always at risk in a power-hungry world. That was what the peaceable Confucians found out as Qin pummeled them in war. It's what infuriated Nietzsche and propelled Donald Trump to power: the one with the will to dominance will dominate over the one with the will to harmony and care. That's why Jesus told his followers to expect death. Because if you're ready for death, you're ready for anything.

But that's also what the resurrection story shows us—that there's been a different plotline all along. Whether you believe we are ourselves in heaven, or that we enter some kind of collective communion with God, or that we live on in the oneness of creation, the story of abundant love goes on.

HEALING OUR VIOLENT STORIES

Living a healing story, a love story, a resurrection story is not some philosophical exercise about whether a person can truly be unselfish. Shalom builds a world where instead of being separate and centered on our own selves, our good is inseparable from one another. When you flourish, I flourish. Humanity will tolerate the suffering of others until there's nothing to be gained from violence, and the gospels remind us that a world burdened by scarcity will never deliver that kind of system. We have to build it.

Context: Nonviolence will look different in different contexts. It doesn't always mean going limp noodle in the face of aggression. It does, however, mean changing our imagination from dreams of conquest to dreams of peace, and drawing from love, not conflict, as our source.

Judgments: We will have to look at unique situations and weigh the ethics, but our core judgment should be that violence and suffering—which almost always flow from the most to the least powerful—is what we are trying to end, not perpetuate.

Trade-offs: We must trade dominance for solidarity, knowing it will cost us something.

Us vs. them: If we identify more with the victims of gun violence than imagine ourselves as the "good guy with the gun," we will have a better chance at ending gun violence.

Distance and compassion: "Feeling with" the life on the other end of the bullet creates a level of intimacy that cannot sustain violence. It doesn't make us vulnerable—it acknowledges the vulnerability built into being human.

Chapter 15

TURNING THE STORY INSIDE OUT

He was a hopeful bear at heart.

—MICHAEL BOND, of his character Paddington Bear
in *Paddington at Work* (I use this quote here because this
is the point in the book where we have a marmalade
sandwich and figure some shit out)

Sometimes I like to ruin my mental health walks by trying to map out arguments in my head. How would I convince an NRA fanatic that reasonable gun regulation is necessary? How would I persuade Greg Abbott and Joe Biden to stop using the southern border as a political boxing ring and instead mobilize some resources to help the people living in tents? How would I convince my childhood friend to get vaccinated? Somehow these imaginary arguments are even more intense if it's summer in Texas and my casual evening stroll has me sweating like a nervous kid in a cartoon.

If I work hard enough, I can return from my sunset stroll angrier and more despondent than I was when I left. My husband loves it when I do this. Sweaty, agitated wives are the best wives.

That's where the arguing gets me. But when I think about the people who have changed their stances on immigration after visiting the camps, I have a little hope. When I think about the compassion my friend's evangelical in-laws showed when she had to travel out of state for an abortion while grieving the impending loss of her baby, I have a little more hope.

The stories of individual people—mimetic stories—have a compassion-generating power that rhetorical jujitsu just doesn't have. This is why activists like Harvey Milk encouraged queer people to come out. It's why theologians like Howard Thurman believed in the power of racially integrated schools.

At the same time, I also believe we need thematic stories to hold those breakthrough moments of mimetic compassion. We cannot limit compassion to the people we know, because in this huge, interconnected world, our actions and votes and advocacy affect people we will never meet. In the healing stories we've analyzed in this book, I think we see some common themes among the elements of story. We see again and again the context of love, the judgment that the suffering of the marginalized should be alleviated, the trade-off of self-protection for taking up our cross, and the idea that we are all one.

What follows is my best stab at a framework to hold our thematic stories. A grand unifying story, if you will. I developed it in dialogue with the mimetic stories encountered while reporting, the issue-specific dilemmas and ethical quandaries addressed in this book, living in an age of deconstruction and interrogation of what Christianity has become, and my own search for themes across religious history and human spirituality.

CONTEXT: UPSIDE-DOWN KINGDOM

The predominant context of any healing story has to be love. Jesus's life and teaching offer an example of how that might look.

Jesus's approach to suffering in the gospels was very human—he sweated blood over it, he was tempted to avoid it—but it was also radical. The stories he told and the stories told about him in the gospels are contrary to the triumphal, kick-ass way we would probably have liked for him to address our suffering. We want to enter the prosperity gospel version of Willy Wonka's Chocolate Factory, with all the macabre justice for the Augustus Gloops and Veruca Salts of our lives. What we get, instead, are stories and riddles and a crucifixion and an ambiguous resurrection that still brings no dead enemies and no rivers of chocolate.

The popular imagery of the "upside-down kingdom" has been used by theologians and pastors to describe the unexpectedness of Jesus's teaching and storytelling—he loved a good ironic turn, chastising the pious and praising the tax collectors—and how it lifts the humble and brings down the proud. The same could be said for the life modeled in the gospels. For those of us who grew up in the age of presidents having to kiss the ring of Billy Graham to get elected, it can be hard to listen to Christians express a longing to bring about the upside-down kingdom "on earth as it is in heaven" all the while amassing as much power as possible. Mostly, these power-seeking, president-defending, celebrity-buddy pastors simply remove the social, political, and economic components of the cross Jesus bore, and the crosses we are supposed to be taking up in turn. They make "taking up your cross" all about either (1) enduring sickness, mishaps, and the natural suffering of life with joy and gratitude, or (2) repenting of our bad attitudes, particularly lust, jealousy, and resistance to their authority.

Finding joy amid sorrow is fine. Gratitude is great for your mental health. Turning from your own harmful attitudes? Fantastic. Go for it. But that's not "taking up your cross." That's not radical love for others at great cost to yourself.

In his seminal book *The Upside-Down Kingdom*, Anabaptist scholar Donald Kraybill refutes these dematerialized, devotional interpretations by pointing out that Jesus was being crucified for specific challenges to economic, religious, and government institutions. He was also being crucified willingly. His cross was neither an accident of nature nor a punishment for sin. It was the consequence of promoting an upside-down kingdom that upset leaders rather than endorse them.

When Jesus talked about "taking up your cross," Kraybill writes, "Jesus wasn't talking about primarily an inner, spiritualized, or mystical cross. Nor was he talking about accidents or genetic disabilities. He was describing expensive decisions with real social consequences (Luke 9:23)."[1]

If we accept its real-world nature, we often corrupt the upside-down kingdom again by making it transactional: humbling ourselves before God so we can be "lifted up." I've written about Senator Ted Cruz saying this sort of thing often enough that I can confidently report there is a quid pro quo going on in his understanding of God's kingdom. Cruz wants more biblical proof texts in the laws of the United States, and he expects to win wars and get money in return. Obviously this preaches on an individual level too. Tithe and you'll get a raise. Abstain from premarital sex and you'll have amazing married sex.

Buyer beware: the Way laid out in the gospel texts doesn't promise any of that, and it's possible you're being scammed by someone who has their eye on your bank account.

The political and religious landscape of Jesus's day suggests that he likely knew the consequences of opposing the religiopolitical powers that be. He knew that rather than amassing riches, he'd likely be killed. Decades later, when his followers penned the gospels and early church epistles, the cost was well established.

It's more radical than a people's revolution though. Kraybill points out that there was plenty of that going on in the Roman-occupied Near East. Groups of political "bandits" were roving the cities and countryside robbing from the establishment, Robin Hood–style. The Zealots were ready to take back the country. There were plenty of opportunities for Jesus to join the resistance, sword in hand, but he isn't on record having joined any of the established movements. He told Peter to put his sword away, and he said, "All those who draw the sword will die by the sword" (Matt. 26:52). Jesus was killed for his opposition to Rome, but that opposition didn't appear to be following the usual trajectory. For those who have studied human history, you know what happens to revolutionaries who see power as the goal of liberation. Over and over revolutionary leaders become dictators. Jesus's revolution seemed to have another layer, a layer that set his messages apart from the many other would-be messiahs crucified by the Romans.

Jesus's Way was not just a material revolution. It, according to the earliest accounts of this movement, was applicable beyond national sovereignty or equal distribution of wealth. I'm not saying those are bad things, or that Jesus would oppose them. But I don't think we need Jesus to cast a specifically political vision for us, because whatever political vision he had was contextual to the aims and issues of the Jews under Roman rule. But the Way that grew out of whatever Jesus was doing in Nazareth, Galilee, and Jerusalem transcended politics.

Faith can inform how we interact with politics, the policies we support or resist—throughout history they were inseparable. But I also believe that we are granted the freedom and wisdom to make political choices that advance larger goals—the goal of caring for our neighbors—and we can and should have lively debate about how best to do that, because up till now, I'm pretty sure no one has found the abuse-proof political system or an economic system that ushers in perfect shalom.

This leads me to the inevitable discussion of Marxism, so let's just take it head on. I think Karl Marx had a pretty good read on the situation. Civilization has been built on people working to produce food they will not eat, on land they do not own. But while Marx concludes that only revolution, possibly even violent revolution, will change the fundamental inequalities of either capitalism or feudalism, Kraybill presents a model in which that's not inevitable. There's no need for violent uprising—increasing the suffering of the oppressed when either the revolution is quashed or the revolutionary becomes the dictator—if we willingly flatten the hierarchy, Kraybill argues.

This isn't the oppressor trying to be the liberator, as Paolo Freire advised against in *Pedagogy of the Oppressed*. It's not the kind of capitalism-serving compromise Frantz Fanon warned us of in *The Wretched of the Earth*. This is an actual willing transfer of power so that the work of social and spiritual liberation can happen without additional violence. It's idealistic though, which is why postcolonial and anti-racist scholars are so wary of the suggestion.

Neither Kraybill nor I have a solution for what a state system would look like if it were truly governed in the Jesus Way. I don't even know if Jesus or the early church had that answer. When the gospels say, "the poor you will always have with you" (Matt. 26:11), they seem to be acknowledging that the material suffering around us isn't going anywhere until the kingdom of love replaces the coercive power of the state, which, in the gospels, was as much a mystery to Jesus as it is to us. That the epic struggle between love and power is not something we are likely to end in our lifetime, though of course we hope to gain some ground. This is why Christian advocates of nonviolence always wrestle with state-centric models of nonviolence. Whether your revolution ends in democracy or dictatorship, capitalism or communism, the state's primary power is coercion. Break rules, get punished. We like the idea of the government enforcing our values, which we believe are the right values, the liberating values, the just values. But coercive power itself, the means of enforcement, is not how Jesus rolled. This is upsetting for my progressive Christian friends who think the opposite of Republican Jesus is Socialist Jesus. (The political goals of socialism would certainly make it easier to behave like Jesus, in my opinion, because taking care of other people is way easier to do if you're not being pitted against them for survival.) But political systems are not the root issue; they are part of the plant that blooms from our root-level relationship to power. Jesus was all about the root.

We can argue about which political or economic system is best, and I believe we should. Our arguments are informed by our priorities and understanding of what it means to be a community, a people, neighbors, earth-sharers. And yes, the gospels' root-level teaching will influence that conversation. But Jesus didn't preach a political system as the means for bringing about a spiritual kingdom (or if he did, his earliest followers struck that from the record, because it clearly did not work out). His Way endured in a form that allows us to love, heal, and liberate when we aren't in power. He was giving us a way of being that was as possible in Roman-occupied Judea as it is in modern Norway.

Ultimately, the paradigm shift I think the Jesus of the gospels was getting at was this: stop making decisions based on gaining power and start making them based on showing love. Which means we're going to have to stop justifying the suffering of others and get serious about compassion. When you take that mindset into the public sphere, you, like Jesus, might trouble the waters.

JUDGMENTS: GETTING OVER THEODICY AND SOCIAL DARWINISM

In healing stories, we focus less on the logic or justification of suffering, and more on how we respond to suffering.

Since the Enlightenment, it's been the favorite pastime of men with beards and cigars to try to make everything in the Bible make sense. Or at least to prove the existence of the Christian God based on cold, hard logic. For these tobacco-loving guardians of orthodoxy, there is no more invigorating logic problem than the reality of suffering in a world where God is all-loving and all-powerful. A real three-cigar conundrum.

Answers to this conundrum even have their own theological name: *theodicy*.

Some posit that suffering, properly understood, can deepen our joy or lead us deeper into relationship with God, so God allows it. This is unsatisfying on its face, and a good example of why theologian John Swinton, who ministers to people with physical and mental health needs in Scotland, insists that theodicies usually "end up silencing the lamenting voice of the sufferer."[2]

Worse, Swinton argues, are theodicies that blame sin for suffering. Here's how that looks: Free will was necessary for creation to be fully good, and thus sin was always a possibility. That possibility came to pass, and all hell (literally) broke loose. Suffering was and is the fault of people who aren't living up to God's standards.

Conversely, the cigar-smokers often argue, aligning with God's will leads to goodness and prosperity. Thus, those who are succeeding are doing so because they are in line with God's will. There's a class element to this argument. The prosperity gospel often uses this sort of logic to keep poor people trying hard to earn some blessings. At the country club, where the generational wealth is in the bag, this is the logic that lets us feel good about it.

That's not how Jesus talked about suffering or prosperity. In the gospels, Jesus cured people, and he forgave people who were in the wrong; but he did not conflate the two. He had tough words for rich folks: their wealth was an impediment to faith, not a reward for the faith. He explicitly identified with the poor, because he was poor. The historical Jesus was a citizen of Roman-occupied lands. The wealth and religiosity around him were widely corrupt and oppressive. The gap between rich and poor was huge. The gospels and epistles certainly connected our physical and spiritual situations, but in the opposite direction of the prosperity gospel preachers or the #blessed influencers or the National Prayer Breakfast luminaries. Wealth and power were not consequences of goodness, they were impediments to it. Jesus didn't hold up rich people as de facto paragons of virtue or explain away poverty as a lack of moral fiber. Humans and the systems we make are more complicated than that, and no one knew this better than the guy whose ministry would end at the hands of a religious system colluding with an empire.

Theologian Stanley Hauerwas takes a system-level view when he challenges the link between prosperity and virtue. Empire logic attributes our world's current allocation of wealth and power to God's perfect love and control, he argues. It's a way to link earthly power to divine will, to baptize the power we have, and to justify our lust for the power we want. Rather than God being God whether or not we suffer, a messy ambiguity to be sure, theoretical solutions to the problem of evil reflect "the metaphysical expression of this deep-seated presumption that our belief in God is irrational if it does not put us on the winning side of history."[3]

It's the theological version of social Darwinism, which I would argue, is at work in many of our deepest divides, anesthetizing us to the suffering of others. Social Darwinism is not something most people explicitly believe, but it's part of the genetic code in our philosophical roots. It's what makes the radishes so tangy. Social Darwinism suggests that "might makes right" and that the ones who rise to the top of society are the ones that *should* (note the judgment word) be there. But scientific Darwinism did not require social Darwinism. Social Darwinism is what happens when power co-opts other people's ideas to justify itself, like the teaching of Jesus and the agenda of Martin Luther King Jr.

"American society saw its own image in the tooth-and-claw version of natural selection," writes Richard Hofstadter.[4] From the rugged individualism of industrial tycoons to nationalist efforts abroad, Hofstadter traces the influence of the "might makes right" thought. Writing in 1944, living in a New Deal world, he saw it on the decline. Surrounded by the benefits of cooperation and social safety nets, Hofstadter could not have foreseen the greed-ridden 1980s, megachurch movements, Silicon Valley, and MAGAism, all claiming that success justifies the successful. The suffering of successful people would be unnatural, and the suffering of those who oppose them is inevitable, if not deserved.

The gospels don't spend time explaining and justifying suffering. They don't offer a theodicy or cite the laws of nature to validate the Roman empire. In those stories of his ministry, Jesus responded to suffering with compassion. Our healing stories can address the spiritual wounds, corrupt systems, and material consequences of life in a hurting world. We go for the long-term roots, but we mind the flowers too, the suffering stories of individuals who share our days. Wisdom traditions like Mohism and Buddhism speak to this too: we have to tend to the renewing of our spirit and mind, but how we take care of the world and our neighbors is inseparable from that renewal.

I want to pause for just a moment to call in both my progressive and conservative friends on the roots and flowers bit. It is true that philanthropy and mercy ministries often fail to get to the root of an issue, because they leave inequity in place and insist that the rich are the best at allocating compassion. Often they even make matters worse. However, progressives can be quick, too quick I would argue, to sneer at efforts to help the desperate and dying if those efforts do not flow through their preferred system, be it the state, collective action, or mutual aid. We might be the ones annoyed at Jesus for restoring sight to the blind, because miraculous intervention let the Roman government off the hook for funding ophthalmological research. We need to be wary of philanthropic paternalism, but we also need to have an answer ready for how we're going to care for people while we wait for the perfect system to emerge and reallocate all the wealth and power. Again, a healing story can be told in Rome, Norway, North Korea, or the United States.

Judgments about (1) what kind of suffering is deserved or natural, and (2) what kind of compassion is ideal, protect me from uncomfortable involvement in the suffering of others. If, in addition to working toward better systems and structures, we use our wise capacity to judge the most compassionate response available in the moment, we are bound to get involved in the suffering of others and it's bound to be messy. That's why we have to be prepared to suffer a bit ourselves.

TRADE-OFFS: THE RED FLAGS OF "TAKING UP YOUR CROSS"

Healing stories require something of us: they require us to reorient or set something aside. And that should raise some red flags.

A red flag likely popped up for you just now. If you have spent any time in a religious hierarchy, you have probably seen calls to love, forgiveness, humility, and joyful suffering misused. You may have even been abused or traumatized by leaders insisting that Christ compels you to "die to self" in a way that harms you. Women and queer people may have been told that being denied a position in ministry or ordination was a chance to practice humility. When you, a spiritually attuned congregant, questioned a pastor's bullying behavior, you may have been told to stop being so selfish and to sacrifice for the church.

The bigger, redder flag hanging over this whole discussion is asking marginalized people to potentially add to their own suffering. This section is long, I'm warning you now, because you may want to go pee or something. We are really going to dig in on this, because in my opinion, if we don't get it right, our healing narratives fall apart.

Just like "turning the other cheek," this idea of "taking up your cross" has a lot of potential to harm people who are already bearing a lot of burdens. If Black, Indigenous, immigrant, pregnant, queer, and poor people take this inside-out view, are they not simply doing what all of society does anyway, tolerating their own suffering? We cannot go further until we answer that question.

To try to get an answer, I reached out to Rebekah Mui, a PhD candidate from Malaysia whose website, Kingdom Outpost, is dedicated to the historical roots and imagination of a Christianity that challenges empire instead of cheering it on. I asked if I could interview her about the idea that Jesus and his followers called colonized, oppressed people to "turn the other cheek" and "take up their cross" as a liberating practice, while obviously those same teachings have been used by enslavers and colonizers to do the opposite.

"The really big question is whether the theology of Christian servanthood is grooming people for oppression," she mused in our Zoom meeting.[5] She can speak with authority on the lived experience of colonial Christianity and finding liberation within Christian tradition, but for Mui, the question of how certain doctrines can be beneficial in a postcolonial world remains something to be considered with care.

Whenever Christianity works hand in hand with empire—for instance, through colonial missions, churches' support of slavery, or white Christian nationalism—the call to take up one's cross becomes a problem for the people in power. Honestly, a historically rooted teaching of the gospels becomes a problem, so the habit has been to decontextualize and over-personalize it. Remember what we do to the "upside-down kingdom"? Well, we do that with "Take up your cross" as well. A preacher could speak to slaves and order them to honor their masters, to turn the other cheek, and to focus on rewards in heaven. A good preacher can make your personal suffering sound like your personal glory and urge you not to do anything about it. "Empire always makes oppression sound really good," Mui said. "People slap servanthood on authoritarianism and call it a day."[6]

In the modern context, where a middle class is entangled in capitalism and democracy, and churches are dependent on donors to build their buildings and launch their initiatives, we continue to decontextualize the gospels' messier messages. Can't have everybody selling all their belongings and giving them to the poor; that wouldn't work. In the church business model, pastors need parishioners to give their money to the church, which means they have to get something in return. The pastor has to meet some need. But the needs that Jesus spoke to don't really mesh with fancy sneakers, flashy tech, and big pastoral salaries, so they do what any good marketer does and create a new need. I didn't grow up going to church to find the daily bread I needed to resist empire and live a life of service to the poor. I went to church twice a week to deal with the real problem: my personal sin.

The thing about this sin-focused religion so many of us know is that it keeps us totally focused on ourselves. We're too worried about our own moral performance to look up and notice that we're tangled up in the suffering of others. Doctrines like total depravity ensure the treadmill never stops and we never experience the abundant life Jesus promised and can't share it with others. We're too wounded to take up any more crosses.

Our current coziness with power has roots in Christianity's foes-to-lovers storyline with the Roman empire and runs through the history of Christendom. It is prevalent in the white American church but is heavily exported through international ministries and missionaries to the global church. After our chat, Mui sent me a link to a 2020 lecture where political feminist scholar Silvia Federici speaks on the way church and state work together to keep people from organizing to undermine them. "A large number of these Evangelical sects financed by the right wing in the United States and other countries are now going across the world spreading a capitalist, neoliberal, individualistic Christianity that basically says 'Jesus wants you to be rich,'" Federici says in the lecture. "'If you are not rich, it is because there's something wrong with you or because people in your community are conspiring against you.' So it's really putting people against each other."[7] Black women I interviewed for my previous book, *Bringing Up Kids When Church Lets You Down*, told me that while the Black church has a rich history of resistance to racist oppression, it is not immune to the siren songs of patriarchy and power, especially when those are the avenues offered as the path to safety and security.

It seems like Christianity is hopelessly useless to all but the most powerful, and yet Jesus was talking to the margins of society. Paul was writing to a persecuted religious minority. "Taking up the cross" is not noblesse oblige. These guys were not padding their own bank accounts either. They preached suffering as inevitable along Jesus's liberating Way. And here is something I know for fact: those who suffer understand the words of Jesus in ways those who do not suffer simply cannot. Jessica Menjivar, an immigrant woman we will meet a few pages from now, held on to the words of Jesus in the detention cell, ministered to the hearts of the others in there with her, and the words of Jesus are what make her determined to get to the United States to see her daughters again. So, what is it that is so freeing, even energizing, about taking up your cross?

Mui pointed to three important elements that make sense of what theologians call the "cruciform life" (a life of service or sacrifice) in a postcolonial or resistance context. First, the cross was a rebuke of power-hungry systems and those who maintain them. The cross was proof that Jesus's Way was an existential threat to the Roman empire and religious authorities, and so corrupt was their understanding that they executed the Son of God and called it justice and virtue. Living lives of service and sacrifice exposes the evil of the system working against you. It's not as satisfying as seeing Violet Beauregarde rolled away to be juiced by Oompa Loompas, but not all of us are living at the cusp of achievable revolution. Sometimes refusing to buy in is the only resistance we get to mount.

The gospels are not asking people to allow systems of oppression to continue unaddressed. Jesus has harsh words for the folks who run those systems. Very harsh. Again, they *killed* him. While postcolonial philosophers like Fanon insist that decolonization must be violent because colonialism is violent, Mui thinks that Jesus is suggesting a different tactic, perhaps a wiser tactic if it's you vs. the Roman empire. Jesus doesn't appear to disagree that empires are violent things, but instead of preparing to fight, like Fanon would say, the gospels call followers of Jesus to be prepared to die for their refusal to accept oppression. Jesus was executed by the systems he criticized. So were Martin Luther King Jr., Dietrich Bonhoeffer, Óscar Romero, and Joan of Arc. For every martyr there are countless lost incomes, broken relationships, sleepless nights, and lives lived in fear. Every person who has led a resistance movement, or even participated in one, knows there will be elective suffering involved.

Being prepared to die is not something that can be demanded of you, which leads to the second liberating component of a cruciform life: agency. Cruciformity is a site of self-determination no empire can control. Jesus's Way was not authoritarian—it was mutual. The hierarchies of the day were rejected and flattened in the earliest Christian teachings, only to be built up again in practice as the church struggled with organizational culture and eventually empire management. But the best safeguard against using servanthood and sacrifice as oppressive doctrines is a commitment to spiritual agency. Crosses are to be taken up in the same way Jesus did, by choice. No one else can interpret for you what it means to take up the cross in your life, nor can they withhold God's Spirit from you if you don't do it the way they think you should. The gospels are pretty clear on this. Don't go policing everyone else's performance.

It seems to be the habit of radical and revolutionary thinkers to want to demand purity from their comrades. I was listening to *Mother Country Radicals*, a podcast produced by Zayd Ayers Dohrn, the son of Weather Underground leaders Bernadette Dohrn and Bill Ayers. He interviews them about the communist practice of self-criticism, in which members would endure hours of berating and interrogation about their private thoughts and biases.

It wasn't self-criticism as much as it was a group pile-on. As I listened, I was reminded not of my time as a Maoist (which never happened) but of my time as a Reformed evangelical, always trying to root out the idolatry in my heart with the help of pastors and pals who, depending on how annoying or threatening they found me, were always happy to help. I was reminded of sitting across the lunch table from friends as they listed off the litany of sins they had observed in my flirting or sarcasm. Cults do this too. They are like speck-removing parties where the whole club gets to have a go at your eyeballs.

Ideological purity is not freedom. Life under spiritual authoritarianism and constant scrutiny is not an abundant life. Society, by necessity, will always have more rules and laws to keep us from harming one another, but just like those laws can cross into authoritarianism, so can spiritual community.

We have to make that critical distinction between how a state functions and how a soul functions. We have to push for the state to pass laws that require more justice. But the state's power will not fully heal us. You can tell that all the legislated progress of the Civil Rights era and the baby steps forward since then did not heal our national "us vs. them" or our suffering stories, because then we went and elected Donald Trump to roll back a few decades of progress with a handful of executive orders and some Supreme Court appointments. There's a dialogue between policy and society—that is true. But sometimes that dialogue goes sideways. If we are going to legislate justice, and I think we should, we also have to work toward healing our communities and the way we interpret the world, and that's not something the law can require. You can require that people stop hurting people, but until they stop hating people, you're going to have to keep plucking that weed. We have to get radical, to the roots. We're going for radishes.

We can't just change what people are allowed to do and have. We have to talk about our desires.

As they witnessed the ravages of stratified agrarian societies and warring empires, peace prophets throughout the world were coming to similar conclusions. Jesus wasn't the only one teaching us how to resist the greed and destruction of power lust. He wasn't the only one suggesting we change our relationship to suffering. Buddhist teaching on suffering seems to be widely mischaracterized. The Western caricature of Buddhism places a monk under a tree with no possessions and no relationships saying that our attachment to the world causes suffering and that the only way to be happy is to sit under a tree with no possessions and no relationships. A different tree. The monk's tree is taken.

In his book *The Heart of the Buddha's Teaching: Transforming Suffering into Peace, Joy, and Liberation*, Vietnamese Buddhist monk and Nobel Peace Prize winner Thich Nhat Hanh is more nuanced. What leads to suffering is not all desire, he explains. It's what we desire.

"Everyone wants to be happy and there is a strong energy pushing us toward what we think will make us happy. But we may suffer a lot because of this. We need the insight that position, revenge, wealth, fame, and possessions are, more often than not, obstacles to our happiness. We need to cultivate the wish to be free of these things so we can enjoy the wonders of life that are always available—the blue sky, the trees, our beautiful children," he writes.[8]

It's possible, as we meditate on our own suffering, as great wisdom traditions encourage, that we realize we feel suffering because we believe that we cannot be happy without more wealth, more power, more *more*. Worse, though, our fight to prevent or alleviate our own suffering has robbed others. We have caused real suffering. If we believe that, say, increasing our profits will alleviate our suffering, we may pay our workers less, increasing their suffering.

I don't get to tell the person I'm robbing that they just need to detach themselves from their belongings. How they relate to desire and suffering is their business, their balance of peace and resistance. I need to make sure that my fear of scarcity, my lust for power, my insatiable hunger for more is not where goodness and harmony are getting all blocked up.

Changing our perspective, if it leads us to action, can reverse the exploitative trajectory of society. If we have seen how increasing our profits never brings us permanent peace, we may be more open to alleviating the suffering of people who are actually struggling to pay their bills because of low wages.

And then comes the wild part. We may find, as Jesus said, that in losing our life we save it. We may find that increasing a worker's wages brings us more peace than increasing our profit. We may find that in welcoming what we once thought of as suffering we find new life.

Which is why the cruciform life, as the apostle Paul said, would be foolish if not for the resurrection. This is the third and final thing Mui pointed to that makes the call to "take up your cross" a call to liberation. The cruciform life isn't giving in to scarcity and nihilism, she pointed out, because there's life, abundant life, beyond the lie we've been told. We've been told this is how it must be, that the lion always has to eat the lamb. The gospels tell us over and over to stop playing the lion's game, and then they show us what happens when we do. We die, but we rise. We have radical—root-level—contentment that yields more joy than the continual striving of power hunger. We are not #blessed with millions and billions of dollars; we are actually blessed—comforted, filled, shown mercy, children of God, and inheritors of both heaven and earth (Matt. 5:3–10).

CHARACTERS AND DISTANCE: WE ARE ONE

Healing stories ultimately move toward healing the deep wound beneath all wounds: our alienation from God, earth, and one another.

Kraybill suggested a vertical reorientation of society, "upside down." I like using radial images for power and love, suffering and compassion, because it makes sense both personally and socially. I am at the center of my own life, and the people least like me—the "them" in our "us vs. them" discussion—are on the furthest ring from the center. It's normal to see things through my own eyes, to consider my own concerns. My vision is the fuzziest when I look at the lives of the people most different from me, those whose lives seem incomprehensible. It's normal to be this way as a person; it's just part of being a self. But a lot of people don't recognize their own subjectivity, and that is where things go awry.

Not every self-centered person is acting antagonistically. Some people just really do not understand that the world as they see it is not the world as it is for everyone. I was making $16,000 per year when a woman in my church asked me to come take weekly tennis lessons with her. It was "only" $30 per hour per person if we got a group of four. She wasn't evil; she just apparently had no idea how budgets work.

The problem gets bigger when we think that this self-centered view of the world is the proper structure of power, comfort, and love. As if all good should flow inward toward us, regardless of the expense to those furthest from us. When "our" perspectives are the only ones we consider, and "their" suffering is the only suffering we will tolerate. The more powerful "we" are, the more suffering gets shoved out onto "them."

In my reporting, activists and social workers talk to me about *the margins*—the people on the outer edges of society. When I was in school studying postcolonial theory, we used the term *subaltern*. Marx would call these people the most *alienated*. It's the people who are making the world revolve—workers and laborers—but it doesn't revolve around them. They are not marginal in an absolute sense—they are still selves—but they are marginal to the people with all the money and the power.

We also talk a lot about whose suffering stories are "centered" when we consider whether a particular issue is worth taking up and how it should be addressed. Example: Is it the missing white women or the scores of missing Indigenous women who motivate us to do something about violence against women?

The gospels' call to decenter our own comfort and move toward others in compassion cannot be understood outside a social context. It doesn't just matter who is most alien to you. It matters where you are in relation to the economic, political, and social power in your society. I have no idea what it would be like to be Jeff Bezos, but it matters much more that I have no idea what it would be like to be Jessica Margarita Menjivar. I met her via WhatsApp after she was deported to El Salvador, leaving her daughters behind in the United States. I'm called to love both Bezos and Menjivar, but when considering whose interests I will promote, whose life I will work to improve, and who would benefit from the changes I work to see in the world, it has to be the latter.

We know little else about Jesus, historically, other than that he was a man of the margins. He was a blue-collar worker living in an unsophisticated town in a Roman-occupied region. As the gospels present him, he was at various times homeless, a refugee, and a wanted man. That was his mimetic story for thirty-three years. His thematic story continues. Unity with him is unity with "them." That's why womanist theology asserts that, in the twentieth and twenty-first centuries, Jesus is a Black woman, because Black women are "them" to the most powerful in the world. One might argue that he is fleeing famine in Africa, crowded into a boat off the coast of Italy, a young woman held in sexual slavery, or a queer child aching to be accepted and safe. He's on the far side of every intersection.

If instead of blame we draw close to the margins with compassion, we're going to literally "feel with" people we used to ignore or despise. For those who have opened their hearts to refugees, you know the pain of investing yourself in the struggle and bureaucratic miasma of bringing someone to safety. For those who help people battling addiction, you know the pain of caring. But emotional solidarity is only part of it. When we spend our time and resources bringing people to safety or organizing for change, we no longer have that time and those resources to spend on enriching ourselves.

The lack of self-preservation among people who have chosen a life of solidarity with the suffering was the main gripe that Friedrich Nietzsche had about Christianity. Because he believed that life was the will to power, any system eschewing power was eschewing life. It was nihilism. "Christianity is the religion of pity. Pity opposes the noble passions which heighten our vitality. It has a depressing effect, depriving us of strength. As we multiply the instances of pity we gradually lose our strength of nobility," Nietzsche wrote.[9]

Nietzsche laments the "noble passions" lost to Christianity. It is noble, in his view, for man to dictate what is right and wrong based on his own interests. "The noble type of man regards himself as a determiner of values; he does not require to be approved of; he passes the judgment: 'What is injurious to me is injurious in itself'; he knows that it is he himself only who confers honor on things; he is the creator of value."[10]

What is injurious to me is injurious in itself. When I read that line as a student, I barely understood it. When I reread it at thirty-eight years old, a real, literal chill ran down my spine, because I now know Nietzsche's noble man. He is in the experience most of us have had with Christian pastoring. The noble man is, in all the hot-button topics we have considered, urging white American Christians to align with a predictable "us." The noble man's will to power is why refugee ministries saw support plummet under Trump, and it is why I get numerous emails about the dangers of CRT and Marxism in schools. The noble man urged churches to continue to meet despite COVID risks, and he nudges politicians to talk about the right to bear arms as "God-given." Nietzsche's noble man is alive and well, and he is always saying, "What is injurious to me is injurious in itself."

When we give that up, turning power and compassion inside out, we have to say, "What is injurious to you is injurious to me."

We must enter this conversation together in good faith. We can't do what white pastors have been doing to Kraybill's "upside-down" kingdom for so long: reframing and equivocating to prove that white Christians don't have the power we know we have, that we are actually the ones on the margins.

Or that we are suffering in ways we aren't. We must stamp out our cigars, stop trying to win an argument, and try to love people. We can't say, "I'll care about their suffering when they care about mine." We must mind our power lust, but also our fear.

In her book *All about Love*, bell hooks goes on to muse about this tension between power, fear, and love several more times, painting a picture of that creative and destructive dance across families, friendships, romance, spiritual devotion, and society. In the introduction she recalls the inciting disturbance that led her on her quest. It happened after the end of a romantic relationship but opened up her query into the idea of love as a possibility. "It had become hard for me to continue to believe in love's promise when everywhere I turned the enchantment of power or the terror of fear overshadowed the will to love."[11]

As we consider how an inside-out relationship to power and compassion might change our response to suffering stories, it's worth considering what might be overshadowing our will to love, and what it means to take up our cross and die to it.

ACKNOWLEDGMENTS

When I was in graduate school, I said to my friend Todd, "I've got a great idea." He replied, "You don't know how my heart stops when you say that, because I know what comes next is going to be incredibly complicated." That might be the most insightful glimpse into what it's like to live or work with me, so a big thanks to my ever-patient family and friends, and possibly even more patient editors of both news articles and this book.

Don Pape, the best agent around, is the reason I get to publish books. And for this book, I'm especially grateful for the Baders of Bellville for offering me a place to hole up and write, and some good late-night brainstorming early in the process.

I love my work because I get to interview the best people in the world, the ones genuinely trying to alleviate suffering and connect us all to one another. You've been lucky enough to meet some of them while reading this book. They're amazing.

NOTES

Introduction

1. Walter Brueggemann in conversation with the author via phone, August 30, 2023.

2. Adam Serwer, *The Cruelty Is the Point: The Past, Present, and Future of Trump's America* (New York: One World, 2021), 91–92.

3. Serwer, *Cruelty Is the Point*, 103.

Chapter 1

1. Will Storr, *The Science of Storytelling: Why Stories Make Us Human and How to Tell Them Better* (New York: Abrams, 2020), 49.

2. Kaitlin B. Curtis, *Living Resistance: An Indigenous Vision for Seeking Wholeness Every Day* (Grand Rapids: Brazos, 2023), 40.

3. Toni Morrison, "The Trouble with Paradise," Moffett Lecture, Princeton University, Princeton, New Jersey, April 23, 1998; printed in Morrison's *The Source of Self-Regard: Selected Essays, Speeches, and Meditations* (New York: Alfred A. Knopf, 2019), 276.

4. Amanda Ripley, *High Conflict: Why We Get Trapped and How We Get Out* (New York: Simon & Schuster, 2021), 4.

5. Ripley, *High Conflict*, 4.

6. Frederick Douglass, "The Color Line," *North American Review* 132, no. 295 (June 1881): 567, https://tinyurl.com/2smc2jam.

7. Shankar Vedantam and Todd Kashdan, "Happiness 2.0: The Only Way Out Is Through," February 13, 2023, in *Hidden Brain*, podcast, 48:45, https://tinyurl.com/9bvscvab.

Chapter 2

1. Amanda Montell, *Cultish: The Language of Fanaticism* (New York: HarperCollins, 2021).

2. Benedict Anderson, *Imagined Communities* (London: Verso, 1983), 7.

3. Douglass, "Color Line," 569.

4. Martin N. Marger, *Social Inequality: Patterns and Processes*, 2nd ed. (Boston: McGraw-Hill, 2002), 329.

5. Karen Armstrong, *Fields of Blood: Religion and the History of Violence* (New York: Alfred A. Knopf, 2014), 14.

6. Armstrong, *Fields of Blood*, 26.

7. Randy S. Woodley, *Mission and the Cultural Other: A Closer Look* (Eugene, OR: Wipf and Stock, 2022), 31.

8. Woodley, *Mission and the Cultural Other*, 14.

9. I had always heard this quote attributed to Desmond Tutu, but when I went to Google to verify it, several sources claim it was actually Kenyatta. I'm giving it to the elder statesman, but given how often I've heard it repeated by other Africans, it's fair to just call it a broad sentiment, regardless of who said it first.

10. Lilie Chouliaraki, *The Spectatorship of Suffering* (London: Sage, 2006), 14.

Chapter 3

1. Bekah McNeel, "SB 4: Political Aims, Personal Consequences," *San Antonio Report*, June 19, 2017, https://tinyurl.com/yjktrjn7.

2. Public Law 414, Sec. 212(e), https://tinyurl.com/4ynbydsj.

3. Maddalena Marinari, "Divided and Conquered: Immigration Reform Advocates and the Passage of the 1952 Immigration and Nationality Act," *Journal of American Ethnic History* 35, no. 3 (Spring 2016): 12, https://tinyurl.com/4nmcdvhu.

4. Immigration and Nationality Act, Sec. 202 (a)(1)(A), https://tinyurl.com/yuv8yv4t.

5. Chigozie Obioma, "The Naked Man," in *The Good Immigrant: 26 Writers Reflect on America*, ed. Nikesh Shukla and Chimene Suleyman (New York: Little, Brown, 2019), 168.

6. Karen González, "In Search of the Good Immigrant," *Christianity Today*, June 9, 2020, https://tinyurl.com/2p847477.

Chapter 4

1. Karen González, *Beyond Welcome: Centering Immigrants in Our Christian Response to Immigration* (Grand Rapids: Baker, 2022), 89.

2. González, *Beyond Welcome*, 79.

3. González, *Beyond Welcome*, 96.

Chapter 5

1. H.B 3979, Sec 1. h-3. 4.B.vii, https://tinyurl.com/2p995w7e.

2. Paige Williams, "The Right-Wing Mothers Fuelling the School-Board Wars," *New Yorker*, October 31, 2022, https://tinyurl.com/4pseh5pj.

3. Krista Torralva, "San Antonio School Districts Still Struggle with the City's Segregated Past," *San Antonio Express-News*, July 27, 2020, https://tinyurl.com/4ca45des.

4. Benjamin Wallace-Wells, "How a Conservative Activist Invented the Conflict over Critical Race Theory," *New Yorker*, June 18, 2021, https://tinyurl.com/3dfmktya.

5. The Inaugural Address of Gov. George C. Wallace, January 14, 1963, https://tinyurl.com/mrutepzv.

Chapter 6

1. Duke Kwon and Gregory Thompson, *Reparations: A Christian Call for Repentance and Repair* (Grand Rapids: Brazos, 2021), 139.

2. Susan Neiman, *Learning from the Germans: Race and the Memory of Evil* (New York: Farrar, Straus, and Giroux, 2019), 267.

3. Lindsey Johnstone, "Holocaust Remembrance Day: How Are Europe's Children Taught about the Holocaust?," *Euronews*, October 2, 2020, https://tinyurl.com/msdbyysa.

4. Kwon and Thompson, *Reparations*, 190.

5. Neiman, *Learning from the Germans*, 269.

6. Neiman, *Learning from the Germans*, 269.

7. Patty Krawec, *Becoming Kin: An Indigenous Call to Unforgetting the Past and Reimagining Our Future* (Minneapolis: Broadleaf, 2022), 159.

8. Krawec, *Becoming Kin*, 149.

Chapter 7

1. Marvin Olasky, "How Americans Got Away with Abortion before *Roe v. Wade*," *Christianity Today*, August 22, 2022, https://tinyurl.com/bdu92j84.

2. Randall Balmer, *Bad Faith: Race and the Rise of the Religious Right* (Grand Rapids: Eerdmans, 2021).

3. Jamal Greene, *How Rights Went Wrong: Why Our Obsession with Rights Is Tearing America Apart* (Boston: Houghton Mifflin Harcourt, 2021), 114.

4. John MacArthur, "The Curse on the Woman, Part 1," June 11, 2000, https://tinyurl.com/4j79835w.

5. MacArthur, "The Curse on the Woman, Part 1."

Chapter 8

1. Bekah McNeel, "Texas Abortion Law Complicates San Antonio Group's Mission to Help Undocumented Immigrants—Even Those Raped En Route to the U.S.," *Texas Tribune*, November 12, 2021, https://tinyurl.com/6zrkaxav.

2. Katey Zeh, *A Complicated Choice: Making Space for Grief and Healing in the Pro-Choice Movement* (Minneapolis: Broadleaf, 2022), 24

3. Bekah McNeel, "Abortion and Faith after 1 Year without Roe," *Sojourners*, June 13, 2023, https://tinyurl.com/yutke6kx.

4. Camila Ochoa Mendoza and Zachi Brewster, "In Conversation with Abortion Doula, Zachi Brewster," April 27, 2021, in *Abortion, with Love*, podcast, MP3 audio, 39:52, https://tinyurl.com/44x3skbv.

5. Greene, *How Rights Went Wrong*, 114–39.

6. Greene, *How Rights Went Wrong*, 129–32.

7. Greene, *How Rights Went Wrong*, 122.

8. L. Ann Jervis, *At the Heart of the Gospel: Suffering in the Earliest Christian Message* (Grand Rapids: Eerdmans, 2007), 81.

9. John Swinton, *Raging with Compassion: Pastoral Responses to the Problem of Evil* (Grand Rapids: Eerdmans, 2007), 87.

10. Katey Zeh, in discussion with Bekah McNeel, interview with the author on June 5, 2023.

Chapter 9

1. Cornwall Alliance for the Stewardship of Creation, *Protect the Poor: Ten Reasons to Oppose Harmful Climate Change Policies*, 2014, https://tinyurl.com/2dzjeyck.

2. Jeremiah Bohr, "The Structure and Culture of Climate Change Denial," *Footnotes* 49, no. 3 (2021), https://tinyurl.com/yckurdy5.

3. Bohr, "Climate Change Denial."

Chapter 10

1. Winkie Pratney, as quoted in Randy S. Woodley, *Shalom and the Community of Creation: An Indigenous Vision* (Grand Rapids: Eerdmans, 2012), 127.

2. Woodley, *Shalom and the Community of Creation*, 127.

3. Krawec, *Becoming Kin*, 138.

4. Woodley, *Shalom and the Community of Creation*, 36–40.

5. Woodley, *Shalom and the Community of Creation*, 86.

6. Douglas Rushkoff, *Survival of the Richest: Escape Fantasies of the Tech Billionaires* (New York: W. W. Norton, 2022), 67.

7. Rushkoff, *Survival of the Richest*, 9.

8. Rushkoff, *Survival of the Richest*, 188.

9. Woodley, *Shalom and the Community of Creation*, 53–57.

10. Vanessa Nakate, quoted in Christina Colón, "A Fight for God's Creation: An Interview with Activist Vanessa Nakate," *Sojourners*, December 2022.

11. Nakate, quoted in Colón, "Fight for God's Creation."

12. Nakate, quoted in Colón, "Fight for God's Creation."

Chapter 11

1. Greene, *How Rights Went Wrong*, 58.

2. "Wearing a Mask Is for Smug Liberals. Refusing to Is for Reckless Republicans," *Politico*, May 1, 2020, https://tinyurl.com/4acvwtx7.

3. Montell, *Cultish*, 21–27.

Chapter 12

1. James Davison Hunter, *To Change the World: The Irony, Tragedy, and Possibility of Christianity in the Late Modern Age* (New York: Oxford University Press, 2010), 103.

2. Hunter, *To Change the World*, 235.

3. Hunter, *To Change the World*, 193.

Chapter 13

1. Louise Penny, *A Fatal Grace* (New York: Minotaur Books, 2007), 164.

2. Philip Bump, "The Economics of Arming America's Schools," *Washington Post*, February 22, 2018, https://tinyurl.com/3ddpzwm7.

3. Bekah McNeel, "In Uvalde Community Struggles for Reform Amid Grief," *The Trace*, November 15, 2022, https://tinyurl.com/kzzte93n.

4. Roxanne Dunbar-Ortiz, *Loaded: A Disarming History of the Second Amendment* (San Francisco: City Lights, 2018).

5. Dunbar-Ortiz, *Loaded*, 127.

6. Ryan P. Brown, *Honor Bound: How a Cultural Ideal Has Shaped the American Psyche* (New York: Oxford University Press, 2016).

7. For more on the religious version of the honor culture, see Kristin Kobes Du Mez's book, *Jesus and John Wayne* (New York: Liveright, 2020).

Chapter 14

1. Kellie Carter Jackson, "The Story of Violence in America," *Daedalus* 151, no. 1 (2022): 19, https://tinyurl.com/mtwscf49.

2. Carter Jackson, "Story of Violence in America," 16.

3. David C. Cramer and Myles Werntz, *A Field Guide to Christian Nonviolence: Key Thinkers, Activists, and Movements for the Gospel of Peace* (Grand Rapids: Baker Academic, 2022).

4. Aaron James, "Preachers, Prophets, and Philosophers: Martin Luther King Jr's Moral Reasoning on Nonviolence," in *The Gospel of Peace in a Violent World: Christian Nonviolence for Communal Flourishing*, ed. Shawn Graves and Marlena Graves (Downers Grove, IL: InterVarsity Press, 2022), 105–19.

5. James, "Preachers, Prophets, and Philosophers," 119.

6. Mae Elise Cannon, "Problematic Pacifism," in Graves and Graves, *The Gospel of Peace in a Violent World*, 237.

7. Carter Jackson, "Story of Violence in America," 20.

Chapter 15

1. Donald Kraybill, *The Upside-Down Kingdom* (Harrisonburg, VA: Herald Press, 1978; rev. ed., 2011), 249.

2. Swinton, *Raging with Compassion*, 21.

3. Stanley Hauerwas, *God, Medicine, and Suffering* (Grand Rapids: Eerdmans, 1994), 56.

4. Richard Hofstadter, *Social Darwinism in American Thought* (Philadelphia: University of Pennsylvania Press, 1944; Beacon edition, 1955), 201.

5. Rebekah Mui, in discussion with Bekah McNeel, March 17, 2023.

6. Mui, discussion.

7. Silvia Federici, "Witches, the Commons, Reclaiming the Body and Discovering Our Power," January 28, 2020, speaking to the Democratic Socialists of America, Sacramento Chapter, https://tinyurl.com/2p8b3bxw.

8. Thich Nhat Hanh, *The Heart of the Buddha's Teaching: Transforming Suffering into Peace, Joy, and Liberation* (New York: Harmony Books, 1998), 34–35.

9. Friedrich Nietzsche, *The Antichrist* (New York: Alfred A. Knopf, 1918), 47.

10. Friedrich Nietzsche, *Beyond Good and Evil* (London: Penguin, 2003), 195.

11. bell hooks, *All about Love: New Visions* (New York: HarperCollins, 2001), xvi.

SELECTED BIBLIOGRAPHY

Anderson, Benedict. *Imagined Communities*. London: Verso, 1983.

Armstrong, Karen. *Fields of Blood: Religion and the History of Violence*. New York: Alfred A. Knopf, 2014.

Bohr, Jeremiah. "The Structure and Culture of Climate Change Denial." *Footnotes: A Magazine of the American Sociological Association* 49, no. 3 (2021). https://tinyurl.com/yckurdy5.

Brown, Ryan P. *Honor Bound: How a Cultural Ideal Has Shaped the American Psyche*. New York: Oxford University Press, 2016.

Bump, Philip. "The Economics of Arming America's Schools." *Washington Post*, February 22, 2018. https://tinyurl.com/3ddpzwm7.

Carter Jackson, Kellie. "The Story of Violence in America." *Daedalus* 151, no. 1 (2022): 11–21. https://tinyurl.com/mtwscf49.

Chouliaraki, Lilie. *The Spectatorship of Suffering*. London: Sage, 2006.

Colón, Christina. "A Fight for God's Creation: An Interview with Activist Vanessa Nakate." *Sojourners*, December 2022.

Cramer, David C., and Myles Werntz. *A Field Guide to Christian Nonviolence: Key Thinkers, Activists, and Movements for the Gospel of Peace*. Grand Rapids: Baker Academic, 2022.

Curtis, Kaitlin B. *Living Resistance: An Indigenous Vision for Seeking Wholeness Every Day*. Grand Rapids: Brazos, 2023.

Douglass, Frederick. "The Color Line." *North American Review* 132, no. 295 (June 1881): 567–77. https://tinyurl.com/2smc2jam.

Dunbar-Ortiz, Roxanne. *Loaded: A Disarming History of the Second Amendment*. San Francisco: City Lights, 2018.

González, Karen. *Beyond Welcome: Centering Immigrants in Our Christian Response to Immigration*. Grand Rapids: Baker, 2022.

Hofstadter, Richard. *Social Darwinism in American Thought*. Philadelphia: University of Pennsylvania Press, 1944. Beacon edition, 1955.

hooks, bell. *All about Love: New Visions*. New York: HarperCollins, 2001.

Hunter, James Davison. *To Change the World: The Irony, Tragedy, and Possibility of Christianity in the Late Modern World*. New York: Oxford University Press, 2010.

Jervis, L. Ann. *At the Heart of the Gospel: Suffering in the Earliest Christian Message*. Grand Rapids: Eerdmans, 2007.

Johnstone, Lindsey. "Holocaust Remembrance Day: How Are Europe's Children Taught about the Holocaust?" *Euronews*, October 2, 2020. https://tinyurl.com/msdbyysa.

Krawec, Patty. *Becoming Kin: An Indigenous Call to Unforgetting the Past and Reimagining Our Future*. Minneapolis: Broadleaf, 2022.

Kraybill, Donald. *The Upside-Down Kingdom*. Harrisonburg, VA: Herald Press, 1978, revised edition, 2011.

Kwon, Duke, and Gregory Thompson. *Reparations: A Christian Call for Repentance and Repair*. Grand Rapids: Brazos, 2021.

Marinari, Maddalena. "Divided and Conquered: Immigration Reform Advocates and the Passage of the 1952 Immigration and Nationality Act." *Journal of American Ethnic History* 35, no. 3 (Spring 2016): 9–40. https://tinyurl.com/4nmcdvhu.

Morrison, Toni. "The Trouble with Paradise." Moffett Lecture, Princeton University, Princeton, New Jersey, April 23, 1998. Printed in Morrison's *The Source of Self-Regard: Selected Essays, Speeches, and Meditations*, 271–79. New York: Alfred A. Knopf, 2019.

Neiman, Susan. *Learning from the Germans: Race and the Memory of Evil*. New York: Farrar, Straus, and Giroux, 2019.

Nietzsche, Friedrich. *Beyond Good and Evil: A Prelude to the Philosophy of the Future*. New York: Dover, 1997.

Obioma, Chigozie. "The Naked Man." In *The Good Immigrant: 26 Writers Reflect on America*, edited by Nikesh Shukla and Chimene Suleyman, 155–68. New York: Little, Brown, 2019.

Ripley, Amanda. *High Conflict: Why We Get Trapped and How We Get Out*. New York: Simon & Schuster, 2021.

Rushkoff, Douglas. *Survival of the Richest: Escape Fantasies of the Tech Billionaires*. New York: W. W. Norton, 2022.

Serwer, Adam. *The Cruelty Is the Point: The Past, Present, and Future of Trump's America*. New York: One World, 2021.

Storr, Will. *The Science of Storytelling: Why Stories Make Us Human and How to Tell Them Better*. New York: Abrams, 2020.

Swinton, John. *Raging with Compassion: Pastoral Responses to the Problem of Evil*. Grand Rapids: Eerdmans, 2007.

Thich Nhat Hanh. *The Heart of the Buddha's Teaching: Transforming Suffering into Peace, Joy, and Liberation*. New York: Harmony Books, 1998.

Torralva, Krista. "San Antonio School Districts Still Struggle with the City's Segregated Past." *San Antonio Express-News*, July 27, 2020. https://tinyurl.com/4ca45des.

Wallace-Wells, Benjamin. "How a Conservative Activist Invented the Conflict over Critical Race Theory." *New Yorker*, June 18, 2021. https://tinyurl.com/3dfmktya.

Williams, Paige. "The Right-Wing Mothers Fuelling the School-Board Wars." *New Yorker*, October 31, 2022. https://tinyurl.com/4pseh5pj.

Woodley, Randy S. *Mission and the Cultural Other: A Closer Look*. Eugene, OR: Wipf and Stock, 2022.

———. *Shalom and the Community of Creation: An Indigenous Vision*. Grand Rapids: Eerdmans, 2012.